WHITNEY HOUSTON!

The Spectacular Rise and Tragic Fall of the Woman
Whose Voice Inspired A Generation

WHITNEY HOUSTON!

The Spectacular Rise and Tragic Fall of the Woman
Whose Voice Inspired a Generation

MARK BEGO

Skyhorse Publishing

Skyhorse Publishing books may be purchased in bulk at special discounts for sales promotion, corporate gifts, fund-raising, or educational purposes. Special editions can also be created to specifications. For details, contact the Special Sales Department, Skyhorse Publishing, 307 West 36th Street, 11th Floor, New York, NY 10018 or info@skyhorsepublishing.com.

Skyhorse® and Skyhorse Publishing® are registered trademarks of Skyhorse Publishing, Inc.®, a Delaware corporation.

Visit our website at www.skyhorsepublishing.com.

10 9 8 7 6 5 4 3 2

Library of Congress Cataloging-in-Publication Data is available on file.
ISBN: 978-1-62087-254-3

Printed in the United States of America

DEDICATION

To Susan Gilbert—
Thank you for coming to my rescue so many times!

CONTENTS

ACKNOWLEDGMENTS

The author would like to thank the following people for their help and encouragement with this book:

Kirsten Borchardt
Angela Bowie
Tom Cuddy
Dan DeFilippo
Jerry George
Michael Glenn
Frances Grill
Isiah James
Bashiri Johnson
John Klinger
Monika Koch
Dave Marken
Nick Mayer
Walter McBride
Scott Mendel
Charles Moniz
Ruth Mueller

Luke Nicola
Mark & Bonnie Olson
David Perel
Pipeline Management
Kenneth Reynolds
David Salidor
Tony Seidl
Barbara Shelley
Andrew Skurow
Marsha Stern
Derek Storm
Val Virga
George Vissichelli
Sharon Weisz
Beth Wernick
Mary Wilson
Patrick Wood

PROLOGUE

"GRAMMY EVE, SATURDAY, FEBRUARY 11, 2012"

It was the day prior to the fifty-fourth annual Grammy Awards presentation in Los Angeles. Without a doubt, this is the most exciting and dramatic weekend of the year in the music business. All week, musicians, technicians, and superstars had been converging on the City of Angels for the parties, the celebrations, and the awards themselves.

With the Grammy Awards presentation set to take place on February 12 at The Staples Center in downtown L.A., master record executive Clive Davis was amidst plans for his own annual celebration at The Beverly Hills Hilton Hotel: his exclusive pre-Grammys party which draws the A–list of music business heavy hitters, and a glittering roster of guest star performers every year. This year was going to feature an elite crowd including Tony Bennett, Jane Fonda, Joni Mitchell, Tom Hanks, Richard Branson, Sean "Diddy" Combs, John Fogerty, Kim Kardashian, Serena Williams, Neil Young, Britney Spears, Brandy, Monica, Alicia Keys, Swizz Beats, Adam Lambert, Ray Davies of The Kinks, and Sly Stone. Also expected at the event was Clive Davis's prized star and dear friend: Whitney Houston.

So that she could have a room right on the site of Clive's party, Whitney Houston took a suite at The Beverly Hills Hilton Hotel. That way she could be in the middle of all the action, and when it came time for her to arrive at the gala party she could simply sweep down on the elevator and make a grand entrance.

On Thursday night, February 9, Whitney was in town, and showed up for a performance by her friend Kelly Price at a local nightclub. The event was billed as: "Kelly Price and Friends Unplugged: For the Love of R&B Grammy Party at Tru Hollywood."

In the middle of Kelly's show, Whitney briefly got up on stage and together she and Price sang part of the song "Jesus Loves Me." The video footage from the event depicts a sweaty and slightly-disheveled Houston in a simple black dress, looking like she was enjoying an evening with friends, and "letting her hair down." No one could have guessed at the time that this would go down in history as Houston's final public singing performance.

On Friday, February 11, Whitney was at The Beverly Hilton Hotel, which is located at the intersection of Santa Monica Boulevard and Wilshire Boulevard. She had made herself right at home there on the luxurious fourth floor. She had taken a spacious corner suite: room number 434.

Usually she was surrounded by members of her personal entourage. This evening, however, she was left alone for a while, and she had decided to take a relaxing bath before the party.

According to the Beverly Hills police reports, it was a member of her entourage and two bodyguards who discovered Whitney Houston's lifeless body in the bathtub. She was unconscious and unresponsive to their efforts to rouse her. The entourage member telephoned "911" for help at 3:43 PM, Pacific Standard Time. Fortunately, the Beverly Hills Police Department and Fire Department were already on the premises, and they responded immediately. The emergency response personnel were completely unable to revive her, and Whitney Houston was officially pronounced dead at 3:55 PM.

INTRODUCTION

"DIDN'T SHE USED TO HAVE IT ALL?"

There are few people in the world of show business who have achieved the kind of career heights that Whitney Houston had attained. She is one of the top recording artists in the history of popular music, having reached her creative high point in 1992 with the phenomenal international Number One hit "I Will Always Love You." At her peak, she was personified as having beauty and talent, and she was one of the most successful women ever to sing and act. She won countless awards, and amassed a vast fortune. She also had one of the longest and deepest falls from grace ever chronicled.

After Whitney married former singing star Bobby Brown in 1992 she began a twenty-year streak of bad luck and self-destructive behavior. Houston had one of the longest career and personal meltdowns ever recorded in the press.

Since the year 2000, every album and every career move she made was viewed as a new "comeback." However, it seemed that for Whitney, every great career resurrection was directly followed by another misstep or another personal tragedy.

Thanks to her 2009 album *I Look to You*, which hit Number One on the charts, Whitney Houston had one of the greatest temporary career revivals ever staged. It was no easy feat, but—for a short period of time—she seemed to pull off an incredible return to form with newfound strength, style, and flair.

However, by the time her 2009–2010 world concert tour came to an end, scathing press reports of lackluster performances, poor voice, no voice, and even no-shows, signaled the true beginning of the end of

Whitney Houston's once glorious singing career, as well as her role as a concert performer.

From 2010 to 2012, Whitney Houston's life became a harrowing roller coaster of temporary triumphs, and of deep disappointments. In 2011 she made one last attempt at rehabilitation for her drug dependencies, and she filmed a role in the remake of the hit '70s musical movie *Sparkle*. However, for Whitney, 2012 began with press rumors that she was about to go broke, and that her drug abuses were worse than ever. Her sudden and tragic death on February 11, 2012 was especially sad and disappointing for her millions of worldwide fans, because she had fallen from such an extreme height of achievement. Since her 1980s debut on the music charts, she had become a recording star, a movie star, and a glamorous show business icon. She had all of the trappings of stardom and success, and still they did not always bring her happiness. What happened? Where did it go wrong? Didn't she used to have it all?

Without a doubt, Whitney Houston had one of the most carefully plotted and planned music careers on record. She was literally born into the music business. Her cousin is the incredibly successful pop icon, Dionne Warwick. Her mother is Cissy Houston, the gifted lead singer of 1960s girl group The Sweet Inspirations, whose background singing has been heard behind such legends as Aretha Franklin and Luther Vandross. Whitney's own career was the carefully-executed dream of music business magician, Clive Davis. Yes, Whitney had the looks and the pristine voice as a teenager, but it was Davis who worked for two years finding the right songs and the right producers to show off her natural attributes.

Her first album, 1985's *Whitney Houston*, hit Number One, and sold an astonishing 22 million copies worldwide. It produced one international hit single after another, and is still acknowledged as the best-selling debut album of all time. Her sophomore release, 1987's *Whitney*, repeated the same alchemy, becoming the first album by a female performer to debut on the *Billboard* album charts at Number One. Her third album, 1990's *I'm Your Baby Tonight* sold 10 million copies.

For the first eleven years of her once-successful singing and acting career she was known around the world as a charming, beautiful, self-confident, and gifted performer with a glorious voice. She wore clothes stylishly, always appeared in public glamorously coiffed, and masterfully headlined prestigious venues like Carnegie Hall.

Whitney Houston placed eleven hits in the Number One position in the United States, including: "Saving All My Love For You," "How Will I Know," "Greatest Love of All," "I Wanna Dance With Somebody (Who Loves Me)," "Didn't We Almost Have it All," "So Emotional," "Where Do Broken Hearts Go," "I'm Your Baby Tonight," ""All the Man I Need," and "Exhale (Shoop, Shoop)." She won six Grammy Awards, twenty-one American Music Awards, an Emmy Award, and Germany's prestigious Bambi Award for excellence as "The Best International Artist." It appeared that there was nothing she could not accomplish.

In 1992 Houston became a movie star, sharing the silver screen with Kevin Costner in the box-office hit *The Bodyguard*. The soundtrack album featured Whitney's all-time greatest hit, "I Will Always Love You," which went on to sell an astonishing 34 million copies worldwide. The soundtrack album for her second film, *Waiting to Exhale* became the singularly most-nominated album in Grammy Award history. And, the soundtrack album for her third film, *The Preacher's Wife*, at 5 million copies sold, became the biggest-selling gospel album ever released. For the time-being, everything Houston touched turned to million-selling *Gold*. She was the embodiment of a real-life Cinderella.

Upon Whitney's insistence, for her 1998 album, *My Love is Your Love*, she shifted gears into hip-hop soul, and created a new harder-edged image for herself. Although it was less successful than her past releases, she still managed to find an international audience. In the year 2000, Whitney released a two disk *Greatest Hits* album which sold another 10 million copies. It would mark her last collaboration with Clive Davis for several years. Many of her critics claimed that this marked the beginning of the end of her musical and performing career. It was the start of seven years of extremely bad luck.

During the years that Whitney was married to Bobby Brown, she dramatically transformed herself into an unpredictable and desperate woman whose life seemed to spin out of control. The effervescent and appealing Whitney the world fell in love with in the 1980s and early 1990s changed into someone the public no longer recognized.

Starting in the year 2001, it all seemed to unravel for her. Piece by piece, Whitney, herself, seemed to sabotage her own carefully crafted and meticulously planned public image. By 2005, around the time that the disastrous TV reality series *Being Bobby Brown* was on the air, Whitney Houston was portrayed in the press as an arrogant, unreliable, substance-abusing, and paranoid person who had eroded both her looks and her voice. Even her once strong fan base seemed to abandon her.

Marriage to talented but trouble-prone "bad boy" Bobby Brown, marked a huge change in her life. It ushered in highly publicized drug use, canceled concerts, public rudeness to fans, problems with the law, and eventually a shockingly thin and dissipated look for Whitney. Her name on a recording used to guarantee a multi-million-selling hit. Suddenly she found herself ignored by radio programmers and the music-buying public as well.

Bobby Brown originally found fame as a former member of the 1980s R&B group The New Edition. Since then he is most commonly known for his drunken public fights, physical battles with Whitney in public, and for his notorious womanizing. He has several out-of-wedlock children in addition to his daughter with Houston. Characteristically, one of his biggest solo hits is a song called "Humpin' Around." His influence drove away her family, her friends, and her fans.

While under Brown's spell, in 2002 Whitney Houston released a dull and misguided album called *Just Whitney*. It sold a dismal 3 million copies globally. The first single from the album was a defensive and paranoid song called "Whatulookinat?" It fell flat on the charts. Instead of lovingly gazing at her once-classic beauty, the public viewed Ms. Houston with same kind of horror and awe one would have watching a train wreck in progress.

Few performers have risen to the show business stature that Houston's career has attained, and few have fallen so far so quickly. Whitney was once heralded as one of the most beloved, heavenly-voiced and cherished singers and actresses of the twentieth century. However since the year 2000, Whitney's life sunk into a quicksand of "tabloid headline hell." She publicly complained that the tabloid papers were doing her in, and "dirtying up" her name. However it was she who was creating the shocking headlines!

She was publicly perceived as being a drug addicted, unpredictable, undependable, unbankable, and haughty has-been of a star. After three very successful Hollywood theatrical films, suddenly no one in the movie business wanted to touch her as an actress. There is also the much-talked-about fact that people had been whispering for years about Houston's marriage to Brown being for "show" only, and that she is in actuality a lesbian.

Whitney Houston's career disintegration had as much to do with her gaunt and tired looks, as it did with the fact that she could no longer hit the musical high notes which had once effortlessly flowed from her throat. Had Whitney Houston fallen under the dark influence of her criminal bad boy husband? Or, was she merely showing us her true colors? The absolute low point in her career was her appearance on the shocking American reality show entitled *Being Bobby Brown*. The notorious duo was seen as an obnoxious pair of substance-abusing desperate characters, who brought each other to newfound depths.

Finally, in 2007 Whitney officially divorced Bobby Brown and she almost instantly began her resurrection. Once Bobby was out of the picture, it marked the return of the one man who always believed in her, and who first made her into an international singing star: Clive Davis. He made it his personal goal to restore Houston to her former glory.

The public loves a success story. What they love even more is to see someone fall apart and then return even stronger and more determined than before. With the 2009 album that Clive fashioned for Whitney—*I Look To You*—she instantly returned to incredible prominence as a survivor, and as a shining superstar. There is no one in show business who has done that better, or more successfully, than Whitney.

At the beginning of her career, Whitney astonished the world with her talent, her looks, and her expressive voice. She became a one-of-a-kind singer, and an award-winning movie star as well. When she lost favor, and everything seemed to fall apart for her, it was uncertain where fate would take her.

When her 2009 album, *I Look to You* hit the top of the charts, and her song "I Didn't Know My Own Strength" became a hit, it looked like she might relive the dream. For a short period of time it seemed that she was starting a new and successful chapter of her career.

However, her disastrous world tour of 2009–2010 demonstrated that she was incomparably undependable, in horrible voice, and in fragile health. She "bombed" in Australia, and she had audiences leaving the concerts mid-show. She began the European leg of her tour by instantly postponing concerts in Paris, France; Manchester, England; and Glasgow, Scotland. Although she sent out a press release claiming to have illness-caused health problems, several sources claimed that it was actually her continued substance abuse that was to blame. After that, American tour promoters were both unwilling and uninterested in taking a chance on booking her for live performances.

Whitney Houston was at the top of the show business world. She had it all, and then she lost it. She had been on a self-destructive path for twenty years, and finally her hard-living lifestyle and her abuse of drugs and liquor had seemingly gotten the best of her. Although the toxicology findings were not immediately announced when she suddenly died, it was instantly suspected that it was her substance abuse which ultimately caused her death at the age of forty-eight. No one in show business had so much talent and so many opportunities handed to her. Her name is Whitney Houston, and this is her story.

CHAPTER ONE

"WHITNEY'S FAMOUS FAMILY"

It is September 1, 2009, and it is a warm summer day in New York City's famed Central Park. In the Rumsey Playfield area of the park, a huge concert stage is set up, with the backdrop of Manhattan skyscrapers behind it. Since 11:00 PM the night before, people have been waiting in line to be the first ones to face the stage the following morning. It is a free concert by someone who was once beloved, disappeared for a while, but is now suddenly back in the public eye. She is someone whom the public first fell in love with in her early twenties. Now, twenty-five years later, she is back and eager to show her fans how she looks and how she sounds. Her name is Whitney Houston.

If you have a good vantage point in Newark, New Jersey, on a clear day you can look across the Hudson River to the East, and see the towers of New York City. It was in nearby Newark that Whitney Houston was born forty-six years ago. As a child in Newark, little Whitney used to dream of one day performing in New York City like her mother, Cissy Houston did, in nightclubs and recording studios. However, for young Whitney, at that time her entire life was all about her close-knit and loving family.

On this day in Central Park, Whitney's main focus is again on her family. It is her first major televised concert in seven years. These seven years have been marked by extreme bad luck for her, and she is here this morning to let everyone know that she has recovered from years of substance abuse, a bitter divorce, and a tumble in popularity that has been upsetting to witness.

Not only have over 5,000 fans assembled to witness today's return of a beloved musical legend, they are here to celebrate her career and her talent. However, there are two key figures in her life who are more important than all of the others. They are her teenaged daughter Bobbi Kristina Brown, and her beloved mother Cissy Houston. They are both her today to cheer Whitney's return to the stage.

Throughout the majority of her life, Whitney has been all about the members of her family. They have protected her, they raised her, they fought with her, and they instilled her with the incredible talent and drive that originally made her a star. On her 2009 *I Look to You* album, in the song "Nothin' But Love" she sings her praises "for the family that raised me." For Houston, being a singing star has been the family business for five decades.

When she began singing professionally as part of her mother's nightclub act in New York City, people didn't say, "See that girl with the big voice, that's Whitney Houston." What they did say was, "Listen to that amazing little girl—she is related to Dionne Warwick and Cissy Houston."

On this triumphant day in Central Park, people have not shown up just to witness the return of Whitney Houston. They are coming to see something much more. They are here to see and to hear the latest chapter of the Houston / Warwick family legacy of singing stars. And, what a history it has been.

To fully examine the whole Whitney Houston story, one has to know about the strong musical legacy that preceded her. She comes from a very famous and very talented family—particularly her first cousin Dionne Warwick; and her own mother, Cissy Houston. Interestingly enough, their lives and their careers have intersected several times throughout the years. Cissy has sung on several of Dionne's albums, and it was through singing with Cissy that Whitney was first discovered by Clive Davis, with Dionne's encouragement. In the 1990s, Dionne and Whitney finally teamed up for a duet recording on Arista Records. Furthermore, Whitney's Godmother is none other than the Queen of Soul—Aretha Franklin herself. Cissy has sung background vocals on several of Aretha's albums, and Whitney and Franklin also recorded a duet together. In addition, Dionne's younger sister, Dee Dee Warwick had hit records of her own.

What is even more interesting to note, is that Clive Davis, the president of Arista Records is single-handedly responsible for reviving both the recording careers of Aretha Franklin, and of Dionne Warwick in the late '70s and early '80s. By the time Whitney Houston was signed to Arista, Clive had already brought Warwick and Franklin back to Grammy-winning hit making status.

Multi-talented, Dionne Warwick has had one of the most illustrious singing careers in show business. Although, today an entire generation knew her mainly for her 1990s infomercials about the Psychic Friends Network, her classic recordings made her one of the most defining voices of the 1960s, the 1970s, and beyond. In many ways, Whitney's early career directly mimicked the ballad-singing success of Dionne's heyday of hits.

Born Marie Dionne "Warrick" in East Orange, New Jersey, Dionne's interest and knowledge in the world of music is deeply rooted. In the early 1960s her mother, Lee Drinkard Warrick, her Aunt Cissy, and her sister Dee Dee, were members of a local family gospel group known as The Drinkard Singers. It was with this group that Dionne gained her first musical experience. While studying under a scholarship at the Hartt College of Music, Dionne formed her own trio, The Gospelaires, with Dee Dee and a cousin.

One night when Dee Dee, Dionne, her mother, and her Aunt Cissy were appearing at New York City's famed Apollo Theater, someone spotted Dionne onstage and offered her a job doing background singing for a recording session. It was through this recording session that Dionne met a then-unknown composer named Burt Bacharach. The brilliant recording career that followed the union of Dionne and Burt is one of the longest hit-making relationships ever, from their first hit recording "Don't Make Me Over" in 1962, to their Grammy-winning Number One hit "That's What Friends are For" (with Stevie Wonder, Gladys Knight, and Elton John) in 1986!

According to Dionne, "I met Burt when he was with another songwriter, Bob Hilliard, and they wrote a song called 'Mexican Divorce' for The Drifters. I was doing background [singing] and that was the year that he and [lyricist] Hal [David] started to become partners. I was doing some demo records and background work on sessions they were involved with. I did a demo for The Shirelles and they wanted the singer, not the song, and that was me. That started our relationship."

Recalls Bacharach, "I couldn't help noticing her. Dionne had something—it was there when I first met her: a kind of elegance, her flow and feeling for the music." It was similar to what Clive Davis years later heard in the music and singing of Whitney Houston.

After that, Dionne changed the spelling of her last name to "Warwick" and went to work immediately, cutting demos for Burt and his partner, Hal David, for the sum of forty dollars per song. Among the early songs that Dionne recorded for the fledgling team was a ballad called "One Less Bell to Answer," which eventually became a smash for The Fifth Dimension, and "Close to You," which became The Carpenters' hugest hit. Eventually, through her gospel background, Dionne, as part of the singing and writing trio of Warwick, Bacharach, and David, came to the attention of Florence Greenberg, the president of a small gospel recording label, Scepter Records. Dionne was offered a recording contract, with Burt and Hal writing and producing. Their first release, "Don't Make Me Over" became a Top Ten hit in December of 1962.

According to Warwick, "It was fabulous. We were all young and tender and didn't know where we were going. I was doing background singing and he [Burt] was just starting to write with Hal David."

The next two years saw unprecedented success as Dionne's lush and expressive voice catapulted hit after hit to the top of the charts with memorable songs like "Anyone Who Had a Heart," "Walk on By," "You'll Never Get to Heaven," "This Empty Place," "Reach Out for Me," and "A House is Not a Home." By 1964 she had attained international acclaim, and in her premiere at the Olympia Theater in Paris, she was introduced onstage personally by Marlene Dietrich.

Throughout the 1960s, Dionne Warwick became the most listened-to female voice over the airwaves. Her forte was for recording love ballads, which found equal popularity with the contemporary "Pop" radio stations, as well as the more traditional easy-listening stations. With Bacharach and David behind her creating the songs, she continued with her string of recording triumphs, which included such classics as "Message to Michael," "Trains and Boats and Planes," "Alfie," "I Say a Little Prayer," "(Theme

From) Valley of the Dolls," "April Fools," "Promises, Promises," and "Do You Know the Way to San Jose?" Several times she was nominated for Grammy Awards, and she won in 1968 for "Do You Know the Way to San Jose?" and in 1970 for "I'll Never Fall In Love Again." From appearances on television programs including *The Tonight Show, The Ed Sullivan Show*, and *The Carol Burnett Show*, Dionne went on to make her motion picture debut in *Slaves* with Stephen Boyd in 1969. However, in the early '70s her vast success suddenly changed.

Urged by the famous author of the astrology best-seller *Sun Signs*, Linda Goodman, Dionne added an extra letter to her last name to become known as "Dionne Warwicke." The spelling change was numerologically supposed to give her extra luck in her life and her career. Recalls Dionne of her disastrous additional vowel, "I know this sounds silly, but all my troubles started in 1971 when I added an extra 'e' to my last name. Linda Goodman, the astrologer, told me it would be a good idea. But it wasn't. In fact, everything went wrong afterward." She finally deleted the extra "e" in 1975—after the damage was already done.

Moving from Scepter Records to Warner Brothers Records in 1972, Dionne recorded her final album with Bacharach and David, entitled *Dionne*. The album represented the creative height of the trio's teamwork, including the definitive versions of "One Less Bell to Answer" and "Close to You." However, the magic was gone, the record-buying public wasn't interested in lovely ballads, and the album didn't sell well. After a decade of recording alchemy, the hot streak was over for the trio. Furthermore, Bacharach and David began feuding with each other, and they both left Dionne and her new contract with Warner Brothers Records high and dry. Dionne ended up suing Burt and Hal for $5,500,000 on the grounds of breach of contract.

Complained Dionne at the time, "It was just a matter, I think, of massive egos. But I was not privy to everything leading up to it, and I should have been, I felt. The two men obviously had gotten to the point where they didn't like each other much anymore. I don't know the reasons. Whatever they were, that was their hang-up, not mine. I don't care. But the least that could have been done after a ten-year relationship was a phone call from either of them saying that there's a little problem, and there may come a time very soon when we won't be existing anymore as a team. That would say, 'Dionne, get your house in order, prepare yourself.' I thought they were my friends. I now question it. But I don't owe them anything. As far as I'm concerned, they owe me an awful lot. A part of me is gone and will never be regained. I was the kid left out in the cold." The icy cold war was to continue into the mid-1980s.

For her subsequent LP's, Dionne went from producer to producer trying to recapture the hit-making formula with the likes of producers Holland, Dozier, and Holland (The Supremes, Martha Reeves & The Vandellas), and Thom Bell (The Spinners, Harold Melvin & The Blue Notes, Teddy Pendergrass). From 1972 to 1977 Dionne released six albums, and although her singing was up to par, the material was not, and none of the songs replicated any of the magic of her smashes of the previous decade.

As though these problems weren't enough for Warwick, in 1973 her marriage to Bill Elliot ended after twelve years and the birth of their two sons, Damian and David. Looking back on this period of court battles and lawsuits Dionne claimed, "Going through two divorces at once was really heavy duty!"

Throughout this slow period there were some rewards though. Dionne's 1975 duet with The Spinners yielded a Number One hit single, "Then Came You," which sold a million copies and received a Grammy nomination. In 1976, anxious to find another winning formula, Dionne teamed with Academy Award-winning soul stylist Isaac Hayes for a national tour billed as "A Man and a Woman." The tour elicited new interest in Dionne, and a two-record "live" album was released by the duo. In 1977 Dionne's sixth and most critically acclaimed Warner Brothers album, *Love at First Sight*, was released, and her contract with the label lapsed.

Pursued in 1978 by Clive Davis, Dionne optimistically signed with Arista Records. When it came time to suggest potential producers for her to work with, Clive proposed someone else who recorded for Arista, Barry Manilow. When Manilow went into the recording studio on January 22, 1979, the match produced one of the all-time biggest albums of her career.

According to Barry Manilow, "She can sing a ballad as well as Streisand. Dionne's one of the all-time best."

Returning the compliment, Dionne boasted, "Working with Barry was one of the easiest things I've ever done. Recording with him was like a big party. Barry's such a wonderful performer, you tend to forget he's also a brilliant producer."

After the release of her Manilow-produced *Dionne* album on Arista, in May 1979, Dionne Warwick stepped onstage at Carnegie Hall to a thunderous standing ovation. That night she ended an eight-year absence from performing in New York City. The standing-room-only event was a triumphant success. That September, by popular demand, she returned for another special night at Lincoln Center, where she was presented with a *Gold* album for her comeback LP, *Dionne*. The following February, Dionne won two more Grammy Awards for her new Manilow-produced Top 10 hits "I'll Never This Way Again" and "Deja Vu." The two Grammy Awards were the frosting on the cake of a year in which Warwick's career came full circle back to the top.

Since that time, Dionne's career in the 1980s continued to be a long succession of new peaks. On and off through the decade she was seen as the hostess and star of the popular television show, *Solid Gold*. In 1982 she went into the recording studio with Barry Gibb of The Bee Gees, and this union produced still another huge best-selling album, *Heartbreaker*. The title cut of that album went on to become a big Top Ten hit as well. In 1983 she was paired with Luther Vandross as her next producer and yielded the exciting album *How Many Times Can We Say Good-bye*. In 1984 Dionne teamed up with Stevie Wonder for the soundtrack album for the film *The Woman in Red*.

On the album she did with Luther, she not only sang the title song as a duet with him, but she also reunited with her old friends The Shirelles on the song "Will You Still Love Me Tomorrow?" And, that album featured one of Luther's favorite background voices singing behind Dionne: her own aunt Cissy Houston.

It looked as if it was a big era for reunions in Dionne's life. However, throughout this long time period, Dionne Warwick, Bacharach, and David had continued their long-running feud. Burt has since married lyricist Carole Bayer Sager, and they had been working together on several compositions. In 1984 Dionne was asked to sing the theme song for a TV show called *Finder of Lost Loves*, dueting with newcomer Glenn Jones. She didn't realize when she accepted the assignment that Burt Bacharach was the composer and producer of the song.

The recording of the song "Finder of Lost Loves" forced Dionne and Burt to patch up their differences. The experience was so positive that they decided to join forces for another song in 1985. The outcome was the incredible Number One hit single "That's What Friends Are For." The song was credited to "Dionne Warwick and Friends." The "friends" on the song were Elton John, Gladys Knight, and Stevie Wonder. The song's proceeds were all donated for research toward finding a cure for AIDS. The single eventually raised over $600,000 for the cause, and Dionne's *Friends* album went *Gold* and stayed on the charts for more than six months. It became the most successful single album of her long career.

For several years, Dionne has been considered part of Hollywood royalty. In fact, when Queen Elizabeth II and Prince Philip of England visited Los Angeles in the early 1980s, Dionne, along with Elizabeth Taylor and Frank Sinatra, was part of the welcoming committee on hand to greet them.

Simultaneously, Warwick has also had both pop and rock & roll credibility as well. In 1985, when dozens of stars—including Michael Jackson, Lionel Richie, Paul Simon, Tina Turner, and Bruce Springsteen—all got together to record the mega-hit song "We Are the World," Dionne was one of the many soloists on the song. A charming and well respected figure in show business, she can hang with Springsteen, and she was still buddies with Sinatra. Now, that's versatile!

No one was more proud of Whitney Houston's initial success than her cousin Dionne. According to Warwick in the 1980s, "It's nice to know the world's recognizing Whitney for the enormous talent that she is. Whitney's got the genes to be a star for a long time!"

Said Whitney of the influence that her famous cousin had on her, "What I got from Dionne was the class and elegance and the radiance, how she commands an audience." At the beginning of her performing career, there was no question that Houston styled herself after her classy cousin Dionne.

In February 1986, at the Grammy Awards presentation in Los Angeles, it was Dionne Warwick who presented the Best Female Pop Performance trophy that night. The winner was none other than her cousin Whitney. According to Whitney, while she was waiting for Dionne to read the name of the winner, "I was hoping my name would be there." It certainly was, and it became a proud moment for this talented family of singers.

In 1988, Dionne returned to the big screen, as one of the stars of the Burt Reynolds and Liza Minnelli detective film, *Rent-A-Cop*. She played the role of Beth, who runs a high-priced call-girl establishment. Her performance was one of the main highlights of the film.

In 1993, when Dionne recorded her *Friends Can Be Lovers* album, she and Whitney at long last teamed up for a duet. It became even more of a family affair when the writer and producer of the cut was none other than Dionne's son, David Elliot—who is Whitney's second cousin. The song was entitled "Love Will Find a Way." On this album, the song "Sunny Weather Lover" was another landmark, as it is the first song that Burt Bacharach had written with his old partner, Hal David, in over twenty years—and it was Dionne who was able to introduce it to the world. The album was "executive produced" by Clive Davis himself.

By 1994, Dionne again came into the spotlight in a big way. As the hostess of a series of the most famous "infomercials" of the decade, she was seen beckoning viewers to dial up The Psychic Friends Network, to have their fortune told. Warwick's presence on television was seen day and night, especially at the height of The Psychic Friends Network's success. She reportedly made a fortune on "hostessing" the infomercials herself. However, by the end of the 1990s she had parted company with the enterprise, and returned her focus to her singing career.

Dionne Warwick has had one of the longest and most glamorous singing careers in the business. With the initial success of Whitney Houston, it made it clear that a family tradition was underway.

Although Whitney's cousin Dee Dee Warrick had a career that was in the shadow of her older sister Dionne, she too had a notable recording streak. To make the association with Dionne clear, she also changed her last name to "Warwick." Signed to Jubilee Records, Dee Dee's first single was the song "You're No Good," which later became a hit for Betty Everett, and in the 1970s for Linda Ronstadt. In 1964 Dee Dee signed to Blue Rock Records, and proceeded to have a nice string of chart hits. Her recordings included "We're Doing Fine," which made it to Number 28 on the R&B charts. Then when she switched to Mercury Records in 1966, she had hits with "I Want To Be With You" (Number Nine R&B, Number 41 Pop), and "I'm Gonna Make You Love Me" (Number 13 R&B, Number 88 Pop). The Supremes and The Temptations later made the song into a bigger hit, but it was always associated with Dee Dee. In 1970 she moved to ATCO Records, and had hits with the songs "She Didn't Know (She Kept On Talking)" (Number Nine R&B, Number 70 Pop) and her version of Elvis Presley's "Suspicious Minds" (Number 24 R&B, Number 80 Pop). Her final chart hit was the song "Get Out of My Life" in 1975. In 1999, Dee Dee's contribution to R&B and Pop music was saluted by The Rhythm & Blues Foundation, as they presented her with one of their prestigious Pioneer Awards, and Dionne was personally on hand to present Dee Dee with her trophy. Sadly, Dee Dee died in 2008, of a long illness, following years of substance abuse problems.

Meanwhile, speaking of this brilliant Houston / Warwick family tradition, we now come to the equally fascinating story of Cissy Houston's own singing career. According to her, "I can express myself better in songs than by talking. Singing gets out all my frustrations and reveals the sadness and joy inside of me." And, "expressive" is exactly the quality her strong and distinctive singing voice possesses.

Although she is most famous for being a background singer, she is confident with her position in the record business. "I've always said, 'You don't have to be a star to be a star, because I was a star in the background!'" she proclaims. "You know, maybe that is one thing that kept my head together. I've been on so many stages and with some really great artists, and I always knew I could out-sing them all." Anyone who has seen and heard Cissy Houston perform live or on record, will attest to the fact that she has a "star" quality uniquely all her own.

Cissy's start in singing began in church. She was just five years old in 1937 in Newark, New Jersey. "I never wanted to sing," she ironically remembers. "I hated it. But with three sisters, two brothers, and a father who were always singing, I was beaten into it, and, of course, I had to sing in church since I was five." Together with her family she was first part of The Drinkard Four.

"When I was sixteen," Cissy continues, "my father died, and I got my first job in a cleaner's—taking paper off the hangers." Back there at the cleaner's, life didn't look too glamorous to teenaged Emily "Cissy" Houston. She later went on to a job making tubes on an assembly line at a toothpaste factory. This was not an occupation that she enjoyed either. Somehow she was always able to forget her troubles when she was with her choir singing.

It was when she was sixteen years old that she first organized The New Hope Baptist Church Young Adult Choir. It wasn't long before she was singing with several gospel groups, developing her own strong voice. After she organized The Drinkard Singers with her sister and her nieces Dionne and Dee Dee, she got a taste of what the show business aspect of the music world was all about. It was much more exciting than singing in church.

After Burt Bacharach and Dionne hit it off so brilliantly in the recording studio, Warwick was off on her own successful career as a singing star. According to Cissy's husband, John Houston, "People thought the group would fold when Dionne left, but with Cissy in the act it was a whole different sound. They began to wipe out all the other background singers."

Cissy's first recording session was singing background on a record with Ronnie Hawkins & The Hawks, who were later to evolve into the rock group known as The Band. Eventually, Cissy and The Drinkard Singers ended up reuniting with Dionne on Warwick's mid-'60s gospel album, *The Magic of Believing*.

Cissy soon realized that as much as she loved singing gospel music, there was little or no financial profit to be made from it, and she was tiring herself out. "I loved singing with my sisters," she explains, "but after a while I found we were being typecasted as a gospel group, and let's face it, there was no money in gospel. I had to continuously work a full-time job in order to make ends meet, and it was just wearing me out."

She struck upon the idea of taking herself and three of the girls from her church choir and starting their own singing group. And so, together with Myrna Smith, Sylvia Shemwell, and Estelle Brown, Cissy formed her own group called The Sweet Inspirations. Their first album, entitled *The Sweet Inspirations*, was released in 1968 on Atlantic Records, and their second single, "Sweet Inspiration," became a huge Top 20 pop hit.

Throughout the 1960s Cissy and The Sweet Inspirations sang background on several records, most notable on some of Aretha Franklin's classic Atlantic recordings. It's Cissy Houston's high voice that you can hear behind Aretha on "Ain't No Way" and countless other Queen of Soul hits.

Among the other singing stars whom Cissy sang behind were Wilson Pickett, Brook Benton, Bette Midler, Seals & Crofts, Neil Diamond, Paul Simon, Connie Francis, Herbie Mann, Dusty Springfield, Buddy Rich, Luther Vandross, Carly Simon, Elvis Presley, Burt Bacharach, Leslie Uggams, and the list goes on and on.

In her years in the business, Cissy has watched people come and go. She has also observed how show business can often destroy people. One of the biggest stars she saw physically abuse themselves and throw their lives away, was Elvis Presley. While he was heavily hooked on drugs, he declined to admit that he had an addiction. Since he heavily medicated himself on pharmaceutical drugs, he justified it by rationalizing that he was taking doctor-prescribed "medicine." According to Cissy, "You can become quite discouraged in this business. But I took a lot when I first started, and I will not let anything crush me. I've seen too many people crushed. I had something more than just this business. I had my husband and my three children and the saved me throughout all my disappointments. I would not let this business keep me down. Before I'd do that, I'd leave it. I believe totally in God. God has guided me through all these years and greatly so." Obviously, her faith has kept her strong all of these years.

The Sweet Inspirations never made any real money, although it seemed they kept working constantly. According to Cissy's husband, John Houston, who was the manager of the group, "The record companies made all the 'bread.' But you see, we're talking about a learning process. You look back and see all the money that went down the chute, the things you should have done."

Finally, in 1970, Cissy had enough of trying to make The Sweet Inspirations work as a singing group, and she decided to try to concentrate on a solo career. Unfortunately, in its first incarnation, it was not very successful. She signed with a small label, Janus Records. One of the songs Cissy recorded was a composition most people thought should have become a huge hit for her. It was a country song in which Cissy slightly changed the lyrics. It was originally called "The Midnight Train to Houston," but she decided to make it "The Midnight Train to Georgia."

According to John Houston, "There was a hit record! Everywhere we turned it was being bought and played. A lousy five thousand [dollars] was all that was needed to kick it over the top, to do the right kind of promotion. You're really at the record company's mercy if they don't have the money to promote it."

The song "The Midnight Train to Georgia," of course, became a huge Number One hit for Gladys Knight & The Pips in 1973. As Cissy recalls, "Then Gladys Knight recorded it, and we all know what happened to 'Midnight Train to Georgia.' But Gladys has been very kind, always mentioning where she got it."

Not everyone was so kind. John Houston remembered, "Time and time again, when record companies have wanted to star Cissy, the big names on their labels—people she's backed—have threatened to split the minute Cissy Houston gets promoted." They feared the competition of Cissy's incredibly strong voice.

One of the records that Cissy was featured on while she was still under contract to Janus Records was a Burt Bacharach album on A&M Records, aptly entitled *Burt Bacharach* (1971). On the album Cissy sings lead vocals on "One Less Bell to Answer," "Mexican Divorce," and "All Kinds of People." The album made it to Number 18 on the *Billboard* charts, and was certified *Gold* for selling over 500,000 copies in the United States. How ironic that these three vocals—which were among her strongest performances as a lead singer, should be on the album of her niece Dionne's producer. Funny how things do eventually come full circle.

However, things weren't going too swiftly for Cissy in the early 1970s. "I really don't know what went wrong," she says. "But whatever happened left me feeling very disgusted. I've been in this business a long time, and it discouraged me immensely to see people who seemingly started yesterday ride straight to the top. I thought about quitting and, for a time I just devoted myself to my family. But inside I knew I'd be back."

Cissy turned her focus back to doing background vocals for a time. In 1972 she got back together with The Sweet Inspirations to sing on Aretha Franklin's exciting *Young, Gifted and Black* album.

The following year Cissy toured with jazz musician Herbie Mann. She recorded an album with him and sang lead vocals on the songs "Be My Baby" and "I'll Be There."

It was about 1976 in New York City that a new kind of high-energy music began to take over the record business. It was something called "disco." Suddenly everyone was recording disco music. When New York City's Studio 54 discotheque opened in spring 1977, a whole new musical era was ushered in, and everyone from Barbara Streisand to Ethel Merman, to Mary Wilson & The Supremes was singing disco. A whole wave of new overnight disco stars also emerged on the scene. All of a sudden Donna Summer, The Village People, Dr. Buzzard's Original Savannah Band, and Gloria Gaynor were among the industry's biggest stars.

In 1977 Cissy had shifted her focus to becoming something of a legend on the New York City cabaret circuit. She was making waves by singing her own soulful version of the theme song from the Broadway show *Annie*, about the comic-strip character Little Orphan Annie. The song was called "Tomorrow," and there was no one in the business who could sing it like Cissy Houston could. Suddenly, people were flocking to see her at small cabaret clubs like Reno Sweeney in Greenwich Village, and the supper club Les Mouches on Eleventh Avenue and West Twenty-Sixth Street. That year Cissy had the most successful album of her career, on Private Stock Records, entitled *Cissy Houston*. On the album Cissy sang "Tomorrow," "He Ain't Heavy, He's My Brother," and "Make It Easy on Yourself," and she quickly made people forget the original recordings.

One night at a small cabaret called Reno Sweeney, Rock Hudson stopped in to catch Cissy's act. It was reported in the press that he looked up at the stage and shouted, "Sing it, sister, sing it!" Even Rock recognized true musical talent when he heard it!

It was inevitable in 1978 that Cissy too would jump into the middle of the disco craze. Nobody was buying ballad albums, everyone wanted to get up and dance. Cissy's biggest disco hit was a record that unleashed as much energy as she used on everyone else's records. The song was "Think it Over," and it was a big disco smash for her. Cissy's album of the same name was quite successful. It seemed that it was only a matter of time before she finally broke through and became the huge star that everyone predicted she would blossom into being. Private Stock Records at long last had been doing everything for Cissy that so many other record labels had only promised. Unfortunately, Private Stock Records went out of business at the same time that it looked as if Cissy was finally going to break through to the big time.

She then moved to Columbia Records and recorded an album entitled *Step Aside for a Lady*, which was basically a disco album. However, by the time it came out in 1980, disco was dead on the charts. So much for Cissy's big leap to the top. It seemed like every time something went right, something else went wrong. She came so close to mainstream stardom so many times, and yet she never allowed herself to become depressed about it. It was hardly the end of the world.

"I've been very fortunate in this business." Cissy claims, "I've never stopped working even without a current hit record. Somehow or other, God has made it so that I could always keep going."

In the 1980s, Cissy kept on working in nightclubs in New York City, eventually spotlighting her young daughter, Whitney, who was singing background vocals for her. Cissy also continued singing background vocals on record, especially on all of Luther Vandross' albums, and most notably on the albums he produced for Dionne Warwick and Aretha Franklin on Arista Records. Little did Cissy suspect, but it was going to be at Arista Records that her little girl, Whitney, was destined to become one of the biggest stars in the record business.

CHAPTER TWO

"A CHARMED CHILDHOOD"

To say that Whitney Houston was born into the music business is an understatement. Her mother was busy doing background vocals at Atlantic Records Recording Studios during the summer of 1963 when she was pregnant with her. According to Whitney, the recording engineers in the studio were concerned about Cissy's working into the final weeks of her pregnancy, but she just kept on singing.

"Mommy said the producers were real jittery, but she just told 'em to quit worrying and get on with it," Whitney says.

Her father, John Houston, laughingly said to Whitney, "You can't remember the first time you were in the recording studio, because your mother was pregnant with you!"

According to Cissy, when she was in the hospital, and in labor, she was passing the time by watching television. The program that had her attention was the Shirley Booth sitcom called *Hazel*. Booth played the part of a maid for a well-to-do family, and the woman she worked for—whom she referred to as "Mrs. B"—was played by an actress by the name of Whitney Blake. Cissy decided right then and there, that if she gave birth to a girl, she would name her "Whitney."

Whitney Houston was born on August 9, 1963, the youngest of three children. Her parents, John and Cissy, had already had two sons. Michael is two years older than Whitney, and her half-brother, Gary Garland is six years older than her. Cissy was never publicly forthcoming about her relationship with Gary's father, but John was always actively a father to him as well.

Growing up in her parents' New Jersey home, Whitney remembers being in an environment of total creativity. With her mother's career, her cousin Dionne's success, and her exposure to gospel music in the church, she always felt as if she was born to sing.

When she was just a little girl, Whitney was nicknamed "Nippy." On the back of the album cover of the *Whitney Houston* LP, she signs some of her personal "thank you's" to close friends as "Nippy." Explaining the name that has stuck since childhood, Whitney says, "My dad gave me that name when I was a little girl. I don't know [why], it's just that he gave me that name: Nippy!"

Raised as the youngest of three children, Whitney remembered mainly the good times. She said of her early life, with her two older brothers to tease her, "Being that I was the only girl, you would think that I had it rough. I did. But I must admit I wouldn't have wanted it any other way! In my family, all of my mother's brothers and sisters can sing, and all their children can sing, so it was nothing new for me to have a voice and be able to carry a tune," she proclaimed proudly.

As Cissy Houston's little girl, Whitney got her exposure to singing since she was a baby. "I grew up in the church, and gospel music has always been the center of our lives," she recalled. "It taught me a lot about singing. It gave me emotion and spiritual things, and it helped me to know what I was singing about, because in gospel music, the words mean everything. Now whatever I sing, whether it's gospel or pop or R&B, I *feel* it. I think I got my emotion from gospel singing, from my mom instilling it in me at an early age. You can't make people feel anything you don't feel yourself."

Whitney fondly remembered her home life: "Music was all around my house. There was the gospel music, but my parents listened to everything else, too—rhythm & blues, jazz, pop."

One of the special things that Whitney was able to do as a little girl that other people could not, was to go into the recording studios with her mother and watch some of the music industry's legends produce hit records. Whitney especially recalls being in the studio in New York City watching her mother singing with Aretha Franklin. She had come across the Hudson River from New Jersey, and she sat in the control booth watching the session from behind the huge panes of soundproof glass.

Said Whitney, "I remember when I was six or seven, crawling up to the window to watch my mother sing. And I'd be talking to 'Aunt Ree.' I had no idea that Aretha Franklin was famous—just that I liked to hear her sing, too!"

Watching Aretha had a lasting influence on Whitney. In the 1980s she stated, "Aretha has such a gut [feeling] about what she was singing. I said, 'I want to feel like that. I want to be able to make people feel like she's making them feel.'"

These trips to the recording studios left a permanent impression on little Nippy. "I'd have all kinds of conversations with Aretha and Wilson [Pickett]," she was later to recall distinctly. "I just remember being in an atmosphere of total creativity. When I heard Aretha, I could feel her emotional delivery so clearly. It came from down deep within. 'That's what I want to do,'" she remembers thinking to herself.

Both she and her older brothers found themselves accompanying their mother into New York City to watch her sing with some of the legends of show business. "Of course, there were people that we knew that other children didn't get the chance to be around. I had no idea then that they were stars. But, we were taught to be grateful for knowing those people," she says. "It was fun, but my mom made sure we didn't star-gaze at any of the successes surrounding her, friends in the business who exposed us to the bright lights and limousines at a young age." Growing up like that, it is easy to see why Whitney, at the beginning of her career, had such a down-to-earth attitude about her initial recording success. She was to admit at the time, "I was lucky because I got 'the star' . . . my mother, who was also 'the friend,' and my greatest teacher."

In one of her very first videos, for Whitney's song "Greatest Love of All," the concept of the video is that of a young girl going to a talent show and being encouraged by her mother. In the clip it is Cissy Houston who plays the mother to the little girl who grows up to be the adult Whitney. Although the video is a fantasy flashback, it is very much a case of art imitating life. Cissy was very supportive and instructive of Whitney when she was a little girl, especially when her interests turned towards a singing career.

Growing up, Whitney also looked up to her father, John Houston. In the mid-1980s he was an administrative secretary for the Newark Central

Planning Board. When Whitney's career took off, he became part of her management team. Said Whitney, amidst her first wave of recording success, "My dad is the backbone of our family. Any problem that I've ever had, he's always been there for me. He looks over all my business deals and everything. Most people don't know that my dad has been in the business for a lot of years. He used to manage my mom's group The Sweet Inspirations."

John Houston at the time proclaimed, "Nobody could beat those Sweet Inspirations." Little did he suspect, that simultaneously, under his own roof, he was raising one of the biggest recording stars of the '80s and '90s.

Like her mother, and her cousin Dionne before her, Whitney Houston's first singing experiences came in church. The first song that she ever sang as part of her local church choir was the gospel standard "Guide Me O Thou Great Jehovah." Thinking back on that hymn, Whitney described it as "a song that will stay with me for the rest of my life."

She remembered at the age of twelve, singing her first solo in church: "I stood there stiff as a board. But I sang this song and the people went crazy." That was where it all began for Whitney.

"When I decided to become a singer, I was twelve. I knew this was what I wanted to do. I knew that God had given me something, and that I ought to use it," she claimed.

John Houston remembered his daughter's first experiments with singing. "I'd hear all this hollerin' and screamin' down in the basement," he claimed. "Whitney'd be down there with one of Cissy's microphones singing along with Chaka Khan and Aretha records. I knew her mother was training her, but I wasn't paying much attention. One day Cissy said, 'Your baby is soloing in church for the first time this Sunday. Be there!' What I heard that day was the voice of a young woman coming from the throat of a twelve-year-old child. It blew my mind!"

How interesting it is to note that Whitney would be practicing to Chaka and Aretha songs. Who could have predicted that in time she would eventually become such a big star, that she would be singing duets with Aretha and with Chaka!

Whitney was later to proclaim, "One of the happiest experiences was finding out I could sing. When you're young, you're not too sure about much of anything. One day you want to be a teacher, the next day you want to be a doctor. When I started to sing in church, I was always singing in the choir, and when I was chosen to sing a solo song, I was scared to death! I wasn't sure whether I could do it. But then I tried it and I found out that there was something inside of me that made me feel like I do whenever I'm singing. It's an incredible feeling. In fact, it's like magic."

Growing up in a rough neighborhood in Newark, New Jersey, Whitney always felt that she wasn't like the other kids. Her mother would dress her up in frilly dresses with bows in her hair. Often as a little girl she would come home in tears, because the other girls had teased her or pulled the bows from her hair. Her mom instructed her that she had to learn to stand her own ground, and fight her own battles. Young Whitney very quickly began to develop her own toughness, and it wasn't long before she was able to stand up and fight for herself. Still, she often felt like a loner, and had few close girlfriends as a child.

Recalls Whitney, "In grammar school some of the girls had problems with me. My face was too light. My hair was too long. It was the black-consciousness period, and I felt really bad. I finally faced the fact that isn't a crime not having friends. Being alone means you have fewer problems. When I decided to be a singer, my mother warned me I would be alone a lot. Basically we all are. Loneliness comes with life."

In 1977, when Whitney was just a young teenager, her parents' marriage crumbled. John Houston moved out of the house. Explained Whitney in the late '80s, "They'd laugh a lot. And when times were hard, they fought, which taught me a lot about love and sacrifice. For a while they stayed together for our sake. Finally they realized that the only way for them to stay friends was to split. It was strange not to have my father there, but he lives just ten minutes away. Besides, even if you're not together physically, the love never dies."

Although he no longer lived in the house, John Houston remained active in Whitney's life. He later explained, "I used to give her flowers. I helped her with term papers in high school—she'd call me on Tuesday for a paper due on Wednesday. She's always been great with that 'Daddy' bit."

The break-up of her parents caused Whitney to become even more sullen and withdrawn than she had been before. To keep her daughter busy and occupied, Cissy took Whitney wherever she went. According to Whitney, "My mother was a major influence for me. When I decided to get into singing seriously, she took me by the hand and taught me how to do it right. I was only twelve when I had made up my mind to get into singing. But I didn't start officially working until I was seventeen. In between those years, I got involved in doing background sessions and working with my mother in clubs on weekends. Having her show me the way helped me to groom myself for the business, as well as grow and understand what it was about," she stated with sincere gratitude.

Other people who grew up with the same opportunities that Whitney had, such as meeting recording stars at an early age, might have ended up spoiled by the experience. Not Whitney. She was able to look back on those days in the studio, in the choir, and touring with her mother, with thanks. "It was lots of fun," she once claimed, "but I wasn't spoiled in any way. I did get to experience a lot of things that maybe other kids didn't, like being around other entertainers. But I got to know them like they were family, and contrary to what other people may think about being a show business brat and all that, it wasn't like that at all."

In the 1980s Whitney spoke of the strict disciplinarian way in which Cissy brought her up. "I don't believe in sparing the rod," she claimed, "My mother didn't. Sometimes she would tell me something and I would walk away mumbling. She hated that, and I got smacked in the mouth many times for it. Now I can appreciate that and I'd do the same thing to my kid."

With regard to her voice, Whitney explained at the beginning of her career, "God gave me this gift. My vocal training was really the gospel singing I did in church because I put inspiration into it and special feelings of emotion."

She further elaborated on her mother instilling a sense of reality in her from the very beginning. "When I told my mom this was what I wanted to do, she prepared me for all the things that would come. She taught me that fame is not all it's cracked up to be. Sometimes you may hate it, and sometimes you may really love it," she said.

Cissy made sure that Whitney went to a school where there was the kind of discipline that she felt her daughter needed. She enrolled her at the all-girl Mount St. Dominic Academy. According to Cissy, "Whitney was a very delicate kind of child, and I thought she needed a certain kind of environment. I thought she could get more education there. I know it can be regimented, but that wasn't my main reason. Besides, I didn't need anyone to enforce my rules. Early dating, cruising around—she wasn't going to do that anyhow. She wasn't going to wear stockings until I said, 'O.K.,' even if her friends did. No make-up, no lipstick, no high heels. And, no discussion! She didn't like it. She hated it. Sometimes she would go to her father, her brothers would too—because they thought he was a little more lenient. But they didn't get around what I told them."

Concerned that Whitney had few friends, and was still a bit withdrawn, Cissy came up with the idea that her daughter should get out and do some things on her own. It was Cissy's idea for teenage Whitney to volunteer to be a counselor at a local camp for children. It was there that she was to meet a lifelong friend, who was to become very influential and very important in her life. This new friend was a girl two years older than Whitney, by the name of Robyn Crawford.

Robyn was more athletic and sports oriented than Whitney. From the very beginning, there were rumors that Houston's friendship with Crawford was much closer than just being social friends. However, Whitney never cared what anyone thought of her relationship with Robyn. The two girls had an instant bond that has lasted throughout the years.

According to Kevin Ammons, in the 1996 book *Good Girl, Bad Girl*, "Kids at camp teased them, calling them 'dykes' and making kissing sounds when they passed by, arms linked and heads together in some private, intimate conversation. But the two girls didn't seem to care. They were both tough, headstrong young women and their relationship was volatile."

When she was in high school at all-girl Mount St. Dominic Academy in West Caldwell, Whitney began modeling, and she had started to sing behind Cissy in her nightclub act. Between school, camera work, and singing, she had a full schedule to contend with at an early age. "It was a sacrifice," she said. "But I was doing something I like to do—sing—and that was my real training after graduation."

This ability to juggle several activities was one of the reasons that when her initial wave of solo success suddenly became hectic in 1985, she was able to handle it. She had grown up learning to deal with working on several projects simultaneously, and she was able to complete all of them with maximum success. When her life became a whirlwind of recording sessions, photo sessions, interviews, video shoots, and traveling, Whitney was ready, willing, and able to accomplish all of her goals. When she was still a teenager, several offers came in for Whitney to drop out of her schooling and become involved immediately in the record business, but her parents made sure that school came first. "I didn't sign a contract to sing until I was eighteen," she was to clearly state. "My parents made sure that I had a childhood and that I was a little girl when I was supposed to be a little girl, and that I was a teenager when I was supposed to be a teenager, and that I finished school."

Cissy Houston was to add, "I wanted her to finish school first, because I knew if she got started in the business, there'd be no stopping her."

Whitney explained of her progression toward deciding on a singing profession, "I was singing in church at around age eight, and that's when I really started singing. I started singing professionally at twelve." Did she always want to be a singer? "No I didn't," she replied. "I wanted to be a teacher, you know, or a veterinarian. But when I opened my mouth [to sing], I said, 'Whoa! Wait a minute. Why not?'" And so, that's exactly what she did.

When Whitney was a junior in high school, Cissy realized her daughter was quite serious about pursuing a singing career. Said Whitney, "My mom realized, 'This is it, she's going for it.'" Again, her parents wanted her to ease into show business and not miss out on her teenage years. Whitney further explained, "They said, 'She's still young—we want her to finish school, be a teenager, act crazy.' And I *was* having fun, so I took their advice and just waited."

While she was in high school, teenage Whitney Houston was already well on her way to a professional singing career. She had the voice; now all she needed was a little firsthand experience, and she was about to get it.

CHAPTER THREE

"THE TEENAGE YEARS"

It was in 1978, when Whitney Houston was just fourteen years old, that she started singing background vocals in her mother's nightclub act. Whitney will never forget that first night in Manhattan at Town Hall on West 43rd Street, when she made her stage debut. Town Hall is a concert auditorium in the middle of the Broadway district, yet it is still small enough of a theater to have an intimate feeling to it.

Cissy Houston had a big record with her version of "Tomorrow," from the Broadway show *Annie*. It was featured on her 1977 *Cissy Houston* album. When she performed the song on stage, she decided that she would have Whitney step forward on the song and sing some of the lead vocals. Whitney remembers being scared to death in the moments before she stepped into the spotlight. But once she started singing, all of her fears vanished, and she realized that right on center stage was where she longed to be.

The *Cissy Houston* album was such a hit that in 1978 Cissy returned to the recording studio in New York City with producer Michael Zager. The year 1978 was a momentous time for disco music, and that year Zager had a big hit of his own called "Let's All Chant" accredited to The Michael Zager Band. Especially in New York City, it seemed like the only kind of music that was selling was pure disco. So, when it came time to record the follow-up to the *Cissy Houston* album, Zager decided to produce her next LP with more of a disco flavor to it.

Cissy Houston's 1978 album *Think It Over* was exactly that—very "up" and disco sounding, especially on the title cut. The album was recorded at Secret Sound Studios in New York City. When Cissy went into the studio to record the vocals, she brought her teenage daughter Whitney, to sing backgrounds on the album. Whitney can be heard on all but one of the cuts on the *Think It Over* album. The song "Think It Over," which is a six-minute disco cut, went on to be a big Top Ten hit on the dance charts when it was released.

In reality, Cissy Houston truly excelled at singing heartfelt ballads. However, since it was disco that dominated the marketplace, she gladly followed Zager's instincts into following the current trends. This ability to really "sell" a ballad to an audience, and then have them up and dancing to the next song, was part of the musical versatility that Cissy instilled in Whitney. She, too, learned to really milk a ballad for its emotional depths one moment and effectively shift gears into an up-tempo number.

During this same period of time, another "Houston" scored an across-the-board smash on the disco and the Pop charts. Her name was Thelma Houston, and her song "Don't Leave Me This Way" became a Number One hit in 1977 on Motown Records. Although many people mistakenly assume that Thelma is related to Cissy and Whitney, she in fact is not a relative.

In 1980, when Whitney was sixteen years old, her life took an un-expected turn. She was in Manhattan one afternoon, walking with her mother near the intersection of Seventh Avenue and West 57th Street. This is the intersection where Carnegie Hall is located, and it is also the neighborhood where a small modeling agency named Click was located as well.

According to legend, a scout for Click Models ran into teenage Whitney Houston and suggested that she make an appointment with the agency, as he thought she would make a perfect model. Confirms the founder and president of Click Models, Frances Grill, "Yes indeed! She ran into someone who works for me, Dean Avedon. He found her in the hallway downstairs, and he asked her if she wanted to be a model. He brought her up, and I loved her. And we started her modeling."

Frances was very impressed with young Whitney. "She wasn't who you see now," she explained in the mid-1980s. "She was a very pretty kid, and she had this wonderful mother with her. You can tell very quickly in these kinds of situations; just put them in front of the camera and something happens. They have a 'language.' The talented ones are really going to do it, and she had that language . . . Everyone adored her. She was 'a very fresh little energy' is all I could call her. And, very 'clean-spirited' is the way I would put it."

The Click modeling agency was instantly able to get Whitney work. Recalls Grill, "She did a lot of 'editorial' modeling. She worked for *Mademoiselle*, she worked for *Seventeen*, and she did a number of products."

Eventually Whitney ended up on the pages of several high fashion magazines, including *Cosmopolitan*, *Young Miss*, and *Glamour*. She also did some work for several print advertisements for Revlon cosmetics, and for the carbonated beverage Sprite. Later she moved from Click Models to another agency called Wilhelmina Modeling Agency.

However, as Whitney was to later confess, "I like modeling, but singing was in my blood." She further explained of her modeling career, "I like modeling, but it's a sideline, really. It's not something like singing, where I really *believe* in everything about it. It was something I could do, so I did. But singing always comes first."

Modeling also carried with it, a certain connotation that it was part of the partying, drugs, and liquor "fast lane." According to Whitney in the mid-80s, "It can be. Well, my mom, she didn't allow that, so I wasn't into that fast life, but it can be." During this era of her fledgling singing and modeling career, she was still Cissy's "good girl."

So, Whitney continued singing with her mother, simultaneously working on her budding modeling career on the side. She not only appeared with Cissy at Town Hall, but she also performed behind her mother at several clubs in Manhattan including gay-oriented supperclub Les Mouches, as well as jazz clubs on West Ninety-Sixth Street, and a famed West Side cabaret club called Mikell's.

Pat Mikell is a friend of the Houston family, and Cissy performed at Mikell's several times, with Whitney singing backgrounds. According to Pat in the 1980s, "Cissy was a great mother. She was tough. That's why Whitney's a class act."

Eventually, Whitney graduated in her mother's act, and she went from just singing a solo on "Tomorrow," to having another spotlight song in the show as well. Apparently, one particular night Whitney was getting a bit too cocky about her own vocal power, and she began to show off for the audience. To punish her for being boastful on stage, Cissy took away her solos for two weeks until she learned to behave. Whitney was later to say, "My mother is my best friend and my greatest inspiration. Of course, sometimes your mother's *your mother*, too!"

Whitney felt as if she was literally growing up on stage before nightclub audiences. As time went on, her mother gave her more responsibilities and shared more opportunities with her. According to Whitney, "My mom taught me everything that I know about this business, about singing, studio work, and things like that." Of performing in her mom's act, she explained, "I had a song to do and then as I got a little older, she gave me two songs to do, and I went on from there."

One singer, whose voice Whitney always admired, has been Chaka Khan. In 1980, Cissy Houston was hired to sing backgrounds on two cuts of Chaka's album *Naughty*. She decided that Whitney had done such a great job on her own *Think it Over* album that she would bring her into the studio to work on Chaka's record as well.

At that point in Khan's career, she had just recorded her first solo album, *Chaka*, in 1978, and she was continuing to record as the lead singer of the group Rufus as well. The hit song on the *Chaka* album was a Nicholas Ashford & Valerie Simpson composition called "I'm Every Woman." The album was produced by Arif Mardin, and Cissy Houston was on the background vocals of several of the cuts. This was another point of sheer irony, in that the song "I'm Every Woman" was a number which Whitney herself was to re-record in the 1990s and turn into a huge hit of her own. Then to bring the song full circle, in 1999 Whitney and Chaka were to sing and record that same song together as a duet on the *Divas Live '99* TV special and album.

In 1980, when *Naughty* was recorded, Arif again produced, and Ashford & Simpson contributed two cuts to the album: "Clouds" and "Our Love's in Danger." Cissy brought along Whitney for the recording session, and the great vocal mother-and-daughter team can be heard behind Chaka on both of those songs. Whitney racked up similar background vocal credits on albums by Lou Rawls and The Neville Brothers which were recorded and released during this same time period.

As Whitney explains of her progression, "First I was singing with my mother and I was in her act—in her club act. Then I started doing some recording here and there and she'd take me into the studio and we'd do background sessions together for other people. Then, when I was eighteen, I signed a contract and I made an album."

The album that she was referring to was an LP by the "studio" group called Material, and the song that she is heard on is a cut called "Memories." The trio—who called themselves Material—were keyboard player Michael Beinhorn, bass player Bill Lasswell, and sound engineer Martin Bisi. Since none of the three guys were singers, they simply hired different lead singers to do the vocals on their recordings so that every record would feature different singers. In 1981, Material went from doing experimental instrumental recordings to scoring a huge dance hit called "I'm Busting Out." The song was also a big smash for the singer they hired for the recording: Nona Hendryx. Nona is most famous as one-third of the incredible trio: LaBelle. Together with Patti LaBelle and Sarah Dash, Nona and the group LaBelle are known for their original Number One smash "Lady Marmalade."

"I'm Busting Out" proved such a big smash that Nona landed a solo recording deal with RCA Records, and Material ended up with their own recording contract on Elektra Records. In 1982, Material produced an album called *One Down* for Elektra. There are eight cuts on *One Down*, and each of the songs has a different lead singer providing the vocals. Nona Hendryx does a song entitled "Take a Chance," Nile Rodgers of the group Chic, plays guitar on "I'm the One," eclectic sax player Oliver Lake is on a cut called "Come Down," and Tony Thompson of Power Station and Chic plays drums on several of the songs.

On the second side of the *One Down* LP, Material enlisted the services of a singer who had not yet recorded a lead vocal of her own. That singer was Whitney Houston. The song is entitled "Memories," and Archie Shepp plays the tenor saxophone solo on the cut. The song is a nice, easy ballad, and Whitney's vocal sound great on it. In fact, when *The Village Voice* reviewed the *One Down* album, they noted, "Guest stars Whitney Houston and Archie Shepp transform 'Memories' into one of the most gorgeous ballads you've heard." The record didn't sell well, but it gave Whitney Houston a nice starting point, and is now known as her first solo recording.

What the *One Down* project also did was to bring Whitney to the attention of Elektra Records, and its then-president, Bruce Lundvall. Apparently, Lundvall was very interested in signing Whitney to a recording contract with Elektra, but the deal never quite came together. However, the song "Memories" brought young Whitney Houston to the attention of other record producers, and it wasn't long before other recording offers were presented to her.

Paul Jabara was known in the industry as a multi-talented guy. He acted in the films *Day of the Locust* and *Thank God It's Friday*, wrote several hit songs, and produced several hit records as well. His major claim to fame was for writing the song "Last Dance" for Donna Summer, which she sang in the disco film *Thank God It's Friday*. The composition won Jabara an Academy Award as Best Song in 1980. He also wrote the disco classic "No More Tears (Enough is Enough)" for Barbra Streisand and Donna Summer.

In 1982, Paul Jabara called up Paul Shaffer and told him that he had a great idea for a new song called, "It's Raining Men." Shaffer is known nowadays as the band leader for TV's *The Late Show with David Letterman*. Jabara and Shaffer completed the song, and the concept alone sounded like an instant hit. Paul Jabara signed two singers to record the song: Izora Armstead and Martha Wash. Izora and Martha had become famous in the 1970s for singing behind Sylvester on all of his biggest disco smashes, and they called themselves Two Tons of Fun. However, for their recording of his song "It's Raining Men," Jabara renamed them: The Weather Girls.

Needless to say, the disco song "It's Raining Men" became a huge hit. Here was Columbia Records with a big smash single, and no album to sell. Hence, Jabara enlisted the services of several vocalists and produced the 1983 album *Paul Jabara and Friends, Featuring The Weather Girls, Leata Galloway, and Whitney Houston*. Again, for Whitney, this was another one-shot recording deal, but she ended up with a second lead vocal under her belt. The song was a beautiful ballad called "Eternal Love" that gave Whitney much more of a chance to show off her expressive voice. After these two solo recordings, it seemed that the whole New

York City record industry was buzzing over Cissy Houston's little girl and her incredible voice.

Whitney was garnering several favorable mentions in the press. Reviewers were showing up to see Cissy's show, and in the process they also wrote glowingly about young Whitney. *The Newark Star-Ledger* proclaimed during this era, "There's no doubt about it, Whitney Houston is going to be a star!" *The New York Times* raved, "She is a talented with tremendous potential!" *Billboard* gave their stamp of approval by stating, "Whitney has the pedigree and the style to be a major vocalist." And, *The Village Voice* heralded, "Sensational word-of-mouth has been going around about Whitney Houston. She has a big voice, the kind that makes you laugh and weep at the same time."

By this time in her career, Whitney had signed a contract with a personal manager, Eugene (Gene) Harvey. According to Harvey, "When she had just turned eighteen, two major labels wanted to sign her, but I felt it was too early. I didn't want her to have a deal with those kinds of pressures at that point."

Columbia Records, which released the Paul Jabara album, and Elektra Records, which released the Material album, were both offering Whitney recording contracts. Another label, Arista Records, had made an offer as well. Ultimately, it was to be the Arista deal which was the one that was accepted.

Remembers Gene Harvey, "Before we signed with Arista, Whitney asked me one day, 'Do you really think that somebody with a nice voice singing nice songs can still sell records today?' She said it very innocently and out of the blue. I said, 'Oh, yeah!'"

Whitney had signed her management contract with Gene Harvey in September of 1981, before she appeared on the Material and Paul Jabara albums. It was in April of 1983 that Whitney Houston signed her solo recording contract with Arista Records, under the watchful eye of her mother. With Whitney's signature on the recording contract, a major chapter in musical history was set into motion. While at Arista Records, Whitney Houston was not only going to make records, she was going to BREAK records!

CHAPTER FOUR

"ENTER: CLIVE DAVIS"

It was quite clear in April of 1983, when Whitney Houston signed her Arista Records contract, that it was a top-priority signing, and that the company had every intention of making sure that she was going to become a major star. Of course, in show business one can package, produce, and present a record, a movie, or a product with every intention of making it a hit, but it doesn't always work. However, when Clive Davis, the founder and president of Arista Records took Whitney under his wing, from the very first day, she was personally being groomed to accomplish great things.

Davis is something of a legend in the record business. He had made his mark in the recording business at Columbia Records by discovering, signing, and developing stars like Santana, Janis Joplin, and Sly & The Family Stone. Arista Records was born in 1974 when Davis left Columbia Records and took over a small company called Bell Records. By taking over Bell, he inherited two relatively unknown singer / songwriters who were under contract to the label. Dropping everyone else's options at the label, he decided to retain the pair of singer / songwriters, who had each released only one album apiece. Clive changed Bell's name to Arista, and proceeded to turn the company into a major hit-making force. He also turned the two relatively unknown singer / songwriters into major-league stars. Their names were Barry Manilow and Melissa Manchester.

Throughout the 1970s, Arista scored one hit after another with its varied roster of stars that included Patti Smith, Ray Parker Jr., Alan Parsons, Air Supply, and Angela Bofill. While he was interested in developing new talent, Clive Davis had also been interested in reviving the careers several of his favorite singing stars from the '60s and '70s, including Melanie, Martha Reeves, and Eddie Kendricks. In the early 1980s he was busily reinventing the recording careers of Carly Simon, Dionne Warwick, and Aretha Franklin.

Aretha had been in the recording business in 1960 when she had been signed to Columbia Records. While at Columbia she recorded several albums, but never really broke through to mainstream fame. When her contract lapsed with that company, she signed to Atlantic Records, and proceeded to launch the most impressive string of hit singles and Grammy Awards in the rhythm & blues realm—with Cissy Houston often singing behind her. From 1967 to 1974 she had churned out hit after hit, including "Respect," "Chain of Fools," "Think," and "Rock Steady." However, when the disco era began, like so many soul stars of the late '60s and early '70s, she found herself left behind. In 1980, when her long reign at Atlantic Records came to an end, Clive Davis signed her to Arista Records, teamed her up with the right producers and collaborators, and suddenly she was selling more records that she ever had at Atlantic.

Acknowledged as having somewhat of a "Midas touch" in the record business, Clive longed to launch the career of a new major female star. For a while it looked like Phyllis Hyman was destined to go on record as his greatest discovery. A tall, statuesque, beautiful woman who excelled at jazz and contemporary ballads, Phyllis became a star on a certain level. Her biggest chart hit was a beautiful Barry Manilow produced ballad called "Somewhere in My Lifetime." In the early 1980s she became one of the stars of the Broadway hit *Sophisticated Ladies*, and she even garnered a Tony Award nomination for her performance. However, in spite of several critically received albums for Arista, Phyllis never really broke through to major international superstardom. Phyllis also—unfortunately—had several personal problems in her life, which eventually led to her career downfall (and her untimely death by suicide in the mid-1990s). But, when Clive Davis saw the raw talent that young Whitney Houston possessed, he was determined to launch her recording career in a huge way. In a very real sense, Whitney ended up with the career achievements which were originally blueprinted for Phyllis Hyman.

After a decade in existence, Arista Records had been so successful, that it enabled Clive to devote a full two years to developing Whitney's look, her sound, and her image. He spent an unprecedented $250,000 planning and recording her first album. Clive made sure that Whitney was seen at the right parties, and that she was heard singing at several key venues and private music industry functions. Every detail of Whitney's career-to-be was meticulously plotted, and personally overseen by Davis himself.

Even before she recorded any songs for her debut album, she made an unprecedented appearance on TV's *The Merv Griffin Show* in 1984. The special episode of the famed variety / talk show was a salute to Clive Davis and his ten years as a star-maker with Arista Records. It was on this particular program that a proud Davis introduced Whitney to the American television audience. In his introduction, Clive proclaimed of his new protégée Houston, "You either got it or you don't. She's got it." Whitney proceeded to take center stage and she successfully brought down the house with her stirring version of the song "Home," from *The Wiz*.

Finally, in 1984, Whitney recorded the first song that was to end up her debut album. The former lead singer of the group Harold Melvin & The Blue Notes, Teddy Pendergrass was concurrently making his return to recording with a new album and a new record label. Following a tragic automobile accident that left him paralyzed from the waist down, Pendergrass had shifted from CBS Records to Elektra Records. Ballad expert Michael Masser was producing seven of the cuts on Teddy's new *Love Language* album, and Luther Vandross produced one song. The song that Luther produced was "You're My Choice Tonight (Choose Me)," which was the theme from the film *Choose Me*. Ironically enough, Cissy Houston is the solo female voice featured on that cut.

Producer / writer Michael Masser at the time was famous for composing the hit ballad "Touch Me in The Morning" for Diana Ross. For Teddy's album, he had written a duet with Linda Creed called "Hold Me." Based on Whitney's performance on the Material album for Elektra, she was invited to do a guest appearance on that particular song for Teddy's album. "Hold Me" ended up being a hit single for Teddy and Whitney as a duet.

Meanwhile, after several years of recording for Motown Records, Michael Jackson's older brother Jermaine left that label and signed a solo contract with Arista Records. The year 1984 literally belonged to Michael Jackson, so when it was announced that Michael, Jermaine, Tito, Randy, Jackie and Marlon Jackson were all going to reunite for the 1984 for a new album and their *Victory Tour*, it was major news. Jermaine needed a hot solo album to support while he was performing on the widely publicized sold-out tour, and that's exactly what he came up with. The 1984 *Jermaine Jackson* album on Arista hit the Top 20 in America, was certified *Gold*, and included a hit single "Dynamite." Also on the album were two hot duets: "Tell Me I'm Not Dreamin' (Too Good to Be True)" with Michael Jackson, and "Take Good Care of My Heart" with Whitney Houston.

In August 1984, Arista Records threw a huge party for Jermaine at a discotheque in New York City called The Limelight. As the entertainment for the party, Whitney Houston performed "Home," and a couple of other solo songs. Then, Jermaine joined her on stage for their duet "Take Good Care of My Heart."

Celebrity photographer Charles Moniz was at The Limelight to take photos of that event. He recalls, "At the time it was Jermaine Jackson who was the huge star. In 1984 all of the Jackson siblings were the focus of the press. I recall Janet and LaToya running around the club to catch their brothers' act. When Whitney came out on stage to sing, she was a relative unknown commodity compared to Jermaine. However, it was clear that she had a bright future ahead of her. She was presented as though she was a star already."

The last weekend in November of 1984, Arista Records threw a party to officially celebrate the tenth anniversary of the company. The party was held at The Museum of the City of New York, at East One Hundred Fifth Street and Fifth Avenue, and it was a beautifully catered formal event. Some of the performers who recorded for Arista Records were there, including Patti Smith, Alan Parsons, and Dionne Warwick. As the entertainment for the evening, Dionne Warwick got up on stage and sang, and Whitney Houston also performed. All of us who were there that evening were very impressed by what we saw and heard.

Throughout 1984, Whitney's talents were constantly showcased by Arista Records, and still she didn't have an album in the stores yet. There was also a musical guest appearance by Jermaine Jackson and Whitney on the popular afternoon TV soap opera, *As the World Turns*.

Amusingly, in addition to this exposure, Whitney Houston's voice was on millions of TV screens every day. Cissy Houston was heard singing the lead on a version of The Pointer Sisters' hit song "Jump," in a Bounce laundry fabric softener commercial. And, it was Whitney's voice that was distinctly heard in the background.

One of the people who was working for Arista at that time, and who was working directly with Whitney at the time, was Kenneth Reynolds. Ken held the position of Head of R&B Product Management during the beginning of Houston's career at Arista. He also appeared in her very first video, as the chef in the restaurant scene in the video for the song "You Give Good Love."

Reynolds explains, "When I joined the company in October of 1983, Whitney had already been signed, and had already been talked up in the company. Everyone was aware of her, everyone was aware of the whole big marketing and promotional campaign that was going to be planned behind her career. It was defined that this was *the* next performer. As opposed to, 'Here's another singer.' We were talking about the next performer in the league with Aretha Franklin, Diana Ross."

There were meetings about where she should be seen, who she should meet, what she should wear, and how her hair should be styled. Every aspect of her promotion was carefully planned, and it was made clear that it was Clive Davis who had the final say on all important decisions.

With regard to the styling and marketing of Houston, Reynolds revealed in 1986, "You can overdo it. And it's hard when someone is as pretty as Whitney, because the thing is that you really have very little to do. I think you just have to style her in terms of wardrobe and the direction in which you want to market her. But everybody at the company had real concrete ideas of how they saw this girl. And, I think it got to the point where Clive then put his two cents' worth in and said, 'I like everybody's ideas, and this is great, but since we're not together, these are *my* ideas." Davis made it clear that he had full "veto" power on all matters concerning Whitney Houston.

Having worked around a lot of stars, Ken Reynolds found Whitney be very charming and professional at the very beginning of her career. Speaking of being on the set for the filming of her first video, he claims, "She came in there like a real polished professional, which is a quality that I noticed in everything that she did. She may have been new to the business, but she conducted herself like someone who had really been around from day one. There's this coolness, always this sophistication about her."

All she needed now was the right album and the right solo debut single. The record turned out to be the *Whitney Houston* album, which was not released until February of 1985. However, several months—in fact almost twenty-four months—were required to produce this landmark of an album. No album in recent record business history had been so meticulously plotted and planned as far as material selection, sound, packaging, and marketing.

To come up with the right producers and songwriters, an unprecedented process was employed. In New York City at Sweetwaters, and in Los Angeles at the Vine Street Bar & Grill, special showcases were held in which Whitney preformed one-hour sets of her strongest songs at that time, and producers and songwriters were invited to witness the legend of Whitney grow before their eyes. After each of these two bi-coastal show sessions were over, Clive Davis and Gene Harvey contemplated the material that each of these producers and songwriters submitted.

According to Harvey, "It was a matter of searching for the right material and producers. It was Clive's philosophy and ours that we not push this girl out there right away. We decided to wait and do the best job that we could, and if it took a little longer, so be it." The process obviously was to work flawlessly.

Clive had so much faith in Whitney all along the way that he wanted this to be the ultimate album for her. He proclaimed at the time, "She has such range, from theatrical to gospel to soul." He wanted to show off all of the sides of Whitney to the best advantage. He didn't care what it cost, he was determined to make this album a smash.

Whitney herself relied on her own instincts as well when it came time to selecting the right songs with which she felt comfortable. After all, she had been watching her mother and other stars like Aretha Franklin making hit records for years, so she knew what to look for in a song that would be right for her. She explained of this process, "Mom knows the business very well, and she taught me real good!"

Cissy once said, "I try to bring feeling to every song I do. I have to *feel* it before I can make anyone else feel it. Everything I do is real." Well, her philosophy must have rubbed off on her daughter, because Whitney was about to follow her advice totally.

Whitney was later to recall of this long two-year process, "I did showcases and invited record-company people. People were interested in me from the time I was fifteen—it was kinda like they were just waiting for me to grow up. Everybody put their bids in. So I sat down with my managers and my parents, and I remember this long, drawn-out meeting: 'What are you gonna do? Who are you going to go with?' I went into another room and sat in a chair, and my mother came in after me and said, 'You know, this is very difficult, but I'm going to tell you the truth: You should go to where you are going to get the best out of it.' Meaning, let's say a company offers you a contract, and they're saying: 'Whitney, you can choose the songs. You can do whatever the hell you want to.' As opposed to Arista, with Clive Davis saying: 'We'll give you this amount of money, and we'll sit down, and as far as the songs you want to do, I will help you. I will say: "Whitney, this song has potential. This song doesn't."' So my mother was saying to me, 'You're eighteen years old. You need guidance.' Clive was the person who guided me."

Whitney and Clive seemed to hit it off right from the start of their working relationship. According to her at the time, "It's uncanny how much Clive and I think alike. If he likes a song, it's almost one hundred percent sure I will, too."

The producers who ultimately worked on the *Whitney Houston* album were all established hit makers. They included Michael Masser, Kashif, Jermaine Jackson, and Narada Michael Walden.

One of the key people who was working at Arista Records during this time of material selection and image development for the *Whitney Houston* LP was Barbara Shelley. She was the head of West Coast publicity of Arista. It was her job not only to publicize the label's newest star-in-the-making, but to organize the listening session / showcase in Los Angeles that ended up garnering Whitney several of the songs with made her a star.

According to Barbara in 1986, "In putting the album package together, there was no rushing this project. Neither Clive Davis nor Eugene Harvey nor anyone involved would settle for second best. So much care went into this album that it didn't seem like it would ever come out. When the album was completed, Clive was still having second thoughts; he was afraid that there were not enough hits to compete with Whitney's talents! He finally succumbed to the pressure of this personal decision. Should he keep this girl's talents under wraps any longer? Or, should he release an album that he knew was good, but was it *good enough* for Whitney's talent? That shows you how much he personally cared about making this the right project."

Shelley also recalls, "It was like two years of preparation. And, Gene Harvey called Clive every day to discuss what Whitney should be wearing on the album cover. Should the art director on the East Coast do the cover? Whitney is a high-fashion model, and she can have many looks. Which would be the right look to put on the album cover? There were like ten album-cover photo sessions. Whitney can look so many different ways. What was the right way to portray her to the public the first time out?"

Not only was she impressed with Houston's singing talent, but she was dazzled by the young girl's manners, and the way she carried herself. Barbara Shelley recounts, "The very first time that I met Whitney Houston was on Jermaine Jackson's yacht, which was docked in Marina Del Rey. We were conducting some interviews with Jermaine to publicize his current album at the time [*Jermaine Jackson*, 1984]. Whitney was in town to record songs off of her debut album which Jermaine was producing for her. I knew that she was Dionne Warwick's cousin, and I knew that my friend Gene Harvey was managing her, so I was especially pleased to meet her. I remember her on that first occasion as a quiet, pretty, young gal who was on the deck of Jermaine's yacht. I was impressed by her sweetness, and the sense of virtual innocence about her. She had the optimistic face of a young child, on the body of a beautiful fashion model. She had such a sincere interest in meeting all of us from the record company, and talking with us, and wanting to know about us. Several times, she sent out 'thank you' notes to members of the Arista staff for help along the way. This is the type of caring person that she is."

One of the most accurate ways to find out what a singing star is really like, is to talk to the musicians she worked with in the beginning. Bashiri Johnson played percussion on the song "You Give Good Love" from her first album, and on "Love Will Save the Day" on the second album. According to him, "When I first met her she was very professional. She was really relaxed, it was a loose situation in the studio. But you can tell with some people who is going to make it big. I worked on Madonna's first record, and I didn't even know who she was at the time. The impression that I got from Madonna was that she was going to be a big, huge star, and she knows it. And, I got the same impression from Whitney, although she was a little more sophisticated, and a little more professional. I would say that Whitney's aura didn't come off as brash. Madonna comes off very aggressive, but Whitney is more of a lady . . . I knew that she was going to be a huge success. I could just sense it from looking at her. For one thing, she's a very attractive girl and she looks like an angel on stage."

These statements, which were made by the people with whom she was working during the 1985–1986 era, truly underscores how important the "image" of Whitney Houston was crucial to her instant success. She was positioned and marketed as the perfect, poised, charming, delightful, church-raised girl next door. In the mid-1990s, when she began to get a reputation for being spoiled, difficult and demanding, it made her fall from grace all the more disturbingly dramatic and tragic.

CHAPTER FIVE

"HER BRILLIANT CAREER"

The *Whitney Houston* album has been heralded as the strongest and most stylistically varied and hit-filled solo debut album that had been released to date. Whitney has to be credited with having the natural vocal dexterity and emotional range necessary to have inspired and successfully performed so many totally different and appealing songs on this album. There is not one un-dynamic or lackluster song on it. Two decades later, it still stands up as the best over-all album of her entire career.

However, the real credit goes to Clive Davis for having recognized Whitney's vocal strengths and for lavishing her with the unprecedented $250,000 production budget that it took to assemble this package. From the first listening, it was unmistakably clear that this was no hit-or-miss album. A lot of forethought obviously went into the process. With so many new pop artists debuting on the international marketplace each year, it really takes a special kind of intuition not only to recognize a singer's "star potential," but to know which producers with whom to match an unproven singer.

Whitney, in her mother's nightclub act, and in her two showcase concerts, inspired her four producers to come up with their most exciting material for this album. Michael Masser is a master at producing ballads. Jermaine Jackson's forte comes on songs with a strong melodic sense and sweet harmonies. Kashif is great at weaving vocals and crisp, clean, energetic music together in an electrifying way. And, Narada Michael Walden is known for creating hit songs that sound like a party set to music—like he did that same year on Aretha Franklin's "Freeway of Love."

According to Whitney, "I listened to the songs first on the demo tapes. I listened to what they were saying and then their melodies. Basically, I look at what I can do with a song and I'll work with the writer and consult him or her on the changes."

The first song on the album, written by a composer who only goes by the name of LaLa, is entitled "You Give Good Love." Whitney's torchy vocal is blended with an ethereal chorus of female voices. The message of this emotional love song is one of dramatic emotional heights. Houston said at the time it was released, "'You Give Good Love.' When I first heard it, in its original form, I really loved it and I wanted to stick close to what it was, because I felt it was so great in its form [as a demo tape]. So, Kashif and I just worked on it. The words stayed the same, but we did change the melody in different parts of the song . . . A young lady by the name of LaLa, she wrote that song. Well, that's her name, but her [real] name is LaForest, but she's 'LaLa.' She wrote that song. I first heard it, [and] I fell in love with it, and I said, 'That's the song I want to do!'"

"Thinking About You" picks up the pace with Kashif's multi-layered and rhythmic musical tracks. The use of male and female voices behind her give Whitney's impassioned singing amply strong support. The effervescent synthesized keyboards keep the crisp, fresh, up-tempo song cracking with energy.

"Someone for Me" starts out slow and delicate for a few seconds, and all of a sudden it blasts off into full gear like a jet plane taking off. A thumping bass line throbs while guitar riffs prod the funky chorus line, repeating the song's title like a chant. Whitney's vocal is all high intensity as she lyrically ponders why she doesn't have a date on a Friday night. The lyric lines about her mother urging her out of the house to have some fun, add to the innocent image that Whitney evoked at the time. This was Jermaine Jackson's best production on the album.

"Saving All My Love For You" is an old-fashioned and romantic torch song—1980s style. Whitney's super-strong voice is literally chilling on this tour-de-force performance. The seductive saxophone work by Tom Scott accentuates the pleas of the determined woman Houston lyrically portrays. In the plot of the song, we find Whitney playing the devoted "other woman" in an obviously scorching love triangle.

The Jermaine Jackson duet, "Nobody Loves You Like I Do," takes Whitney back to an innocent kind of devoted love. A classic love song, the use of pedal steel guitars give the harmonic medium-tempo song an almost country-western flavor to it. The pair's voices work exceedingly well on this cut, especially when their voices harmonically entwine.

The powerhouse cut on the album is the full-throttle dance number "How Will I Know." Narada Michael Walden produced this hot cooking lesson in looking for love. Whitney's voice virtually erupts with excitement. The wailing sax, sledgehammer beat, and call-and-response background vocals—including Cissy Houston—make this a surefire hit.

"All at Once" lets up the power to provide a strong ballad. Written by Michael Masser and Jeffrey Osborne, Whitney shows off the beauty of her voice on the extended notes, which are lushly set off by a full backing orchestra. This Masser-produced number is a perfect showcase for Whitney's uncompromising and gorgeous voice.

The Jermaine Jackson duet "Take Good Care of My Heart" continues the duo's collaborative work with peppy aplomb. Again, the production is fresh and exciting, showing off Jermaine's years of hit making expertise at Motown.

"Greatest Love of All" was originally used as the theme song for the Muhammad Ali 1977 autobiographical film, *The Greatest*. It was originally recorded by George Benson, and it was written by Michael Masser and the late Linda Creed. The conviction with which Whitney delivers this song is filled with such passion that it is presented like an anthem of the self-realization of personal worth. Whitney's mesmerizing singing and the message of the song is the reason it eventually became such a universally appealing hit when it was released as a single.

A confidential source revealed to me that there were several versions of this song recorded. The source proclaimed that Clive Davis was seriously torn between which recording of the song was ultimately going to be included on the *Whitney Houston* album. Apparently, it was Arista vice president Dennis Fine who persuaded Clive to release the version of the song in which Whitney's voice peaks in dramatic crescendos. Fine made his decision while listening to Whitney's three different versions of the song. Hearing it played over the stereo tape player of his car made him realize which "take" on the song would sound the best on the radio.

Whitney's debut album ends with her duet with Teddy Pendergrass, the Michael Masser-produced "Hold Me." The juxtaposing of Teddy's low, smooth singing and Whitney's higher and more innocent voice yields an exciting performance that showcases both performers to maximum success.

When Whitney's album was finally shipped to the stores in late February of 1985, the debuting performer breathed a strong sigh of relief. Whatever the outcome was to be, it was now up to the public. According to her at the time, the stress of producing this ultimate album was out of her hands. "I'm grateful," she said, "It takes the pressure off. I know some people say I'm going to be a star, and all that, but I don't even have to think about that because I know everything's been done, and what's going to happen will."

The press was overwhelmingly positive from the very start. *Billboard* claimed of the *Whitney Houston* album, "This auspicious debut for the young, full-voiced Houston has the soul of the old school and the smarts of the new . . . Done with a great deal of panache, and more than a casual attempt at 'star quality.'"

Rolling Stone glowed, "Whitney is en route to a big career—those pipes, and those looks are not to be denied . . . You get more than a hint of her smooth power in 'How Will I Know' and intermittently throughout the album, but 'The Greatest Love of All' is the track that builds the most convincingly. With the right songs and settings she could be an earth-shaking performer."

USA Today found it to be: "A sparkling self-titled debut album . . . Not only does she resemble a modern-day Nefertiti, but she's also making music waves with a passionate voice that mixes searing Sunday-morning gospel and a kind of rhythm & blues pop!"

The New York Times said of Houston, "Artistically, her debut album is a personal triumph over material that, generally speaking, hews to conservative pop formulas . . . One of the hallmarks of Miss Houston's singing is a continuing tension between a poised self-assurance that one would normally associate with singers ten years her senior, and a compressed youthful exuberance . . . An extraordinary singer whose flexible, rangy pop-gospel voice has a core of steel, she is heir apparent to the female soul tradition of Aretha Franklin, Gladys Knight, and her first cousin Dionne Warwick!"

The Desert News in Salt Lake City, Utah illuminated, "Her vocal abilities on her first LP are electrifying . . . Whitney employs a vocal style not at all different than Diana Ross, and she applies those crystal-clear vocals to a wide range of emotional love songs, ballads, and soul . . . it is a dynamite combination!"

Fashionable *Cosmopolitan* called the album "A dazzling study in cool . . . this gorgeous girl who Gives Good Love is merely sensational with a song!"

While, *Newsweek* proclaimed, "[On] her debut album of pop love songs . . . Houston does bring a charming combination of innocence and seductiveness to the glitzily produced arrangements . . . the years she spent in a Newark, New Jersey, Baptist choir, which her mother directs, are evident in the emotional wallop she can deliver when singing full blast . . . an impresario's dream!"

Amusingly comparing her to her prime rival at the time, Madonna, *People* magazine raved, "With her powerhouse voice, arresting looks, and unspoiled demeanor, she's a classy firebrand who appeals to those grown weary of material girls!"

The ultimate success that Whitney Houston's debut album achieved startled everyone involved with it. "You Give Good Love" was the first single that was released from the album, and it was really the test. In America when it shot up to Number One on the R&B charts, and made it to Number Three on the Pop charts, it looked like she was well on her way. However, when the singles "Saving All My Love For You" and "How Will I Know" rocketed consecutively up to Number One on the Pop charts, it was evident that Whitney was a major success story in the making.

According to Whitney, "I love singing ballads. I really love ballads, but I like singing up-tempo stuff too, so, it's great to do both."

Up until 1985, Donna Summer, Connie Francis, Brenda Lee, Roberta Flack, Cher, and Olivia Newton-John were the only female soloists to rack up two back-to-back Number One Pop hits. In 1986, when Whitney's "Greatest Love of All" hit Number One, dropped out of that slot, and again jumped to Number One spot, she became the first female singer ever to accomplish that feat! Likewise, the *Whitney Houston* album continued to break records by eventually logging in over ten weeks at the top of the American pop album charts. Whitney was so appealing to the whole music world that she also became a Top Ten artist in Canada, England, Australia, Holland, Japan, and Germany.

Whitney also found herself swept up into a trend that was finding more black artists crossing over to the top of the Pop charts, which had previously been dominated by white rock & roll groups. *Thriller*-era Michael Jackson, Lionel Richie, Prince, and Tina Turner were paving the way for Whitney, all benefitted by the concurrent advent of MTV and its nonstop video programming. According to Whitney's manager, Gene Harvey, "It worked out great, because pop radio became more accepting of black music. As Whitney debuted, all the circumstances were there."

Clive Davis was also surprised at the speed with which Whitney's momentum built in the short span of a year and a half. He was to point out, "From a marketing point of view, we kept things very low-key, knowing there's a potential backlash in how the public and critics can eat up artists after a certain amount of commercial success. We wanted to establish her in the black marketplace first. Otherwise, you can fall between the cracks where Top 40 [radio] won't play you and R&B won't consider you their own."

Davis further explained at the time, "We felt that 'You Give Good Love' would be at the very least a major black hit, though we didn't think that it would cross over [to the pop charts] as strongly as it did. When it did cross over with such velocity, that gave us great encouragement."

To support the sales of her album, Whitney hit the concert road in the spring to drum up support, and let live audiences know what she was all about vocally. During May 1985, she spent much of her time doing intimate club dates. Among her first engagements were appearances in Los Angeles at The Roxy (May 22–23), in Dallas at Judges Chambers (May 24–25), in Chicago at Park West (May 29), in Atlanta at Moonshadow (May 30), and in Washington, D.C. at the Warner Theater (May 31). Right afterward, Whitney spent the summer opening Jeffrey Osborne's concert dates across the country.

She then showcased her singing talents at prestigious Carnegie Hall, where she sold out two concerts in the autumn of 1985. From that point onward, she was strictly a headliner. In the summer of 1986 her first major solo tour of American was one of the most successful and popular events of the entire season.

Although she could sing like a goddess on stage, from the very beginning, critics did note that she was quite stiff in performance. While her videos were quite lively and visual, they cleverly depicted her surrounded by dancers, so that the viewer could not tell that she had no natural sense of rhythm and movement. This was especially evident on the large stage at Carnegie Hall, where she stood particularly still and sang center-stage throughout her show.

After her initial wave of success, Whitney was approached by her father, John Houston, wanting to take a role in her career's management. She agreed to that plan, and from that point forward, for the next several years he took part in managing her career, making it something of a family business.

Her phenomenally successful solo album and the public performances weren't the only exposure outlets for Whitney's talents. Since soundtrack albums were suddenly hot on the charts in the mid-'80s, in the summer of 1985, when the album from the John Travolta / Jamie Lee movie *Perfect* was released, Whitney was one of the stars featured on it. She again teamed up with Jermaine Jackson to record the exciting song "Shock Me," which was produced by Michael Omarian. The film and the album were substantial hits that summer, and the album put Houston in an elite setting, sharing album cuts with new and established artists The Pointer Sisters, Wham!, The Thompson Twins, Dan Hartman, Nona Hendryx, and Lou Reed.

Also, in the spring of 1986, Jermaine Jackson released his second Arista album, *Precious Moments*. For it Whitney joined him on the song "If You Say My Eyes Are Beautiful," which is the lushest song that the duo recorded together.

As though all of this exposure wasn't enough to make the public aware of who Whitney Houston was, she also signed a contract to do a television commercial to promote Diet Coca-Cola. The advertisement was the hottest sixty-second spot to air on TV since Michael Jackson did the

Moonwalk for Pepsi-Cola in 1984. In the Diet Coke spot, Whitney looked bewitchingly beautiful, and sang with unbridled energy. Commented a writer for *The New York Daily News,* in an article about singing stars plugging commercial products, "How could I watch Whitney Houston sing her heart out for Diet Coke and then consider drinking something else?"

On top of all this exposure that Whitney's music was making on the radio air waves, from 1985 to the first half of 1986, she also filmed and released four video versions of her top hit songs. In June of 1986, each of these four songs were released on a videocassette entitled *Whitney Houston: The #1 Video Hits,* which became an immediate sales hit. In America, it entered *Cashbox* magazine's Music Videocassette Chart at Number One. Unquestionably, the appealing look and sound of these four videos, and their constant rotation on MTV, truly cemented her stardom. Her videos not only enhanced the public's awareness that a new star had arrived on the scene, but also suggested that she might have a huge future in front of the movie cameras as well.

The *You Give Good Love* video takes place at a Greenwich Village nightclub / restaurant during an afternoon rehearsal session. It opens with the operator of a video camera adjusting his lens, when he is enticingly distracted by the sounds of a beautiful singer onstage in another room. He proceeds down a long corridor, and there is Whitney mid-song. As she sings the lyrics to the heartfelt song onstage, everyone in the place, including the cooks in the kitchen, all of them stop whatever they are supposed to be doing, and they wander out, mesmerized, into the dining room of the club to watch Whitney, and to get into her singing. She is alluringly dressed in a tight-fitting hot-pink Spandex pantsuit, and a black leather jacket, and the video is rife of full-frame close-up shots of Whitney's pretty face and her luscious lips. There was no question that this video was as much about her beauty as it was about the song.

The *Saving All My Love For You* video was filmed in London, England, and was directed by Stuart Orme. In the plot of this particular video, we find Whitney caught up in a love triangle. The video opens with a mysterious-looking young woman giving Whitney the "evil eye" in a London nightclub. Whitney is laughing and talking with friends, and the mysterious woman in question clearly doesn't approve of Whitney's presence. Amid the song, as the plot unfolds, we find that Whitney portrays the part of a recording artist who is in love with her handsome record producer.

Whitney's *How Will I Know* video offered an excitingly colorful change of pace. Plotless, funky and bursting with energy, we find gorgeous Ms. Houston dancing about seductively in a skintight low-cut metallic mesh dress. Together with a troupe of young dancers clad in black, Whitney is seen running through a maze of multicolored paint-splattered panels, asking the musical question: "How will I know I am in love?" There is one particular shot where she asks, "How will I know?" and the image of Aretha Franklin appears like a fairy godmother.

When questioned about Aretha's brief "cameo" in the video, Whitney explained, "I've known Aretha since I was a little girl. She's like a part of the family: my Auntie. I call her 'Aunt 'Ree.' [She's] an inspiration to me musically; I love Aretha so much, I thought that would be great to have her in that slot in the video." The footage of Aretha had been lifted from Franklin's "Freeway of Love" video—which was also a smash hit from this era. Continued Houston, "Brian Grant directed, and he came with the concept of all of that. He does all that stuff, which is great!"

Taking the filmed format to the point of "art imitating life," gave rise to the *Greatest Love of All* video. Filmed onstage and backstage at Manhattan's famed Apollo Theater in Harlem, the video is a complete scenario of Whitney Houston and her famous mother in the past and the present. In it we see Whitney as a little girl about to make her stage singing debut.

According to Cissy, who co-starred as herself: "The video is like a dream. It goes back to when she was a little girl. Whitney is part of the 'Amateur Hour.' She's afraid and I encourage her to go on: 'You can do it,' that kind of thing. It's really a wonderful concept."

The video begins with present-day Whitney wandering around onstage singing the lyrics of the song while musicians, set designers, electricians, lighting people, and other behind-the-scenes people are getting the stage ready for the show. Amid the song Whitney flashes back to herself as a little girl preparing for her stage debut, and being encouraged by her mom. Young Whitney was played by ten-year-old actress Keara Janine Hailey.

In the present-day sequence, Whitney is seen in her dressing room touching up her make-up. She is clad in a white beaded gown with spaghetti straps. Her hair is spiked up on top of her heard, and she is wearing a pair of exotically bejeweled large earrings. As she touches up her lipstick, she again flashes back thirteen years to her mother helping her in the dressing room prior to the children's talent show.

At the song's end, grown-up Whitney rushes offstage to embrace her mother, who is waiting for her daughter in the wings, just like in the old days. The whole effect of the video concept is sheer "magic," and it presents a touching image of a devoted mother and daughter, on this incredibly inspiring song.

According to Whitney at the time, she really enjoyed making each of the four videos that were contained on her *#1 Hits* video cassette: "They're fun. They're really a lot of fun: almost like silent movies with just singing, but it's fun!" These first forays in front of the camera were definitely previews of coming attractions for young Whitney. It wasn't long before the push was on to direct her into a full-fledged film career.

CHAPTER SIX

"THE GLAMOROUS LIFE"

As 1985 drew to an end, it was time to begin tallying the year's biggest successes. When the press and the record industry heralded the most triumphant hit-makers of the past twelve months, the name of Whitney Houston was repeated time and time again. It was clear that within a relatively short period of time, she had made an indelible impression on music critics and record buyers alike.

Billboard magazine, in its annual year-end issue, ranked Whitney Houston and her recordings on sixteen of its "Top" listings. Among them, she was named the publication's Number One "Top New Pop Artist," and the Number One "Top New Black Artist."

In early 1986, the awards began sweeping in, and Whitney seemed to be on everyone's list as one of the hottest new stars on the musical scene. On January 27, she took her first two American Music Awards, in the categories of "Favorite Video Single, Soul / R&B" for "Saving All My Love For You," and the "Favorite Single, Soul / R&B" for "You Give Good Love."

Next came *Rolling Stone* magazine's annual Reader's Poll. In that 1986 issue of the publication, Whitney was declared the "Best New Female Singer—1985."

Now it was time for the most prestigious award of all: The Grammy Awards. In January of 1986, when the twenty-eighth annual Grammy Award nominations were announced, Whitney was mentioned in three categories, and LaLa was nominated as the songwriter of "You Give

Good Love." The awards she was up for, were "Album of the Year," "Best Pop Vocal Performance—Female," and "Best Rhythm & Blues Solo Performance—Female." Conspicuously missing from the nominated categories was Whitney's name under the heading "Best New Artist."

Nominated in that category were the names of A-Ha, Freddie Jackson, Katrina & The Waves, Julian Lennon, and Sade. Predictably, Clive Davis, after all of his work on developing Whitney's talent and "image," went totally ballistic over the fact that his brilliant new protégée was omitted from that particular category. The whole music industry was talking the following week, when Davis wrote a blistering editorial in the January 18, 1986, issue of *Billboard* entitled, "What Does 'New Artist' Really Mean?" According to the National Academy of Recording Arts and Sciences (NARAS)—which presents the Grammy Awards—Whitney had appeared on Teddy Pendergrass' album and Jermaine Jackson's album, both in 1984, so she was not eligible to be nominated in this category.

Davis's fiery editorial began with, "How is it that a recording artist can be voted 'Favorite New Female Artist' by the readers of *Rolling Stone*, named 'Newcomer of the Year' in music by *Entertainment Tonight*, 'Top New Artist' [in both Pop and R&B] by *Billboard*, sell nearly 4 million copies worldwide of her very first album and not be considered a candidate for 'Best New Artist' by the National Academy of Recording Arts and Sciences?"

Whitney herself took the whole issue quite maturely, shrugging her shoulders and commenting, "These things happen." According to her at the time, the omission was quite inconsequential, and she felt the most important thing for her to do at the time was to "keep my feet on the ground no matter how big things get."

She further commented of the Grammy Awards, "If I win, I win. It's an honor of course, but I feel the same as I did before. I feel like a real Cinderella. It's a very emotional time for me."

The Grammy Awards presentation was held on February 25, 1986, and when it came time for the reading of the nominees in the category of "Best Pop Vocal Performance—Female," it was Whitney's famous cousin, Dionne Warwick who presented the award. When she read off the name of the winner, her face lit up when she announced that it was Whitney's performance of "Saving All My Love For You" that was the recipient. In that category she was competing against Madonna ("Crazy For You"), Linda Ronstadt (*Lush Life*—album), Pat Benatar ("We Belong"), and Tina Turner ("We Don't Need Another Hero.")

Accepting the award onstage, Whitney hugged Dionne and thanked "God, who makes it all possible for me," and her mom and dad, whom she called "the two most important people in my life!"

The week of March 8, 1986, after a year on the *Billboard* album chart, finally the *Whitney Houston* album hit Number One in America. It had been a slow build, but now with a chart-topping album, a Grammy Award, and two American Music Awards, little "Nippy" had really arrived. She was now one of the hottest female singers of the year, and there was much more to come.

The next honor that was bestowed upon Whitney was to come from her very own hometown of Newark, New Jersey. In April of 1986 at a gala concert, Whitney was presented with the Key to the City of Newark by Mayor Kenneth Gibson. Since her father, John Houston, worked at City Hall, she had known Gibson, and had been to the governmental building several times before. However, on that particular day she commented, "It feels different now. I've got the keys!"

The success of the *Whitney Houston* album grew at an astronomical rate during the first half of 1986. In the United States, the Record Industry Association of America (RIAA) awarded the LP "Sextuple *Platinum*" honors for having sold in excess of 6,000,000 copies domestically. At that point, it became the biggest-selling debut album by any artist in the history of recorded music.

After it finally hit Number One, the *Whitney Houston* album logged an astonishing fourteen weeks at the top of the *Billboard* charts in America. At the time, only one other person had surpassed that record, and it was Carole King and her incredibly appealing *Tapestry* album. For Ms. Houston, this was just the beginning her success.

That particular year, Whitney's life hit such a fast-paced stride that it was hard for her to catch up with herself. For the moment, it seemed that she had everything in perspective. She was determined to remain the same person she was before fame swept her into a whole new fast-paced existence. From the outside, she seemed very self-confident and grounded.

She did her best to keep a modest stance. She recalled, "You know, it gets to the point where the first couple of million you go, 'Oh, thank you, Jesus!' I mean let's face it, you make a record, you want people to buy your record—period. Anybody who tells you, 'I'm makin' a record 'cause I want to be creative' is a fucking liar. They want to sell records. As it went on—and it went on—I took a very humble attitude. I was not going to say, 'Hey, I sold 13 million records—check that shit out.' My mother always told me, 'Before the fall goeth pride.'"

Interestingly enough, when Whitney's career began to take off, her mother and father were often photographed together with her, even though they had been divorced for several years. She moved out of her mother's house, and took her own apartment, located close-by. To celebrate her newfound success, she bought herself a black 1986 Mercedes-Benz. Other than that one extravagance, for the time-being she remained pretty much the same young girl she had been before fame found her.

According to her, most of her relationships with her friends pretty much remained unchanged for the time-being. What she didn't care for, was suddenly being treated like a "star" by some her friends. "They no longer call me 'Nippy,' but 'Whitney,'" she said at the time. "When I go to visit I'm treated like some kind of goddess. I'm the same kind of girl I was five years ago, with the same morals and values. I do have a lot more money, and I'm a lot busier, but that's basically it."

She also explained that she had suddenly become much more worldly. According to her, "What is exciting for me is to be able to do whatever I want to do, like traveling for instance. I recently enjoyed a trip to Europe, and Paris was 'the best!' I did a lot of shopping. I also love escaping to the Caribbean for a relaxing break. And I'm starting to get into writing music."

Painted a distinctive shade of purple, she referred to her new residence as her "lavender apartment." Since her apartment in Woodbridge, New Jersey was in such close proximity to her parents' house, she explained, "Being close to my family is very important."

According to Cissy, "One of her brothers [Gary Garland] sings in her act, and the other one [Michael Houston] manages her, so, 'yes,' you'd have to say we stay close."

Whitney reinforced that by explaining at the time, "My parents—the love and patience and security they wrapped us in—have been most beneficial to my career. My mother's input is major. She's been a part of this business for many years, so I get professional advice and motherly guidance from her. In the past year my father insisted that I get more into the business end of my career."

She explained at the time, "In this business, I think sometimes people are moving too fast. So, I'm taking it slow. Sometimes when you're going in one direction, people want to pull you in another direction. It's taken me eight years to get to where I'm at now. I have been enjoying this business longer than people think and much longer than the public has known me. Longevity is what counts in this business, though, and I just hope and pray I'm still here, alive and singing in twenty years."

However, the first signs of stress were beginning to show. According to her in 1986, "While I was doing shows this summer, I deliberately scheduled only four days a week. I need private time. I don't necessarily do anything with it—maybe I just clean up my apartment or take a walk—but I need it. On the road, I have so much fun with the band, laughing and kidding around during sound checks, and my assistant is always telling me to stop it, cause I'll use up my voice. I don't think I could do it, though, if I couldn't have that kind of fun."

Already she had experienced a mishap with her voice, coming down with swollen glands, which rendered her unable to sing. She explained, "I did it one night in Los Angeles, and the next morning I couldn't say a word. I finally called Dionne in a total panic. Her doctor told me I couldn't sing for a week. I had to cancel a show, which I hated to do. It felt totally unprofessional, even though I wasn't faking. It was the worst night of my life."

On July 4, 1986, when America is celebrating Liberty Weekend, and commemorating the one hundredth birthday of the Statue of Liberty in New York City's harbor, Whitney Houston was one of the celebrities to be chosen to perform during a gala televised celebration. In Liberty

Park, in Jersey City, New Jersey, in the shadow of The Statue of Liberty, Whitney sang her Number One hit, "Greatest Love of All." According to her, that song was personally very important, especially with the message it imparted: "I was born just a few short miles from here in Newark, New Jersey. This has been a wonderful year for me, and being part of this fantastic night of music is the icing on the cake. As the youngest performer of the evening, I'd like to sing a special song which I feel has something to say to all of us, especially to you young people," she said that night. "Our young people need to hear that song and realize that it's about loving yourself. If you can love yourself through all your rights and wrongs and faults, then that's the greatest love of all. That's the message."

Her performance of "Greatest Love of All" on the Statue of Liberty television special was so excitingly popular, that it brought her further accolades. In August of that year she won an Emmy Award for "Outstanding Individual Performance in a Variety Program" for her appearance on the TV special. It seemed like there was nothing she could not do. Furthermore, she spoke publicly against drugs, she praised her parents, and she sang emotionally patriotic songs about America. She was a clean and wholesome pop icon who seemed to appeal to everyone. At this stage of her career, her image was every bit as important as her singing ability.

There was all kinds of talk at the time about Whitney Houston being heralded as a "role model" for young girls. Barbara Shelley of Arista's publicity department stated in 1986, "Dionne Warwick, who is Whitney's cousin was, is, and has been a 'role model' to young black women all over this country who grew up in the last twenty years. Dionne is a sophisticated, highly-educated, very talented woman whose persona certainly crossed over all racial lines in furthering the progress of black women in America. To this next generation, Whitney Houston will surely be an important 'role model,' and not just the next generation of young black women growing up, but of all young women growing up, because of the standards of excellence that she has strived for and achieved. To think that two women from two different generations of the same family could have this impact on the world is quite phenomenal!"

However, Whitney wasn't 100 percent comfortable with the whole "role model" issue. She, herself stated, that she was "not wild about people looking at me as a 'role model.'" Instead she offered this advice to her peers, "Before you get into something, know what the consequences are. Take your time. You're young and you're supposed to be having fun. But set your goals. Don't just do what everybody else is doing. I never wanted to be like anybody else. I always wanted to be an individual. I always wanted to have a unique perspective."

And, at the time she considered herself a "good girl" who avoided the wild life. She claimed, "Some of my friends even did drugs, but I avoided it because I don't need it; I'm already high. I just don't want drugs to be a part of my life, because I know that eventually they will ruin you. Drugs kill you mentally and physically. You'll die one way or another." How fascinating this statement is indeed, from the perspective of what we know about Whitney today.

She also said of her spiritual beliefs, "I believe in God the Almighty. My parents raised me in such a way that I don't have to do all those things that others are doing around me. You just anchor yourself with God; you can resist a lot of temptations. Prayer helps a lot." Her image at this point was that of a church-going, pure, All-American girl.

The wonderful thing about squeaky-clean Whitney during this era, was that she also appealed to members of the rock and pop worlds as well. On September 15, 1986, she performed the song "How Will I Know?" at the third annual MTV Video Music Awards. Ms. Houston won the MTV Award in the category of "Best Female Video" for "How I Will I Know?"

In November 1986, Whitney journeyed to England where she completed her first European concert engagements. A roaring success on the other side of the Atlantic, all of Houston's shows in the U.K. were sold-out affairs.

Kenneth Reynolds, who worked with Whitney at Arista, claimed in 1986, "I think acting is a natural move in her career, just watching her persona in the Diet Coke commercial. I don't know how true it is, but I had heard rumors that she had auditioned for Bob Fosse's *Big Deal* on Broadway, and that her representatives had been talking to Fosse. Well you know how the rumors go in the business, that she's constantly in California talking with major producers and directors. So, I think that her film career is inevitable."

Now that Whitney was an overnight sensation, and a huge star, everyone wanted to know about her love life as well. According to her at the time, the only love of her life, who shared her lavender apartment with her, was her Turkish Angora cat, Misti Blue. She announced of the feline roommate, "He's the only man in my life at the moment." She further claimed, "I don't have the kind of time it takes to nurture a relationship the way I'd like to right now, and I'd never attempt to jump into one unless I had that time. Besides I'd always be worried about what he was thinking when I was gone. My time is so bottled up into 'me' that it would be very selfish for me to start something with somebody and then just say, 'Hey, I gotta go!'"

With regard to finding a man of her own and settling down, she said that she would "love to have children, and I know that I can have a career and a marriage someday, but I don't think I'm experienced enough to do that yet."

However, in the music business, already, rumors were swirling around her which claimed the reason there was no man in her life, is because she wasn't interested in men—at all. There were stories of all-girl late-night parties, and an insistence that she demanded that all of her limousine drivers were female as well.

For the time-being, she stayed very fixated on her career. She insisted, "There's so much I want to accomplish and so many talented people I would like to work with. Someday I would like to do a gospel album, and record with my mother and Dionne!"

As a solo stage performer, she was just finding herself. With regard to her concert performances she said, "I don't think there's any 'expected thing' for me. Every show, I can feel there are people in the audience who are surprised, who are saying, 'Who is that skinny girl with those skinny legs making those great big sounds?'"

After the release of her first album and all of the awards it won, percussion player Bashiri Johnson said of Whitney, "She's very poised, and she's kind of like a cat: a panther. A panther will only strike when it needs to, but it has the capacity to be real powerful. That's the way she is. She's so powerful and awesome, and it's all under harness. She has control of it. Whitney's family background makes her have to be very professional and upstanding with it."

Regarding how she was handling her first wave of success, Bashiri claimed in 1986, "I think she's handling it well, and it's not overwhelming her. I think that she's on top of it all. For one thing, she's getting enough rest, she's taking care of her health. She doesn't have any vices like a lot of other musicians, so she is able to take care of herself. She's very health oriented. Her schedule might be a bit demanding, but I think that she's learning to pace herself."

Well, when her second album was released, she was about to be moving at "warp" speed. The recording sessions for her second album were already well underway. It wasn't long before she was able to begin to feel the pressures of overnight fame.

CHAPTER SEVEN

"CONFLICTING RUMORS"

In 1987, Whitney Houston's wave of garnering of awards was still underway. She was being saluted for her phenomenal performance on the record charts, on television, and on the radio airwaves. On January 26 of that year she experienced an incredible sweep at The American Music Awards. She took home trophies for: "Favorite Pop / Rock Female Vocalist," "Favorite Pop / Rock Female LP," (*Whitney Houston*)," "Favorite Soul / R&B Female Album," (*Whitney Houston),* "Favorite Soul / R&B Female Artist," and "Favorite Soul / R&B Female Video." And, *Rolling Stone* magazine declared the *Whitney Houston* album their "Best Album of the Year."

On February 24, 1987, Whitney performed her hit, "Greatest Love of All" at the twenty-ninth Annual Grammy Awards, which was held at the Shrine Auditorium in Los Angeles. In April of 1987 Houston was in Montreux, Switzerland, where she performed at the prestigious Montreux Jazz Festival. It set the scene for the release of her second album.

According to Whitney, the recording to her second album was much easier and smoother than her first one. One of the reasons was the fact that she was working with many of the same producers. "It was kind of like coming home again, like old friends," she claimed. "Each producer was more comfortable and more personal this time. Since the first album, we've gotten to be closer."

The 1987 *Whitney* album was far more energetic than its predecessor, but it didn't move far away from the same formulas as her *Whitney Houston* debut disc. Opening with the smashing dance number "I Want to Dance With Somebody," the young diva sounded excitingly energetic on this out-and-out dance song about finding a romantic dance partner. Slowing the pace down for one of her classic ballads, Whitney follows it up with "Just the Lonely Talking Again," a slow and whispery love song. Both of these songs were produced with Narada Michael Walden, so seemed to have a special feel for Houston's fun side, and her melancholy side as well.

The album's only new producer was John "Jellybean" Benitez, who contributed the fast pace and exotic disco-flavored song "Love Will Save the Day." Benitez is famous for having produced Madonna's first Number One hit, "Holiday." Known in New York City at the time as the star DJ at the discotheque The Funhouse, Benitez had carved out a career for himself as a dance record producer, and this song was by far the *Whitney* album's most dazzling and exhilarating cut.

Contributing the album's most touching and dramatically brilliant ballad, Michael Masser brought to the table a song which oddly enough seems the theme song for Whitney's life—especially from a 2004 perspective. The song is "Didn't We Almost Have It All." At the time, it seemed like a song about a lost love. To listen to the song during Whitney's later trouble era, it seemed like a lament about losing much more than just the love of one person.

"Didn't We Almost Have It All" is the kind of ballad that became Whitney's career-peak trademark. The kind of drama, and vocal pyrotechnics that she demonstrates on this song makes it the kind of recording which gives the listener chills.

"So Emotional" is a powerhouse of a rock number, suitable for the likes of Pat Benatar or Madonna. However, Whitney makes this skyrocket of an up-tempo tune all her own, singing about the shocking things that love can make you do. "Where You Are," is the only contribution to this album by Kashif, and is the lightest and least dramatic song. However, after repeated listenings and the song grows on you, like the "quiet storm" kind of radio programming that was popular on "urban contemporary" radio stations at the time.

On the up-tempo numbers of this album, Whitney seems like she is genuinely having fun in the studio. One of the most exciting dance numbers on this album is without a doubt "Love is a Contact Sport." Paralleling love with sports proved a fun image idea on this rhythmically pulsating number.

"You're Still My Man" is another very sentimental ballad from Michael Masser, which Houston seemed very comfortable singing. She also did well reinterpreting The Isley Brothers' jazzy "For the Love of You."

"Where Do Broken Hearts Go" is the perfect smooth and velvety ballad, which Whitney excelled at singing. This beautiful song is about a love that is lost and then reconciled, and the singer turns it into a dramatically effective musical outing.

The most talked-about song on the album was "I Know Him So Well." Written by Tim Rice and Abba singer / songwriters Benny Andersson and Björn Ulvaeus for the hit Broadway musical *Chess*, this song proved a perfect showcase for Whitney to duet with her mother Cissy. Originally, in the context of the musical play, the song is sung by two women: a wife, and the mistress of the same man. Here, however, Whitney and Cissy seem to be talking about a distant husband and father. With so much made in the press about Cissy never getting the chance to show off her expressive lead vocals on record in years, it seemed a perfect and magnanimous way for Whitney to share the spotlight with her famous mother. "I Know Him So Well" is not only an effective, and brilliant way to end the *Whitney* album, it also offered this celebrity mother-and-daughter team the prefect showcase of both their vocal talents.

Singing the song "I Know Him So Well" was the cut that Whitney claimed was her favorite one on the new album. "I would have to say that's the song I will treasure the most," she said at the time. "I love them all, but that one is closest to my heart."

To further add to the glamorous image of Houston, the cover photo and interior shot of the singer were taken by famed fashion photographer, Richard Avedon. On the cover, she is depicted in what looks to be a simple sleeveless shoulder-strapped cotton tee shirt. The effect is one of glamorous youthfulness. The interior shot, in black & white, she is wearing a full-length black gown, looking very much like a high-fashion model. The photos effectively accentuated the whole "funky but chic" feeling that the music on the album conveyed.

When it was released, the critical reviews for the *Whitney* album were decidedly mixed. Several high profile publications found the album to be stiff and devoid of surprises. Vince Aletti in *Rolling Stone* found, "On one hearing, it's easy to dismiss Whitney Houston's new album as over-calculated, hollowed-out pop product, so suffocated by professionalism that only the faintest pulse of soul remains. But after several listens, it's nearly impossible to dislodge *Whitney* from your brain . . . the formula is more rigorously locked in than before and the range is so tightly circumscribed that Houston's potential seems to have shrunk rather than expanded."

Likewise, Jon Parales in *The New York Times*, in a review headlined, "She's Singing by Formula," proclaimed, "Her producers or Ms. Houston herself has much confidence in that voice. Instead of finding (or demanding) material to reveal her individuality on both albums Ms. Houston submits to pop formulas designed for lesser singers—and she executes them with good grace and little heart . . . Even the album title fits in with Arista Records custom of separating female singers—'Dionne,' 'Aretha,' 'Carly'—from their last names . . . Ms. Houston's vocals, with their gorgeously-shaped but arbitrary crests and hollows, have a peculiar undercurrent; they suggest that the feelings she sings about are strictly surface phenomena, just something to say while preening her voice . . . her producers keep emotion at bay."

However, John Milward in *USA Today* loved it, and exclaimed, "*Whitney* clicks with classy style . . . increased emphasis on up-tempo tunes . . . The multi-format formula that worked so well on the debut and was brought back for the new LP doesn't diminish its cushy pleasures . . . Whitney's duet with mother Cissy Houston ('I Know Him So Well') offers an intriguing contrast. While Whitney's voice is perfectly poised, her mom's effortless tones resonate beyond the notes."

The *Whitney* album was obviously critic-proof. The second it was released it was an instantaneous across-the-board smash. Based on the overwhelming appeal of her incredibly successful debut album, *Whitney* became an overnight hit. In fact, it became the first album by a female artist to ever debut at Number One in *Billboard*. Up to that point this had only happened three times. The other recording stars to have an album debut at the top were Bruce Springsteen, Elton John, and Stevie Wonder.

In addition, that same week the first single off of the *Whitney* album, "I Wanna Dance With Somebody," hit Number One on *Billboard's* Hot 100 singles chart. This made her only the fifth recording artist to place five consecutive singles at Number One. When "I Wanna Dance With Somebody" hit the top, it put her in the same league with The Supremes (five in a row), Elvis Presley (five in a row), The Bee Gees (six in a row), and The Beatles (also at six).

Suddenly, Whitney Houston was being looked at in a whole different light. Already hers was a career for the record books, and she had only been a household name for two years. Rarely had a career launch and follow-up album been so strategically plotted, and so successfully received.

At the same time, Madonna was certainly more revolutionary and daring. Tina Turner was far livelier on stage and on record. Anita Baker had a much more effective emotional ability to interpret a song in a way that made it all her own. And, Cyndi Lauper was certainly more emotionally evocative on record. However, Whitney was trouncing them all on the charts. That same month, in an effort to support the demand for more of Houston, the young diva of pop / soul hit the concert road.

Touring through the summer and fall, Houston was one of the hottest concert draws of the season. Catching her act in Columbia, Maryland; *USA Today* reviewer Edna Gundersen enthusiastically called her "The greatest voice of all," and insisted, "Bottle her voice and the potion would tame tornadoes, melt steel, sweeten vinegar. Whitney Houston puts the average nightingale to shame. The twenty-three-year-old siren overcomes occasionally insipid material and awkward pacing to deliver one of the summer's most riveting performances . . . Some songs bear stylistic tracings to cousin Dionne Warwick, and the bouncy 'Love Is a Contact Sport' is too strong an impersonation of family friend Aretha Franklin. But most of Houston's material is solely and soulfully hers . . . Houston milked every note and left fans quaking in the thrill of her trill."

When the press claimed she was a "manufactured" star, and the creation of Clive Davis and Arista, she didn't hesitate to verbally protest. She boldly told *Time* magazine in 1987, "They didn't have to make me over. There would be no 'Whitney Houston' without Whitney Houston." In July of 1987, Arista Records signed a "development deal" with TriStar

Pictures that would last for two years. The goal behind this alliance was to actively seek to find Houston an appropriate project in which to make her film debut.

While Whitney Houston was the toast of the music business, she was also the subject of much gossip and speculation in the press. The rumors that she and Robyn Crawford where in fact lovers, continued to surface.

It was publicly known that Robyn was not only her friend, and on the payroll as her assistant, and that she was also Whitney's constant companion and roommate. In the liner notes of her debut album she had several "thank you's" including one which read, "Robyn, What an assistant! I love you and I guess all you need to do is stay in my life, Nip." In the second album, Whitney inscribed a message to her buddy Crawford: "Robyn, you are my friend and you are also quite an assistant. Be strong, for you are a child of the Almighty God and you walk in his love and in his light. I love you, Whitney."

Several times in the press Whitney was pressed to make a response, and she often became defensive about the issue. "No, I am not a *lesbo*," she announced to one reporter. "Guys that say that about me are the same ones who want to jump into my pants."

Whitney defiantly claimed, "Why should people know everything? There have to be surprises."

She further attempted to deflect all of the speculation by stating, "I really do very ordinary things with my life. I eat, sleep, sing, play tennis, play with my cats. Being alone is very important to me, but when I'm with friends I laugh, joke, fool around—act normal." Still, the rumors persisted.

According to the book *Good Girl, Bad Girl*, both Whitney and Robyn's most common response to the rumors were, "If you don't understand our relationship, fuck you!"

It was one thing when the tabloids or the gossip columns printed gay rumors about Whitney, but when *Time* magazine pressed her about the rumors, and reported their findings, Houston's sexuality became a regular target of interviewers. In the July 13, 1987 issue of *Time*, Richard Corless interviewed Whitney and she referred to Robyn as the "sister I never had." The article claimed that Robyn dropped out of Monmouth

College, where she had a scholarship to play basketball. She then became Whitney's personal assistant. "The tattle mill has ground out the story that they are lovers," Corless reported.

Both of them denied the rumor. First Robyn claimed, "I tell my family, 'You can hear anything on the streets, but if you don't hear it from me, it's not true.'"

Whitney stated even more strongly, "My mother taught me that when you stand in the truth and someone tells a lie about you, don't fight it. I'm not with any man. I'm not in love. People see Robyn with me, and they draw their own conclusions. Anyway, whose business is it if you're gay or like dogs? What others do shouldn't matter. Let people talk. It doesn't bother me because I know I'm not gay. I don't care." But, for some reason she did seem to care, a lot.

On September 11, 1987 Whitney preformed at the fourth annual MTV Video Music Awards, which were telecast from Universal Amphitheatre in Los Angeles. That month her latest single, the ballad "Didn't We Almost Have it All" hit Number One on the *Billboard* singles chart in America. It also reached Number 14 in England.

In late 1987, Whitney herself continued to chip away at her perfect, polite, girl-next-door image. There were recurring reports of her acting haughty and conceited on more than one occasion. Still hounded in the press to give out details of her personal life, on a number of occasions she blasted back rudely, "I don't owe anybody anything but a good performance."

She was also reportedly rude to other celebrities. While in London, Whitney met Culture Club star Boy George. Publicly, Boy George proclaimed of Houston, "What a rude cow! I've met most of the Royal Family, including Princess Diana. Yet, royalty wouldn't even treat people like that. She made me feel like nothing." Apparently, Whitney crossed the wrong "queen" that time around!

There were times in which Houston was downright disrespectful to her concert crowds as well. According to record producer Andrew Skurow, "During her stop in Las Vegas on the 'I Want To Dance With Somebody' tour, it was obvious Whitney did not want to be there. She sang her songs, never cracking a smile. People were tossing roses and screaming 'Whitney!

We love you.' She didn't acknowledge the audience with so much as a 'thank you.' When Houston finally left the stage, several people in the audience began booing."

In a sudden move, Whitney purchased a massive $10 million estate for herself in Mendham Township, New Jersey. Located on a five-acre plot of land, it would afford her the privacy that she longed to have. She bought the house without telling her mother, which sources claim did not sit well with Cissy. Furthermore, she moved her friend Robyn Crawford into the house as well.

According one inside source, Cissy wanted Whitney to get rid of Robyn. She didn't approve of the girl, and she wasn't happy about their relationship—whatever the nature of it was. However, Robyn proved to be just as determined to remain in the picture, and apparently Whitney wanted her to be there. End of discussion.

While all this was brewing, her mother did her best to diffuse the rumors in an *US* magazine cover story from 1987 entitled, "Worrying About Whitney." According to Cissy at the time, "Whitney does want to get married and have babies. It's just a matter of finding the right time and the right person. She's got to find someone who loves her for herself, not for her money or anything. She's a loving, feeling girl, and I know she wants a normal life. Because of her position it's going to be harder to find it. I hope she can. And I think she will. She's a good judge of character." If Cissy only knew then who it was whom Whitney was going to end up marrying, she might have packed her up for a convent at this point!

In 1987 *The New York Daily News* reported the annual earnings of the most popular performers of the year. Madonna earned $47 million, while Whitney Houston brought in a close $44 million. And, both pop divas surpassed Michael Jackson, who lagged behind at $43 million.

Whitney began 1988 with her sixth consecutive Number One single in America, "So Emotional," which also made it to Number Five in England. On January 25 she proceeded to win another pair of American Music Awards, this time around in the categories of "Favorite Pop / Rock Female Vocalist" and "Favorite Pop / Rock Single" for "I Wanna Dance With Somebody." On March 2, in front of a glittering star-studded audience she won the "Best Female Pop Vocal Performance" Grammy Award for her song "Saving All My Love For You." And on March 30, at the second annual Soul Train Awards she picked up a trophy in the category of "Female Album of the Year," for *Whitney*.

In April of 1988, when her next single, "Where Do Broken Hearts Go" hit Number One in the United States, Whitney shattered the record for the longest string of consecutive chart topping hits. With the success of this particular song, she broke the record previously held and tied by The Beatles and The Bee Gees. Houston was no longer just that era's "flavor of the month," her glitteringly successful career was even more definitively one for the history books.

June of 1988 found Houston again in London. She was busy making concert appearances, just as "Where Do Broken Hearts Go" peaked on the British charts at Number 10. On the eleventh of that month Whitney headlined a gala celebration at Wembley Stadium in London, in honor of Nelson Mandela's seventieth birthday.

Her next single from the *Whitney* album, "Love Will Save the Day" finally broke her solid streak of back-to-back Number One hits, when it peaked in America at Number Nine. In autumn of that year, her latest single, "One Moment in Time," peaked on both sides of the Atlantic, at Number Five in America, and Number One in England. The inspirational song, was taken from an Arista Records album also called *One Moment in Time*, as a multi-artist salute to the 1988 Olympics. The album was certified *Gold*.

During this era, with regard to her rumored film career in-the-works, she admitted, "It's just an exciting part of the entertainment world that I could be good at."

The advent of the TriStar film "development deal" ushered in a whole new side of Whitney. While Whitney was formerly presented as the lovely, charming, and spiritual easygoing girl-next-door, gossip columns began to circulate news of a bitchy competition between Houston, and the legendary egotistical diva to-end-them-all: Diana Ross.

Diana had found herself in a similar situation to Houston, in the early 1970s. Ross had scored instant film success when she starred in *Lady Sings the Blues* (1972). However, her subsequent movies, *Mahogany* (1975) and

The Wiz (1978), lost so much money, her film career ended as quickly as it had started. She was also reportedly difficult to work with.

When it was announced that TriStar was looking into starring Houston in a big-screen version of the Broadway show *Dreamgirls,* Ross became incensed. Since the scene-stealing lead character of the musical was a thinly disguised version of Ross, Whitney would essentially be playing Diana. Apparently Ross thought that the role would be offered to her. This tipped off a battle chronicled by the gossip columns. According to one report, with regard to Ross playing the lead in *Dreamgirls,* Houston snapped out a catty retort stating, "Then they'd have to retitle it *Dreamgrannies*—how old is she, anyway, about fifty?" Ross was only forty-four at that time.

Ross also had long harbored the idea that she should star as 1920s international sensation Josephine Baker in a biographical film. However it never got off the ground for the former-Supreme. When it was announced that TriStar was trying to launch a Josephine Baker film starring Whitney, Ross saw red. Diana was apparently furious that Houston—who was nearly twenty years younger—would be awarded the two roles Miss Ross most wanted for herself.

While Whitney and Diana were dueling as divas, during this era, the press still seemed to be having "a field day," speculating about the personal life of Whitney Houston. In spite of the charming, delightful and girly image the press created for Houston, it seemed that she was never linked with any men. If she was on the arm of a man, it was either her father, her brothers, or Clive Davis. The lesbian rumors were now a standard and dreaded question in every press interview that she gave.

Finally, Houston decided that being photographed on the arm of several male celebrities, to quell the rumors once and for all. She went out a couple of times with actor Eddie Murphy. There were also press items linking her with athlete Daryl Strawberry, actor Arsenio Hall, and even Prince. There was even talk that Robert DeNiro was pursuing her. However, she reportedly made it clear that she had absolutely no romantic interest in DeNiro. Prior to her connecting with Bobby Brown, she was seen with football player Randall Cunningham. However, she publicly dismissed it, claiming "We're friends! It was nothing intimate. Nothing romantic. Everybody wants to put me with somebody, you know."

While the press continued to speculate about Whitney's private life, her career by now had a life of its own. On January 30, 1989, she won another pair of American Music Awards. This time around they were in the categories of "Favorite Female Artist, Soul / R&B" and "Favorite Female Artist, Pop / Rock." On February 22 she performed her Olympics song "One Moment in Time," at the thirty-first annual Grammy Awards, held at the Shrine Auditorium in Los Angeles.

That year Aretha Franklin released her latest solo album, *Through the Storm*. Three of the cuts on the album were produced by Narada Michael Walden, with whom both she and Whitney both regularly recorded. On the album, Franklin performed duets with James Brown, Elton John, and on a song with The Four Tops and musician Kenny G. It seemed like a natural move for her to record a song with Whitney as well. The resulting number was an amusing "cat fight" between two women vying for the attention of the same man. An energetic and amusing song, with lots of bitchy ad-libs, "It Isn't, It Wasn't, It Ain't Never Gonna Be," was a successfully "fun" song for the pair of soul divas. Released as a single, this sassy and upbeat Aretha / Whitney duet made it to Number 41 in America, and Number 29 in the United Kingdom.

One of the most interesting events of the year was Whitney Houston meeting Bobby Brown for the first time. Reportedly, they had met when they were both attending The Soul Train Awards in 1989. According to Brown, "It was like love at first sight. Her birthday was coming up, and she was having a party, and she invited me. After that we started dating." Who knew at the time that this social event would have a huge impact on her later career.

As the decade of the 1980s came to an end, there was talk about her making her film debut in separate movies starring Robert DeNiro, and Eddie Murphy. Neither of the discussed films happened. And, besides, she was already busy working on her third Arista album.

CHAPTER EIGHT

"ONE TOUGH DIVA"

As the 1990s dawned, Whitney Houston was already actively at work on her next album. As per usual, she was still picking up awards right and left. On May 30 she was presented with the year's "Hitmaker Award" at the twentieth annual Songwriters Hall of Fame. She was also a presenter that evening at the New York Hilton Hotel, personally inducting Smokey Robinson into the Hall of Fame for his years of songwriting accomplishments.

On October 3, Whitney was one of the celebrities who attended a National Children's Day celebration, held at the White House in Washington D.C. Houston was in New York City on October 19 to receive an award from *Essence* magazine, at a gala event at Radio City Music Hall.

Fall of 1990 is when her next album and single hit with a tidal wave of publicity. Starting with the title cut, Whitney's third album, *I'm Your Baby Tonight* borrowed heavily from it's two multi-*Platinum* predecessors. It also kicked off her first work with producers L.A. Reid and Babyface, with whom she would have a long hit-making association throughout the '90s. A harder edged, but upbeat dance number, "I'm Your Baby Tonight" found her in great voice, sounding energetic and youthful.

The song "My Name is Not Susan" is one the sassiest up-tempo songs that Houston has ever tackled, and she seemed to really connect with the lyrics. In the plot of the song, Whitney's lover has said the name of "Susan" by accident, and a worked-up and incredibly strong-sounding Ms. Houston vocally sets the record straight.

Reid and Babyface's two other Houston productions on the album include the fun and funky "kiss off" song, "Anymore." Again, taking a sassy and self-confident stance, she sings of telling her ex-lover "goodbye." On the duo's composition, "Miracle," it is Whitney's turn at fielding the heartbreak in this ballad of sadness.

Narada Michael Walden and Michael Masser are the only two producers who were on all three of Whitney's first trio of albums. Here Walden contributes the exciting and torchy "All the Man That I Need," the rhythmic "I Belong to You," and medium tempo "Lover for Life." The song "All the Man I Need" had been originally a hit in 1982 for Sister Sledge. Masser brought to the table the slow and romantic "After We Make Love."

Two of the album's most memorable cuts came from a pair of "guest" producers: Luther Vandross and Stevie Wonder. Stevie wrote, produced and dueted with Houston on the medium-tempo song, "We Didn't Know." A pleasant ballad, Wonder's presence seems to add a charming sparkle to Whitney's own expressive voice.

Luther Vandross, really came through with one of his trademark dynamic productions on the effervescent song "Who Do You Love." Interestingly enough, it was Luther who also produced 1980s Arista albums by Aretha Franklin, and Dionne Warwick. On this upbeat and exciting song. Whitney sings with vibrant energy. As on many of his productions, Luther utilized the background vocals of the one and only Cissy Houston. She was clearly his favorite background singer, and on this cut her presence is unmistakable.

The final song on the album, 'I'm Knocking" represents Whitney's first foray at producing her own songs. Teamed up with Rickey Minor, she cut her teeth on having a hand on the recording studio control board. A stripped down, up-tempo song, "I'm Knocking" was a snappy rock-styled number, on which she sounds very loose and spontaneous.

It had been three years since her last album release, and Houston admitted that she had taken some time off for herself. After four years on non-stop exposure, she admitted that it was time for a break. "I think the public had about enough of me, and I had enough of me too." According to her, she spent a lot of time just hanging out at home for a change. "Just to get to know 'me' again."

She also confirmed that she had absolutely no plans to move to Hollywood, or to Manhattan. Whitney said at the time, "With my family at home in New Jersey, I can be myself. I love the business, but I don't want to live it. I'm able to go out. I can go to the mall. People don't bombard me. It's important to me to be human. Everybody thinks I'm a superstar, but I know the real deal."

In addition to having critics pry into her private life, several comedians began to make fun or her. On the satiric 1990s comedy show *In Living Color*, she was ridiculed in a skit for being "too white." Defensively, Whitney claimed, "I don't sing music thinking this is black or this is white . . . I sing songs that everybody's going to like."

Again, on *I'm Your Baby Tonight* Clive Davis was the album's "Executive Producer," meaning that he had input in every aspect of the material on it, and the look of it. However, Whitney was quick to mention that she was not shy in adding her own opinion to the project. "There's no possible way I could sit back and not be involved . . . I always had input in choosing songs, in what the video concept was, and how I looked."

The first single from the new album, "I'm Your Baby Tonight," peaked at Number Five in England in October 1990, and it hit Number One in America in December. The album itself only made it to Number Three in the United States. Since the release of Whitney's first two albums, there was a new sound that was suddenly hot on the charts: rap music. With the Number One and Number Two spots on the *Billboard* album chart dominated by Vanilla Ice and M.C. Hammer, this was her first album not to top the charts.

With her debut album—*Whitney Houston*—selling a global 22 million copies; and it's follow-up—*Whitney*—selling 19 million copies, *I'm Your Baby Tonight* was something of a disappointment at a worldwide 10 million copies sold. However, despite decreased album sales, she still raked in awards, and produced hit songs from the album.

At this time, America was involved in the Gulf War military conflict. As this was the first time in decades that the United States had really gotten in the middle of a new war, patriotic feelings were at a fever pitch. On January 27, 1991, the annual Superbowl football game was televised, and is traditionally the most-watched American TV sports event of the year. When Whitney Houston took the stage and sang an incredibly inspiring version of the American National Anthem, a groundswell of public interest rose to a fever-pitch. By popular demand, a CD single version of the song, and a video cassette of her TV performance were both rush released. The CD alone sold 750,000 copies in America, and landed at Number 20 on the *Billboard* charts.

People loved Whitney's version of "The Star Spangled Banner" so much in fact, that it caused a whole wave of publicity—since her performance consisted of her lip-syncing the song, and not singing it live. The fact of the matter is, that on the Superbowl telecast, the National Anthem is always "prerecorded" by whomever is singing it so that there aren't any audio problems. In spite of this highly publicized revelation, the single sold like hotcakes. The proceeds of the CD and video singles were donated to the Gulf Crisis Fund.

Suddenly, Whitney was looked upon as the most patriotic American diva around. It changed the perception of the singer and her career instantly. On March 31, she headlined an HBO televised special called *Welcome Home Heroes with Whitney Houston*. The event was also simulcast on Westwood One Radio Network. Houston was at the Norfolk Naval Air Station, where the American troops were returning from their time in the Persian Gulf. The concert Whitney gave that night was a huge hit for her, and—naturally—the most anticipated apex of her show was her sparkling version of "The Star Spangled Banner," which she *did* sing live.

Prior to the breakout of war in the Middle East, Whitney had a planned concert tour of Europe. However, the advent of the Gulf War forced the cancellation of that trek. Instead, she embarked on a tour of the United States. On April 18, 1991 she opened her series of U.S. dates at the Thompson Boling Assembly Center Arena, in Knoxville, Tennessee.

In an odd twist of events, Whitney got into her first conflict with the law, when she was accused of assaulting and threatening a man in Lexington, Kentucky. The incident happened on April 19 in the Radisson Plaza Hotel. Apparently her brother, Michael, got into a fight with a man named Kevin Owens. Proving that she is not a diva to be crossed, Whitney apparently slugged Owens as well, causing him to seek medical attention for twelve stitches near the vicinity of his eye. She also verbally assaulted him, and was later accused of "terroristic threatening."

Thankfully, the complaint was handled swiftly. On May 7, Judge Lewis Paisley, upon the recommendation of the District Attorney of Fayette County, Norrie Wake; dismissed the assault charges filed against the patriotic songbird. Just like she used to defend herself from the tough girls in her neighborhood, Whitney wasn't afraid of a good battle. She may have had a "girly" image on stage and on record, but underneath it, she was one tough "broad."

That same month, the *I'm Your Baby Tonight* album was certified Triple *Platinum* in America. The single version of "Miracle" hit Number Nine in the United States in June, and in July "My Name is Not Susan" peaked at Number 29 in England. Meanwhile, she continued her concert tour of America.

On July 23, 1991 Whitney headlined Madison Square Garden in New York City. After the show that evening, at The Grolier Club, she was presented with a commemorative plaque for achieving worldwide sales of 7 million copies for her third Arista LP. Claiming "throat problems," not long afterward she canceled the remainder of her concert tour. For Whitney Houston, some major changes were about to take place in her life. Some of these changes were for the better, and some of them were not.

CHAPTER NINE

"BOBBY BROWN AND *THE BODYGUARD*"

When she first started her career, Whitney publicly claimed that her mother had been a strict disciplinarian, and that she was glad she was raised in such a way. However, inside sources claim that Cissy got involved in her daughter's career much more than Whitney wanted. Her way to rebel against her mother was to repeatedly demonstrate her independence. Part of her protest seemed to be her relationship with Robyn Crawford—regardless of the dynamic of that friendship. Robyn, too, constantly voiced her opinion as to what she thought Whitney should do, and the pair often argued.

What was the way in which Whitney could best protest both her mother's and Robyn's constantly telling her what to do? How about dating and getting pregnant by a bad boy recording star? Well, that was exactly what happened. Enter: the notorious Bobby Brown.

Unbeknown to the public, Bobby Brown had been in the picture for quite some time. In May of 1992 Whitney claimed of their budding relationship, "We were instant friends" who "didn't get romantically involved for two years."

She was later to elaborate, "Bobby and I met at the *Soul Train* Music Awards. He was kicking 'Don't Be Cruel'—he was hot; he was on fire. I and some friends of mine were sitting behind him. I was hugging them, we were laughing, and I kept hitting Bobby in the back of the head.

Robyn said, 'Whitney, you keep hittin' Bobby, he's goin' to be mad at you.' I leaned over and said, 'Bobby, I'm so sorry.' And he turned around and looked at me like 'Yeah, well just don't let it happen again.' And I was like 'Oooooh, this guy doesn't like me.' Well, I always get curious when somebody doesn't like me. I want to know why. So I said, 'I'm going to invite Bobby to a party.' And I did. And he called back and said, 'I'd love to come,' which was a surprise. He was the first male I met in the business that I could talk to and be real with. He was so down and so cool, I was like: 'I like him.' Then we saw each other again, like four months later at a BeBe and CeCe Winans show. After the show, CeCe had a party, and we all went out to dinner. At the end of the dinner, Bobby walked up to me and said, 'If I asked you to go out with me, would you?' At the time I was dating someone, but it was kind of 'ehhhh.' So I said, 'Yeah, I would.' And he said, 'You really would?'—he's so cool—'I'll pick you up tomorrow at eight.' And we've been friends ever since. See, our whole relationship started out as friends. We'd have dinner, laugh, talk and go home. It wasn't intimate. And then it kind of dawned on us, 'What's going on here?'" Well, something was obviously going on, indeed.

Bobby Brown was never a major star in the same league with Whitney Houston, but he certainly had achieved his own distinct claim at music industry fame. He was just a teenager when he first became famous as one fifth of the early 1980s R&B / Pop group New Edition. Bobby established his own solo recording career towards the end of that decade, and was at the peak of his solo fame around the time he met Whitney Houston. Since that time, his own musical career has been on a slow sinking descent, to the point where he soon became famous as "Whitney Houston's husband" than for his own career.

He was born Robert Baresford Brown on February 5, 1969 in Roxbury, Massachusetts. His musical career began when promoter Maurice Starr assembled a teeny-bop, hip-hop act, and named them New Edition in the early 1981. Starr was later to follow-up his creation of all-black New Edition, with an all-white group of teenagers, whom he named New Kids on the Block

As New Edition, the five singers—Bobby Brown, Ralph Tresvant, Ricky Bell, Michael Bivens and Ronald Devoe—almost instantly clicked with R&B and pop teenage audiences alike, with their sugary ballads including "Candy Girl" and "Cool It Now." With Bobby emerging as the front man of the group, Bobby began to launch his own solo career, soon departing New Edition. He was replaced with charismatic Johnny Gill, and the group continued to produce hits. Then Johnny Gill signed his own solo deal, and three of the others formed a successful trio they named Bell, Biv and Devoe.

Bobby Brown's debut solo album, *King of the Stage,* enjoyed moderate success, making it on the charts to Number 88. However, his second release, 1988's *Don't Be Cruel,* ushered in what was to be dubbed the "new-jack swing" sound—with the major production help of hit-making producers L.A. Reid and Babyface. Thanks to the new sound, Bobby scored hits carrying a harder beat, included the Number One smash "My Prerogative" and the Number Three hit "Every Little Step." These two hit singles propelled *Don't Be Cruel* to hit Number One on the album charts. For a while, Bobby won over radio airwaves, and created an R&B movement.

In 1989 he scored a Number Two hit, with "On Our Own" from the soundtrack of the film *Ghostbusters II.* He was also seen in a cameo in the film, as a doorman. Later that year, an album of his re-mixed hits called *Don't Be Cruel . . . Ya Know It* hit Number Nine in America, and Number 26 in England.

In 1992 Brown not only married reigning pop-diva Whitney Houston, he released his next album, entitled *Bobby,* produced by Babyface. The hit single from it was, "Humpin' Around." The album hit Number Two and the single—Number Three in America. Its follow-up, "Good Enough" made it to Number Seven that same year.

Starting in the late 1980s, Bobby Brown began getting a lot of bad press exposure from his onstage and offstage antics. Even then he was making newspaper headlines, which seem to herald every new arrest, or each new jail sentence. It quickly evolved into a situation where his scrapes with the law became more famous than his singing career. On January 25, 1989, nineteen-year-old Bobby was performing in concert at the Columbus, Georgia Municipal Auditorium, when he was arrested for simulating sex during his act on stage.

He was also known for not being dependable. On January 12, 1990, he was scheduled to be awarded a Martin Luther King Jr. Musical Achievement Award in Boston at the Symphony Hall in front of Tony Bennett and The Count Basie Orchestra. Bobby was simply a "no-show" that evening. When he first started dating Whitney Houston, he was not at all popular with her friends, nor her family. Six years younger than Whitney, by the time he became her fiancé in 1992 he was only twenty-two years old, and he had already fathered three out-of-wedlock children. Whitney's legion of fans were equally floored by their affair. How could the singing "good girl" of R&B / pop fame, hook up with a notorious "bad boy" like Bobby?

From the time they got together, both Whitney and Bobby were very verbal and very public in expressing their love for each other to the press. Whitney seemed to be in a quick hurry to do away with her previous "good girl" public image. She told *Time* magazine, "People think I'm Miss Prissy Pooh-Pooh. But I'm not. I like to have fun. I can get down, really freakin' dirty with you. I can get raunchy. I've learned to be freer just being with Bobby. I've learned to be a little more loose—not so contained, ya know? Since I've been with him, I've gotten—you know—a little bit freer with my shit." So much for her "lady-like" public persona!

Whitney's statements now seemed to carry a petulant taste of brattiness to them. From the minute she linked up with Bobby, she seemed to instantly speak with less dignity, and a newly emerging tone of unflattering bitchiness.

Stoking his own ego, Brown said to a reporter for *The Los Angeles Times*, "I may be a 'bad boy' and she may be 'America's Sweetheart,' but it's love. When it happens, you have to grab it. You can't let it go no matter what anybody else thinks. Whitney is a proud black woman. That's what really drew me to her. She's beautiful, not just outside, but on the inside. When we finish a show, she puts on jeans and we roll."

In August of 1991, Bobby Brown asked Whitney Houston to marry him. Also, Whitney was pregnant with his child at the time. During this period, her career was about to soar to new heights, and she was determined to make Bobby part of the new scenario.

Although she had canceled much of her American summer concert tour in 1991, Whitney was back in shape by September, when she played a series of sold-out concerts at London's massive Wembley Arena, from the third to the fourteenth of the month. On September 19 she spoke in London's Hyde Park, at the "Reach Out & Touch People With HIV and AIDS Rally." That same month "My Name is Not Susan" peaked at Number 20 in America, while "I Belong To You" hit Number 54 in the UK.

On December 3, 1991 The Whitney Houston Foundation sponsored a Christmas party at Newark, New Jersey's Symphony Hall. It was a benefit event, and the proceeds went towards the support of 150 children from the charity called Parents Anonymous.

While all of this was going on in her personal life, she was preparing to finally make the big leap into becoming a movie star. She found herself actively pursued by Kevin Costner, who was set to play the title role in an upcoming film called *The Bodyguard*. He was convinced that Whitney was perfect for the part of fictional singing star Rachel.

Houston claimed, "I kept saying to him, 'What makes you think *I* can do this?' And he used to say to me, 'Whitney, *listen*. Every once in a blue moon you get this person who just comes around and has this *quaaality*. When you thought about that it had music in it, you used to think of Barbra [Streisand] or Diana [Ross]. But now it's you.' And I'm like, 'That's what I want. I want it to be *meeee!*'"

One of the most bizarre aspects of this film, was the fact that *The Bodyguard* was originally written in the 1970s, specifically for Steve McQueen. However, when McQueen suddenly died of cancer, it was retooled, and it was announced that the film would star Ryan O'Neal and Diana Ross. However—partially due to the amount of money *The Wiz* had lost—Diana never seemed bankable as a Hollywood actress after that. Then, suddenly in 1992, by portraying the role of Rachel in *The Bodyguard*, Whitney was effectively taking away a role that was supposed to belong to Ross—similar to their mid-'80s press feud which had implied that this might have happen.

Whitney was one of the guest performers on the ABC-TV Special to commemorate *Muhammad Ali's 50th Birthday*, broadcast March 1,

1992. At that same time she had already begun filming *The Bodyguard* with Kevin Costner.

What the public didn't know at the time was that she was pregnant with Bobby Brown's baby when filming began. It was reported that in late March of 1992, less than a month into the filming schedule, Whitney suffered a miscarriage.

When she was cornered by the press she cryptically and defensively stated in *USA Today*, "Let's say I did have a miscarriage—that's my business. You know what I'm saying? It just so happened to have happened. If I was doing a movie on a movie set, people get word and people call up the papers I guess, and say it. But it was really something like that, that would happen, is a very normal situation. It happens to women all the time. It's just that I'm this person: Whitney Houston: 'She's like us. I guess, she miscarriages too.' But when I'm ready to talk about it, I will. I'll straighten it all out. The way it's looking now it's such a sensationalized situation and it was a very simple one. It's not all that dramatic. So I'd rather not deal with it now. I'll deal with it at another time." Other than that, the filming of *The Bodyguard* went without a hitch.

On April 19, 1992, Bobby Brown was stopped by the Metro Police on Route 138 in Canton, Massachusetts for driving an uninsured vehicle, and for driving without a driver's license. It turned out to be Whitney's 1991 Porsche. This was just the beginning of the scrapes with the law that Bobby would have, and inadvertently Houston would end up with the bad press reflected on her.

On May 6 of that year she was the star of her own ABC-TV special: *Whitney Houston: This is My Life*. It was on this TV special that she first publicly confirmed that Bobby Brown had proposed to her the previous August and that they were to be married that summer. She could now concentrate on two of the biggest events of her life: her upcoming wedding, and her major motion picture debut.

The wedding was to be held at Whitney's Mendham, New Jersey, estate. It was a gala affair, and Stevie Wonder was to sing at the ceremony. The thematic color of the ceremony was to be white and purple, from the shades of the bridesmaids dresses to the floral arrangements.

The press was having a field day speculating on what this union between Whitney Houston and Bobby Brown was all about. Was she just marrying him to prove to the world she was heterosexual? Or, was it all just for show? And, was he just marrying her for her money?

Regardless of Houston's sexual persuasion, there was evidently a strange triangular relationship between Whitney, Bobby and Robyn. "Whitney Houston is precious," Robyn Crawford told *USA Today* in May of 1992. "I think once she's married she'll feel a lot more complete. I think that'll be a 'self' phase where she'll be doing something for *her* life."

However, insiders at the Houston compound painted quite a different story. According to Kevin Ammons, who worked for Whitney at the time, Robyn Crawford was inconsolable about the upcoming wedding. Ammons recalls a heartbroken Crawford saying to him, another employee, and John Houston, "If Whitney goes through with this marriage, I'll hold a press conference and tell everyone I'm Whitney's lover, that we've been lovers for years, then I'll kill myself."

However, there was no changing Whitney's mind. She was going to marry Bobby, and that was it. Brown did his best to downplay his troublesome reputation. He told *USA* Today in 1992, "I'm not on drugs. I've never been on drugs. I drink beer. I might take a little glass of Courvoisier on the rocks."

Robyn's pre-wedding hysterics caused Whitney to have Robyn find a place of her own to live. Houston herself told *The Los Angeles Times*, "Robyn is my best friend, who knows me better than any woman has ever known me. We have been tight for years, but when I met Bobby, Robyn and I had had enough time together. We used to be roommates, but now that I'm getting married, she moved into her own place, about thirty minutes away."

In addition to the wedding plans, Whitney still continued to make special public appearances that spring. At a gala presented by the New York Friar's Club, Clive Davis was named the organization's "Man of the Year." During the June 12 presentation ceremony Whitney joined her cousin Dionne Warwick, as they sang the song "That's What Friends Are For" to honoree Davis. The event was held at the Waldorf Astoria Hotel on Park Avenue in New York City.

On June 27 an all-star roster of guests, including Dionne Warwick, actress Jasmine Guy, and gospel singer CeCe Winans gathered at the Rihga Royal Hotel in New York City, for Whitney Houston's wedding shower. The wedding of Whitney Houston and Bobby Brown—as unlikely as it seemed at the time—was planned for July 18, 1992.

At the insistence of Whitney's lawyer, and her parents, the duo signed prenuptial agreements before the wedding could take place. Said Brown at the time, "If anything ever happens in this relationship, we both want to be protected." Then he added, "I'm going to be with this woman for the rest of my life." Or so he thought.

The wedding party consisted of Robyn Crawford as the maid of honor, and her bridesmaids were CeCe Winans, singer Pebbles, Bobby's two sisters, and a cousin. On Bobby's side, his groomsmen included Whitney's two brothers, and Brown's own brother—who was also his manager. According to one source, John Houston was so afraid that Robyn was going to do something that was going to disrupt the wedding, that he hired bodyguards just to watch out for how Crawford was going to act at the ceremony.

At this point in her career, Whitney was something of a fairy tale princess. The wedding ceremony reflected this image. To complete the picture, the gown that she walked down the aisle wearing, was designed by Marc Bauer, and reportedly cost $40,000.

According to one wedding eyewitness, "When it came time for Whitney and Bobby to say to each other, 'Til death do we part,' both Dionne Warwick and Patti LaBelle, who were sitting together, began giggling uncontrollably to themselves. It was like they both thought the idea of Bobby and Whitney ever being faithful to each other was utter nonsense."

As the disc jockeys for her reception, Whitney had David Cole and Robert Civilles, who were better known as recording stars C + C Music Factory ("Everybody Dance"). As mementos of the event, the guests were given bottles of champagne, cards with words of love printed on them, and a piece of the massive wedding cake. It was by far the summer's biggest and glitziest wedding ceremony. With that, the married couple went off on a European holiday, paid for by their respective record labels.

In the fall, Houston was back in the spotlight. Whitney attended a benefit for the Children's Diabetes Foundation, on October 3, 1992. It was held at the Beverly Hilton Hotel, in Los Angeles. At the time she had several European tour dates planned for the fall. However, since she was again several months pregnant, her doctors advised her to cancel the tour, which she did.

Finally, on November 25, 1992, Houston's debut film, *The Bodyguard* opened in theaters across America. It was almost unanimously trashed by the film critics, but ultimately—audiences flocked to theaters in droves. Part of the reason was out of curiosity to see what kind of on-screen chemistry Whitney and Kevin Costner exuded together. Another key element to the film's success was the fact that every non-religious Houston recording on the soundtrack album subsequently became a hit!

The Bodyguard is the story of Frank Farmer, a former Presidential bodyguard, who was off duty the day that Ronald Reagan was shot. Sought out by the manager of a popular singer who is besieged by death threats, Farmer comes to meet the threatened star, Rachel Marron. As Rachel, Whitney appears very comfortable in the role. Essentially, she represents the haughty side of the real life Whitney. Rachel is verbally short with people, and is every inch a "diva." In other words, she is pretty much playing an extended version of herself.

Frank isn't sure that Rachel is serious about deflecting these death threats, as she insists upon continuing to appear in public like nothing is wrong. Unfortunately, much of the gravity of the matter is unknown to her, until things become particularly frightening. Naturally, Frank and Rachel fall in love in the middle of the movie, making for romantic complications.

Several of Whitney's biggest scenes come while performing music, so she is treated to many loving close-ups as the glamorous singing icon Rachel. Some of her dramatic sequences are relegated to mysterious reaction shots of her, rather than pinning the success of her scenes to dramatic speeches. However, she fares remarkably well throughout the film. The chemistry between Costner and Houston is a bit far-fetched, but the idea that she is a damsel in distress, and he is the guardian knight in shining armor, makes the plot believable.

However, not all of the critics agreed. *Washington Post* reviewer Rita Kempley dismissed it by saying, "*The Bodyguard* is a great silly mess of a *luv* story, a multimedia circus of music videos, entertainment journalism, action thriller, and '60s movie melodrama carried by the dream couple of the '90s, Whitney Houston and Kevin Costner. As plushly appointed as it is thinly drawn . . . Though we thought he had modeled himself after a mollusk, Costner acknowledged that it was a homage to McQueen . . . Houston, who is doing nothing more than playing Houston, comes out largely unscathed if that is possible in so cockamamie an undertaking. *The Bodyguard* is a classic of show-business hubris, a wondrously trashy belly-flop, proving that no amount of glittering sets and star power can save a story that should have been buried with McQueen."

Deeson Howe—also of *The Washington Post*—claimed, "At first, the movie's [an] enjoyable, MTV-deep collision of opposites . . . It's only a matter of time before love arises between Mr. Earphone and Ms. High Note. By that time, *Bodyguard* has slumped to the ground. Originally written in 1975 with Steve McQueen in mind, Kasdan's script may make updated references to Ronald Reagan, but it's boneheaded, no matter how old it is . . . As the romance segues into thriller mode, the movie becomes increasingly ridiculous, culminating in a finale at the Academy Awards ceremonies. With the killer still at large, Houston, who has been nominated for an acting award (yes), insists on attending."

Entertainment Weekly referred to it a "disastrously languid romance about a pop singer-turned-actress (Whitney Houston) and the bodyguard (Kevin Costner) hired to protect her from a deranged fan." Reviewer Leonard Maltin pointed out that it was an "Overblown dual-star vehicle [which] makes no sense but has many crowd-pleasing ingredients—as well as moments of high-kitsch." He however admitted, it was a "Solid film debut for Houston."

Roger Ebert of *The Chicago Sun-Times* was one of the few major reviewers to find the film enjoyable. According to him, "The ads for *The Bodyguard* make it look like a romance, but actually it's a study of two lifestyles: of a pop music superstar whose fame and fortune depends on millions of fans, and of a professional bodyguard who makes his living by protecting her from those fans . . . The star is Rachel Marron, played by

Whitney Houston, and is as rich and famous as: Whitney Houston . . . There's an odd, effective dating scene where she leaves her mansion to visit his cluttered, grim little apartment (and a peculiar moment with a samurai sword and a scarf that is undeniably erotic) . . . This is Houston's screen debut, and she is at home in the role; she photographs wonderfully, and has a warm smile, and yet is able to suggest selfish and egotistical dimensions in the character . . . The movie was made as a thriller, I suppose, because of box-office considerations. I felt a little cheated by the outcome, although I should have been able to predict it."

Being as *The Bodyguard* was a film with music, much of Whitney's screentime was spent simply playing a projection of herself in long music-video numbers. This ushered in the reason for a hot soundtrack album with many original songs on it. In addition to six new songs by Houston, the LP was also filled out by five other acts singing one song apiece. The other acts included Lisa Stansfield, Kenny G and Aaron Neville, The S.O.U.L. S.Y.S.T.E.M., Curtis Stigers, and Joe Cocker with Sass Jordan.

The first half of the album, that was all Whitney songs, was handled much like her own albums. First of all, the whole project was Co-Executive Produced by Clive Davis and Whitney Houston. This was the beginning of her stepping into the forefront more, when it came to the production of her albums. For *The Bodyguard*, Narada Michael Walden was the only producer who had been on all of her three previous albums as well as this one. He is responsible for Houston's recording of the song "I'm Every Woman." This song is a lively cover of the 1978 Chaka Khan hit of the same name. It was an overlooked classic written by Ashford & Simpson, and Whitney breathed new life into it.

L.A. Reid and Babyface contributed the exciting danceable rocker "Queen of the Night." And, Whitney Houston and BeBe Winans (CeCe's brother), co-produced the version of the traditional hymnal song "Jesus Loves Me."

However, the real big news here was the addition of master ballad producer David Foster into the Whitney Houston mix. Throughout the rest of the 1990s Foster would continue to provide Houston with some of her most memorable ballads. The three songs that David Foster brought to the table of this landmark soundtrack album included the songs "Run

To You" and the dramatic and sweeping "I Have Nothing." On the album, Whitney breathed an awesome amount of emotion into both songs.

But, the single song that made this project really significant was Whitney's incredible recording of the Dolly Parton-composed song, "I Will Always Love You." Dolly herself had already twice recorded the tune, both times landing it at Number One on the Country hit charts. The first time she recorded and released it was in 1974. When Dolly became a movie star in the 1980s—due to the success of *Nine To Five*—she was signed to star in the 1982 film version of the Broadway musical, *The Best Little Whorehouse in Texas*. Although the musical had a full score of its own, wise Dolly wanted one of her own songs to be included in the film— and she chose "I Will Always Love You," to again record and place at the top of the Country charts. Although the song hadn't really become a huge Pop hit (it made it to Number 53 in 1982), Parton often used the number as her theme song.

"I Will Always Love You" didn't seem like the kind of composition to become the most famous single song of Whitney's entire career, but that is exactly what it was to become. Beginning slow and *a capella*, she milks the touching lyrics for all that they are worth. The song builds up to a sweeping crescendo, with Houston's magnificently powerful voice sustaining high notes that were at once dramatic and stunning.

As the first single released from *The Bodyguard* soundtrack, "I Will Always Love You" hit the Number One spot in the United States and in England in December 1992. It went on to sit at the top of the charts a stunning fourteen weeks in the U.S.—setting a new record. In addition, the song also hit Number One in Australia, Austria, Belgium, Canada, Denmark, Finland, France, Germany, Greece, Holland, Ireland, Italy, Japan, New Zealand, Norway, Portugal, Spain, Sweden, and Switzerland.

According to Dolly Parton, the song's lyrics are "about change and separation and love. And I guess that's why it's still a favorite after nearly twenty years." For penning the song Dolly reportedly earned well over $3 million in publishing royalties.

Whitney explained in 1993, "I talked to Dolly Parton by phone not too long ago. She said to me, 'Whitney, I just want to tell you something. I'm just honored that you did my song. I just don't know what to tell you, girl.' I said, 'Well, Dolly, you wrote a beautiful song.' And she said: 'Yeah, but it never did that well for me. It did well for you because you put all that stuff into it.' I think Dolly Parton is a hell of a writer and a hell of a singer. I was concerned when I sang her song how she'd feel about it, in terms of the arrangement, my licks, my flavor. When she said she was floored, that meant so much to me."

By the time *The Bodyguard* sensation was over, and it finished its run on the airwaves, the soundtrack album sold an astonishing 34 million copies worldwide, making it one of the most successful albums in recording history. Needless to say, the success of the album, ushered in ticket sales for the movie at the box-office, and *The Bodyguard*, became a hit with movie goers. The first weekend it opened, *The Bodyguard* took in an impressive $16.6 million at the box-office. By February of 1993, *The Bodyguard* had grossed $106 million, certifying it as one of the most successful films of the year.

The album was such a smash that every additional Whitney Houston song on it—except "Jesus Loves Me"—became a chart hit. "I'm Every Woman" made it to Number Four in the U.S. and the U.K. "I Have Nothing" peaked at Number Four in America, and Number Three in England. "Run to You" reached Number 31 in the United States, and Number 15 in the British Isles. And, "Queen of the Night" was released in England only, hit Number 14.

While all of these hits were being placed on the international record charts, 1993 was a very busy year for Whitney Houston. As *The Bodyguard* film and album were peaking, Whitney was busy with her pregnancy.

Lounging in her vacation home in Florida, she told *Entertainment Weekly* magazine, "I almost wish I could be more exciting—that I could match what is happening out there to me. I wish I could tell you, I wake up in the morning and play 'I Will Always Love You.' Sometimes I sit around and go, 'You're a bad entertainer. Bad, bad. You're supposed to be into this shit.' But I'm not. These days, the first thing I think about when I get up is labor."

Whitney claimed that she didn't care whether or not the critics liked the film. "The public is intelligent enough that they are willing to say, 'I want to see it for myself.' I worked so damn hard on that movie, and I put a lot of time into it, as everyone else did. I'm grateful that people get it, that they're open enough to understand it," she said.

One of the most interesting aspects of the film's success, was that it found an accepting audience who never questioned that fact that Whitney was black and Kevin was white. "I don't think it's a milestone that a black person and a white person made a movie together. I think for people to look at this color-blind *is* a milestone," Houston claimed. "The black community sees [*The Bodyguard*] as something larger. Black women tell me, 'This is something we've been waiting for, for somebody to kick it down so we can play these roles. We can be powerful independent women.' Black men have a sense of pride too. They say, 'It's so nice to see a good-looking sister playing a part that has intelligence.'"

And then, there was the issue of the most brilliant marketing ploy of all—the mega-success of the song "I Will Always Love You." According to Whitney, "You hear the song, you think of the movie. I think about people who have passed away; people in my family I've been close to. Certain parts make me think of my husband. Whose heart can't this movie touch? We've been missing that level of, 'Oh, God, I can lose myself in this movie.' That's the key element. It's not offensive to anybody."

Suddenly Whitney had a hit film in theaters and the most successful single album of her career. She was now a married woman. Robyn Crawford no longer lived in her house. And she was pregnant, and expecting her first child. Did this make the "gay rumors" blow over? Not at all—the press was still convinced that where there was smoke, there surely must be fire.

According to *Entertainment Weekly* magazine in early 1993, "There have been a few questions about her marriage. Brown, who is five years younger than his wife, already is the father of three children born out-of-wedlock to two other women; he and Houston are rarely together for more than a few weeks at a time."

However, in that same cover story on Houston, she again did her best to defuse questions insinuating that she and Robyn were lovers. She claimed, "Once someone gets to be a success, there are a number of things that are going to be said about you automatically. One is that you are gay. One is that you've got a drug problem. The other one is that you have no idea what the hell you're doing. At one point it hurt me to have dignify

Whitney comes from a very famous musical family. Her mother, Cissy Houston, was not only a member of The Sweet Inspirations, she also had a solo recording career of her own. (PHOTO: PRIVATE STOCK RECORDS / MJB PHOTO ARCHIVES)

In the 1980s, Cissy and Whitney Houston enjoy a night on the town with friend and singer George Benson (right). (PHOTO: CHARLES MONIZ)

Whitney's cousin is the famed pop music singer Dionne Warwick. It was Dionne who set the tone for classy hit-makers in the 1960s and 1970s. (PHOTO: MARK BEGO)

At the New York City dance club The Limelight, Whitney shared the spotlight with Jermaine Jackson. Here they are performing their duet: "Take Good Care of My Heart." (PHOTO: CHARLES MONIZ)

When Clive Davis first met Whitney Houston, she was not only singing background vocals in her mother's act, she was also a teen model who had graced the cover of *Seventeen* magazine. (PHOTO: STEVE PREZANT FOR ARISTA RECORDS / MJB PHOTO ARCHIVES)

For the cover of her second album, *Whitney*, the goal was to come up with a photo that showed off the singer's beauty in a way that made her look like the lovely girl-next-door. (PHOTO: RICHARD AVEDON FOR ARISTA RECORDS / MJB PHOTO ARCHIVES)

Whitney's father, John Houston (left) worked for the city of Newark, New Jersey. He is shown with his wife Cissy, and his daughter Whitney who is flanked by a pair of John's business associates. John is showing off the model of a new city development project. (PHOTO: ARISTA RECORDS / MJB PHOTO ARCHIVES)

For Aretha Franklin's 1989 *Through the Storm* album, producer Narada Michael Walden (left) teamed The Queen of Soul (center) with that era's hottest new diva, Whitney Houston (right). Together they created the snappy hit song "It Isn't, It Wasn't, It Ain't Never Gonna Be." (PHOTO: ARISTA RECORDS / MJB PHOTO ARCHIVES)

She not only sold out concerts wherever she went, in 1991, she was the star of her own HBO television special, *Welcome Home Heroes with Whitney Houston*. (PHOTO: HBO TELEVISION / MJB PHOTO ARCHIVES)

Angela Bassett and Whitney Houston were two of the prime reasons why the film *Waiting to Exhale* was such a huge box office hit in 1995. (PHOTO: CHARLES MONIZ COLLECTION)

Television star Brandy in the title role as *Cinderella*; Whitney Houston portrayed the role of her Fairy Godmother. (PHOTO: CHARLES MONIZ COLLECTION)

It was on the set of the 1997 production of *Cinderella* that Whitney really started to gain a reputation for being difficult to work with. (PHOTO: CHARLES MONIZ COLLECTION)

People were startled by Whitney's haughty portrayal as the Fairy Godmother in Cinderella. One reviewer called her acting characterization "vaguely hostile." (PHOTO: CHARLES MONIZ COLLECTION)

In 1998, when Mariah Carey and Whitney Houston recorded the duet "When You Believe," they were two of the most successful recording artists of the twentieth century. (PHOTO: CHARLES MONIZ COLLECTION)

Although she was known to arrive immaculately dressed at formal events, by the late '90s and early 2000s, photos of Whitney looking disheveled in public regularly graced the pages of tabloid newspapers. (PHOTO: DEREK STORM)

Once she married Bobby Brown in the early '90s, Whitney began to take her role as a demanding diva seriously.
(PHOTO: DEREK STORM)

Diane Sawyer and Whitney Houston on *Good Morning America* in 2009 constituted something of a reunion for the pair. It was during a Sawyer interview in 2002 that Whitney made her infamous drug use proclamation: "Crack is wack!" (PHOTO: DEREK STORM)

On September 1, 2009, Whitney Houston gave a free concert in New York City's Central Park for the morning TV show *Good Morning America*. This was the performance that was to kick off her "comeback" tour, and her album *I Look to You*. (PHOTOS: DEREK STORM)

Whitney Houston sharing the stage with Robin Roberts (left) and Diane Sawyer (right) on *Good Morning America*. With a new attitude and a new album, it seemed like her career was finally back on track. (PHOTO: DEREK STORM)

Bobbi Kristina Brown and her famous mother Whitney, in Central Park, September 2009. Both Bobby Brown and Bobbi Kristina were devastated by Whitney's sudden death in February 2012. (PHOTO: DEREK STORM)

what I *wasn't* with an answer. It used to fuck me up, to be honest with you. I used to go to my mother and say, 'Why, why, why is this happening? I can't be friends with women?'"

Even Cissy Houston defensively proclaimed, "It's because Whitney doesn't wear clothes up to her behind with her tits out—excuse my French! Either you're the biggest whore, or you're a lesbian."

She was an incredibly successful singing star. She was now a bona fide movie star. She was now the wife of another singing star. And, she was about to add still another new role to her biography: that of "mother." Finally, on March 4 she gave birth to her daughter, Bobbi Kristina Houston Brown. Whitney Houston was officially amidst the greatest single phase of her career.

CHAPTER TEN

"LIFE AS A MOVIE STAR"

Finally, in 1993, Whitney Houston seemed to have it all. She declared that she was completely in love with Bobby, even though he was often on the road touring and promoting his own album releases and singles.

Performing in Honolulu, Hawaii, at Neil Blaisdell Arena, Bobby Brown made the final performance on his current concert date. Pleading high blood pressure, and throat problems he subsequently canceled the entire European leg of his tour.

On June 3, 1993, Whitney made her first public appearance since having given birth. She went to a charity gala held in Los Angeles at the Century Plaza Hotel. The event was a fundraiser for St. Jude's Children's Research Hospital, which is located Memphis, Tennessee. People were astonished at how thin she appeared, and how quickly she had lost the weight which she had gained while she was pregnant. There was all kinds of talk about the sudden post-natal birth weight loss being diet pill induced.

In fact, on June 28, *The New York Post* ran an item claiming that Whitney was in the hospital, having overdosed on diet pills. Whitney's lawyers threatened to sue the newspaper, asking for $10 million in compensatory damages and an additional $50 million in punitive damages. They were forced to print a retraction two days later. This was the beginning of Whitney Houston being related to substance abuse problems in the press—drugs both of the prescription and of the illegal sort.

Further bad press came from a disastrous Whitney concert in Miami. Reportedly, the show started an hour and a half late, and Ms. Houston was apparently in a bad mood from the second she set foot on stage. After she had finished her opening number, a fan rushed the stage and pushed an autograph book in her direction for a signature. Houston looked down at the girl and said in her microphone, "Your ticket definitely says 'seat' on it, doesn't it?" When the appalled crowd began booing, she replied, "Look, I've been booed before and it really doesn't phase me."

In *The Miami Herald* the next day, reviewer Leonard Pitts reported, "Houston took the stage with an attitude that smelled like rotting fish. It was the *Hindenburg* of pop concerts. Her behavior was tacky, unprofessional, arrogant, and beneath the dignity of a singer of her talent and stature." Reportedly, representatives at Arista Records had a little talk with Whitney about the bad press she was receiving from that particular concert. The rest of the tour went much more smoothly—at least in terms of her onstage attitude problems.

September 30, 1993, Whitney and Bobby were riding in a limousine at Kennedy International Airport in New York City, when they were stopped by nine police officers who were looking for a group of wanted drug dealers, they had reason to suspect that they were associates of the Browns. Although they were released, it was just the beginning of a series of such drug-related incidents.

The first recorded Bobby Brown and Whitney Houston duet, "Something in Common," was released as a single during this era. It was included on Bobby's most recent album. The song only made an impression on the European side of the Atlantic, peaking at Number 16 in the United Kingdom in January of 1994. The duet single was met with the same kind of audience enthusiasm that Cher and Gregg Allman had when the recorded the duet album *Two the Hard Way* in 1977. It was like Whitney fans viewed Bobby Brown in much the same way that Beatles fans felt when John Lennon married Yoko Ono.

Whitney at this point was still working at maintaining her "good girl" image. She also took time to complain about the notorious misogyny of rap music. She told *TV Guide* magazine that winter, "I don't particularly think it's real cool to call a woman a 'bitch' or a 'ho,' but I don't consider myself that and I don't treat myself that way. That's not my way of life. But a lot of young people identify with this form of expression. You have to listen to it and say, 'Well, I can dig that, but I can't dig this.' You have to weigh it."

She was also verbally supportive of Michael Jackson, who during this era was accused of sexual misconduct with young boys. Said Houston, "This is something that is 'alleged.' It has not been proven that Michael has done this. I hate the media for doing it to him—I really do. In the long run, in the United States of America, you're innocent until proven guilty. That's what I think stands. I just pray for Michael, and he knows he has my love."

As 1994 began, so did a new avalanche of awards being heaped upon Whitney Houston, via her work in the film and on the soundtrack of *The Bodyguard*. On January 5 she was named the Entertainer of the Year, the Outstanding Female Artist, and the Outstanding Music Video (for "I'm Every Woman"), at the twenty-sixth annual NAACP Image Awards. The ceremony was held in Pasadena, California.

At the twenty-first annual American Music Awards, on February 7, 1994 she picked up five more trophies. They are in the categories of "Favorite Pop / Rock Female," "Favorite Pop / Rock Single," and "Favorite Soul / R&B Single" for "I Will Always Love You," and "Favorite Pop / Rock Album" as well as "Favorite Adult Contemporary Album" for *The Bodyguard*.

Whitney looked dazzling when she appeared on the awards telecast that evening. According to Edna Gunderson in *USA Today*, "The night's big winner was Whitney Houston, who swept the awards and stole the show with a classy medley that included 'I Loves You Porgy' (from *Porgy and Bess*) and 'I Tell You I'm Not Going' (from *Dreamgirls*)."

When she accepted one her awards that night, she was carrying Bobbi Kristina with her. As Whitney spoke her acceptance speech, the baby grabbed at the microphone. "I couldn't leave her," apologized the star, "she started cryin'."

The accolades just kept on coming for Whitney that year. Seven days later, and an ocean away, *The Bodyguard* was named the "Best Soundtrack Album" at the thirteenth annual BRIT Awards, which were handed out at Alexandria Palace in London.

On March 1, 1994, Whitney performed her new signature song, "I Will Always Love You" at Radio City Music Hall in New York City at the thirty-sixth annual Grammy Awards. She then proceeded to pick up her next three Grammys, for "Record of the Year," "Best Pop Vocal Performance, Female" for "I Will Always Love You," and "Album of the Year" for *The Bodyguard* soundtrack.

At the eighth annual Soul Train Awards, held at the Shrine Auditorium in Los Angeles on March 15, Whitney won the R&B Song of the Year Award for "I Will Always Love You." She was also presented with the Sammy Davis Jr. Award, and she performed on stage with Bobby Brown. In Canada, on March 20, she won a Juno Award as *The Bodyguard* was named Album of the Year. At the music industry's annual NARM convention, *The Bodyguard* is named the "Best Selling Soundtrack," and the "Best Selling Chartmaker Recording of the Year."

Although she was now "Mrs. Bobby Brown," the lesbian rumors continued to swirl around her. Whitney became even more vehement about the rumors about she and Robyn when she declared in *Rolling Stone*, "I'm so sick of this shit. People want to know if there is a relationship between me and Robyn. Our relationship is that we are friends. We've been friends since we were kids. Robyn is now my employee. I'm her employer. You mean to tell me if I have a woman friend, I have to be having a lesbian relationship with her. That's bullshit. There are so many female artists who have women as their confidantes, and nobody questions that. So I realize that it's like, 'Whitney Houston, she's popular, let's fuck with her.' I have denied it over and over again and nobody's accepted it. Or, the media hasn't. People out there know I'm a married woman. I mean, what kind of a person am I—to be married and to have another life? First of all, my husband wouldn't go for it—let's get that out of the way, okay? He's all boy, and he ain't goin' for it, okay? But I'm so fucking tired of that question, and I'm tired of answering it." Regardless of her statements, the rumors never did go away.

While Bobby and Whitney and Robyn were all staying at the Peninsula Hotel in Beverly Hills, reportedly a huge fight erupted between all three parties. Not only were Whitney and Bobby fighting among themselves, he was also arguing with Robyn. Early in the morning of March 24, Robyn summoned security guards to complain that she had been physically attacked by Bobby Brown.

According to the book *Diva: The Totally Unauthorized Biography of Whitney Houston*, by Jeffrey Bowman, one of the security guards was interviewed and reported, "Mr. Brown was cursing and threatening Ms. Crawford and we asked Ms. Houston if she would like us to stay until the police—who had also been summoned—arrived. But she said she could handle the situation from here. We noticed by his behavior that Mr. Brown had apparently been drinking. It seemed that Brown, Houston, and Crawford had all been involved in some sort of physical altercation."

On April 9, 1994, Whitney was one of the featured stars to headline Carnegie Hall in New York City, as part of the fifth annual *Save the Rain Forest* benefit concert. Also on the bill that night were Elton John, Tammy Wynette, Sting, James Taylor, Aaron Neville, Branford Marsalis, and Luciano Pavarotti. On the fourteenth of the month Whitney began her South American concert tour by performing at San Carlos De Apoqundo Stadium, in Santiago, Chile.

Meanwhile, on April 26, Bobby was arrested and charged with beating up a bar patron at the Disney World nightclub, Mannequin, in Orlando, Florida. According to reports, Brown and three of his friends were partying, when a businessman from Chicago started talking to a particular girl Brown and his group were conversing with. Bobby hit the man over the head with a bottle, and beat him to the floor. The police were called to take care of this brawl. Brown and his friends were asked by police officers to sit on the outdoor streetside curb and answer some questions about the incident. Bobby refused to comply, and was promptly arrested. In the backseat of the squad car he proceeded to urinate, and to carve the word "fuck" into the upholstery of the car. The man who had been attacked was taken to the hospital to reattach his partially severed ear to his head. Bobby and his boys spent approximately five hours in jail, paid $5,000 in bail money, and were released. It was just another night on the town with Bobby Brown.

Next up on Whitney's global award-winning sweep came winning several trophies at the sixth annual World Music Awards gala, held at the Sporting Club in Monte Carlo, in Monaco. At the May 4 event Houston was named: "Pop Artist of the Year," "R&B Artist of the Year," "American

Recording Artist of the Year," "Overall Recording Artist of the Year," and "Female Recording Artist of the Year."

That spring it was announced that the next film role Whitney Houston was signed to portray, was that of the title role in a remake of Rodgers and Hammerstein's *Cinderella*. It had originally been filmed in 1957 for black & white television, and in the 1960s it was remade with an all-star cast, also as a TV special. This too was to be a made-for-television film.

In June she was in the news for filing a lawsuit against a company of concert promoters named Pro Rok, who had handled her April 24 concert in San Juan, Puerto Rico. According to her representatives, she was defrauded her out of her agreed-upon percentage of the ticket sales.

On June 14 Houston was the star of a news conference held in New York City. It was held to announce that she had signed a contract with telephone company AT&T to advertise their new voice enhancing equipment, dubbed "AT&T TrueVoice." She was to be paid a cool million dollars to be part of the company's ad campaign.

At the high-profile sporting event, The World Cup Final in Pasadena, California, Whitney was the headlining act for the pre-game show on July 17, 1994. The teams playing were representing the countries of Italy and Brazil.

For Whitney, the year was not without its odd moments. In Morristown, New Jersey, on September 2, a second restraining order had to be served against a man by the name of Charles Gilberg. An overzealous fan, he proclaimed that it was he who was actually the father of Whitney's child.

Later that same month, Whitney headlined Radio City Music Hall—September 16–17, 20–21, 27–28, and 30—and sold out the entire engagement. She grossed an astonishing $2,668,940. On October 4 she performed at the Rose Garden at the White House in Washington, D.C. Her performance followed a state dinner honoring Nelson Mandela. Reportedly, she showed up extremely late for her performance at the White House that evening, without explanation. This was to become a regular occurrence for her.

On November 12, HBO presented the special concert event, *Whitney—Concert For a New South Africa*. The concert was broadcast live from Ellis Park in Johannesburg, South Africa. It was a part of her concert tour of South Africa, to help celebrate that country's recent unification and the end of apartheid.

In the 1993–1995 era Whitney Houston had become an even bigger star than she was before. With her increased stature, her demonstrations of "diva-like" behavior only increased. On March 2, 1995, Whitney and Bobby and their entourage swept into the Hollywood Palladium where she was scheduled to present her mother with a Pioneer Award from The Rhythm & Blues Foundation. I was personally present that night, and I couldn't believe Whitney Houston's cold behavior. The event began with a cocktail party that was absolutely star-studded. Bonnie Raitt, Fred Schneider of The B-52's, Mary Wilson, Martha Reeves, Mavis Staples, Little Richard, and several other celebrities were present, and were all accessible to the press. Whitney and Bobby arrived late, with a complete posse of assistants. Someone was hanging onto Bobbi Kristina, another was carrying what looked like a diaper bag. They all seemed to be waiting on Whitney and Bobby "hand and foot." I was seated at a table with two very big celebrities, and a security guard came to our table and said very politely, that no one was to approach 'Miss Houston's table, at Miss Houston's request.' We were horrified at how rude this comment was, since the room was filled with dozens of recognizable singing stars, graciously speaking with everyone. One music industry insider said to me that evening, "I can't believe what a conceited bitch Whitney has become."

Meanwhile, *The Bodyguard* was such a successful film, that almost instantly there was a search for new scripts for Whitney's return to the big screen. One idea that kept resurfacing, was a proposed remake of the Cary Grant, Loretta Young, David Niven comedy, *The Bishop's Wife*. However, before that could be put into motion, Whitney was asked to be one of the stars of the filmed version of Terry McMillan's best-selling novel *Waiting to Exhale*.

Much of the spring of 1995 Whitney spent in Phoenix, Arizona filming *Waiting to Exhale*, in which she portrayed the role of Savannah. The film teamed her with Angela Bassett, Loretta Devine, and Lela Rochon, and a stunning, mainly black cast. The film was directed by actor

Forest Whitaker. Whitney was to report to *Ebony* magazine, "In just two weeks, Forest has taught me a lot about acting. In *The Bodyguard* I was just simply playing a character that I was familiar with because she and I had the same kind of world. With Savannah, it's more like me without the fame. She allows me to be a lot more like myself. The great thing about it is that I have three other beautiful ladies who are all great actresses and whom I can play off of."

While Whitney was busy working, her husband was busy playing. In August of 1995 Bobby threw a party for his friends in West Hollywood. When he was told by a security officer that the party was getting too loud, Brown responded by kicking the guard. He was charged with misdemeanor assault for the incident.

On September 21, 1995, a press release was issued, confirming that Whitney and Bobby were officially separated. Houston's fans all breathed a sigh of relief. But the split was only temporary, unfortunately.

The Bobby Brown antics continued that month, to the point where he was nearly caught in some deadly crossfire. Bobby had just hired a new personal bodyguard named Steven "Shot" Sealy. The pair had just left a bar in the Roxbury area of Boston, when someone opened gunfire on the pair. Sealy was killed.

When Whitney was asked about her troublesome husband, in 1995 she replied, "We all have our problems and troubles. All I want to do is to be able to work them out in private . . . They say he cheats on me. I haven't caught him yet. If I had, I'd break his fucking neck." Always the lady, that Whitney!

She was not too fond of the press she and Bobby were generating either. According to her, "The media are demons. They're devils and they're out to eat my flesh." She somehow never took into account the fact that her husband was usually in trouble with the law, and she was rapidly getting a reputation for being "a bitch." She defensive claimed, "I don't take as much shit as I used to, and if that makes me a bitch, then so be it." Well, as the old saying goes: "If the shoe fits, wear it."

According to workers on the set of the film *Waiting to Exhale*, Whitney didn't exactly do anything to repair her new hard-as-nails reputation. *Entertainment Weekly* quoted one member of the film's production staff as saying, "The people that she surrounds herself with are not as cultured as she is. They're kind of gruff. And I think that's her interior. There's something cold about her. She's tough."

On November 2, 1995 at the twenty-fifth annual Soul Train Awards, Whitney was inducted into their Hall of Fame. By November 17 she was reportedly back with Bobby, having publicly reconciled at the Bar None nightclub in Miami, Florida. By the end of the month her latest single, the theme song from *Waiting to Exhale*, "Exhale (Shoop Shoop)" peaked at Number One in the United States and at Number 11 in England.

With this latest hit, Whitney became only the third person to have had a single debut at Number One on the *Billboard* charts in America. In addition, with the song "Exhale (Shoop Shoop)" hitting the top of the chart, she tied Madonna with 11 American Number Ones. That distinction put the pair of divas in league just under The Beatles (20), Elvis (17), and The Supremes (12)—for the all-time record on Number One pop hits.

The film *Waiting to Exhale* was released during the Christmas season of 1995, and it was an instant hit at the box-office, especially with women—of all races. In fact *Waiting to Exhale* is similar to the kind of "women's picture" you would see in the 1930s and 1940s starring actresses like Bette Davis, Miriam Hopkins, Claudette Colbert, and Joan Crawford.

The sensitive and often funny film was indeed unique on the marketplace. It was the very first film made for contemporary black women, and about contemporary black women. Like the best-selling book upon which it was based, the film was entirely racially blind. The four women in the film just happened to be "of color," and the plot has nothing to do with black and white society as a whole. Its entire focus was the story of four women who were friends, and their troubles with the men in their lives.

Set in Phoenix, Arizona, *Waiting to Exhale* took time to tell of each of the women's adventures and misadventures. The plot centered on the four lead women, and showed them cocktailing, partying, and complaining with their relationship problems. All four of the characters were attractive and educated women who were—by choice or not by choice—single and *hating* it.

Whitney plays Savannah, a television station executive who finds herself in an ongoing relationship with a married man, who for years has promised to leave his wife for her. Angela Bassett is Bernadine, who finds herself with a fabulous house in Scottsdale, two adorable children, and dozens of wonderful possessions. However, when her husband walks out on her, she shifts into revenge mode. Loretta Devine is Gloria, whose husband has also left her—when he announced that he was gay. This makes raising her teenage son Tarik even more challenging for her. And pretty Lela Rochon portrays Robin, is a successful business woman, but her lovelife is populated with men who are either too conceited, or too goofy to consider as serious husband material.

Without a doubt, of the foursome, Angela Bassett is the one who really infuses her scenes with snap and electricity. After she discovers her husband is leaving her for his white secretary, she has a glorious scene in which she sets his prize sports car on fire in the driveway—just to piss him off. If one had to give the girls titles according to type, Angela is the feisty one, Loretta is the sweet one, Lela is the cute one, and Whitney is the bored-with-it-all one.

In an effort to act frustrated and blasé, Whitney often seems to wander through her scenes with disinterest. Her charms aren't always shown off at their best. She is the liveliest when she is surrounded with the other principal women, dishing and having some girl talk. There is one scene of Houston's in particular where she is alone on camera, and appears uncomfortable. It comes while having a phone conversation with her character's mother, and she seems to be unemotionally reciting her lines from a cue card.

The press reviews for *Waiting to Exhale* were basically very positive. Barry Walters of *The San Francisco Examiner* claimed, "*Waiting to Exhale* positions itself as the first official you-go-girl film black women can call their own. It's proudly a she thing, perfect for a night of 'just us' female bonding." However he pointed out, "The film doesn't tell the story as well as the soundtrack album, a diva marathon that fleshes out the book's themes better than its author does on screen."

In *The Washington Post* Desson Howe found, "In the ensemble story, four women—played with competitive pizzazz by Bassett, Whitney

Houston, Loretta Devine and Lela Rochon—have suffered the gamut of undesirable experiences with men . . . With such a plurality of developments, *Exhale* could easily lose itself in the shuffle. But it's fluid and emotional, thanks to a crisp, witty script . . . tremendous performances by the principals (playing emotionally wounded seems to come easily to all of them—take that Bobby Brown) and sensitive direction by Forest Whitaker."

Edmund Guthmann in *The San Francisco Chronicle* found it inconsistent. According to him, "It's hilarious in patches . . . [it] is also lifeless and flat in spots. You want the movie to stomp and rejoice and cry like a fool; instead it meanders and lollygags . . . Houston, who hasn't made a movie since *The Bodyguard* (1992), handles the central part here, but she underplays so much that she comes off bored and removed, as though she had better fish to fry."

And, Roger Ebert in *The Chicago Sun-Times* found himself intrigued in the story from the very start. "These are not real women so much as fictional creations carefully designed to embody dreams and desires. Many of the women in the audience would be happy to be like any of these women, man or no man," he wrote. "However, the movie does work. I was never bored . . . for the most part, the movie's content to be an entertainment with a women's magazine angle; its patron saint could be Mae West, who wanted more men in her life, and more life in her men."

In January of 1996 the soundtrack album for *Waiting to Exhale* also hit Number One. In addition to "Exhale (Shoop Shoop)," it contained two more Houston recordings, as well as new songs by Aretha Franklin, Patti LaBelle, TLC, Toni Braxton, Brandy, Mary J. Blige, Chaka Khan and several other soul divas. The entire album, track by track, was produced by Babyface.

Playing on the rhythmic feeling of the 1990s catchword "shoop" came Whitney's most instantaneous hit, "Exhale (Shoop Shoop)." The group Salt-N-Pepa in 1993 had a big Top Ten hit with another song called "Shoop." And, Cher in 1991 had one of her hugest international hits with "The Shoop Shoop Song (It's In His Kiss)." Houston proved that "shoop" lightning could strike three times, with this simple but catchy pop ballad. It features some of Whitney's most restrained yet effective singing.

Her second solo on the album, "Why Does It Hurt So Bad" is one of her smoothest ballads. A simple song about the heartbreak of love, Whitney sounds like she seems to know what it feels like on this effective Babyface composition. She sounds wonderful on the subtle violin-laden, slow-building ballad. And her third performance on the album was her duet with gospel's CeCe Winans, the song of friendship and devotion, "Count on Me."

While Babyface produced all of the music, the album also carries the credit, "Executive Album Producers" as being Kenneth "Babyface" Edmonds, Whitney Houston, and Clive Davis. Although she was flexing her own independence in many ways, Clive was clearly still the person who was setting the tone of how Whitney should be presented to the public. It wasn't long before she began to rebel against his authority as well.

No sooner than *Waiting to Exhale* was safely in the theaters, in January of 1996 principal filming on *The Preacher's Wife* began. According to *Entertainment Weekly* magazine, Whitney was paid a cool $10 million to star opposite Denzel Washington in this family-oriented movie.

The week of February 24, "Count on Me," the Whitney Houston / CeCe Winans duet from *Waiting to Exhale* peaked in England at Number 12. At the tenth annual Soul Train Music Awards, the song "Exhale (Shoop Shoop)" won Houston the "Best R&B / Soul Single, Female" award, on March 29. Then, on April 5, Whitney and Denzel Washington hosted the twenty-seventh annual NAACP Image Awards presentation in Pasadena, California. That night the *Waiting to Exhale* was named the year's "Best Album," and "Exhale (Shoop Shoop)" was named the "Outstanding Song of the Year."

Meanwhile, the Bobby Brown hi-jinks were continuing to make headlines. On April 22, 1996 Bobby was booked for driving under the influence of alcohol in Atlanta. He was so drunk, he was unable to successfully recite the alphabet. It was also noted that the woman who was in the automobile with him was not his wife. While Bobby Brown's career seemed to be falling apart, Houston's remained rock solid.

In May, Whitney's song "Count on Me" peaked in America at Number 8, and in August the third Houston cut from *Waiting to Exhale*, "Why Does It Hurt So Bad" made it to Number 26 in the U.S. On September

13 she was feted by B.E.T television network. Houston was the recipient of their second "B.E.T. Walk of Fame Award," which was bestowed upon her at their United Negro College Fund benefit in Washington D.C. On November 17 she sang at the TV taping of *Celebrate the Dream: 50 Years of Ebony Magazine.* That special was broadcast on the twenty-eighth of the month.

On August 17, 1996, while driving Whitney's Porsche in Hollywood, Florida, Bobby Brown crashed the automobile into a sign. He was treated for neck and leg injuries at a local hospital, and he was released. Fortunately for him, there were no legal charges filed.

The inspiration and the plot of *The Preacher's Wife* was an almost direct re-make of the delightful 1947 comedy, *The Bishop's Wife*. In the original film, the wife in question was played by Loretta Young, her befuddled husband was portrayed by David Niven, and the charming angel, Dudley, was played by Cary Grant. It remains a popular holiday film which still holds up well as charming Christmas entertainment—along the lines of Jimmy Stewart's *It's a Wonderful Life*.

In the updated 1996 version of *The Bishop's Wife*, Courtney B. Vance plays Rev. Henry Biggs, who is the head pastor of St. Matthews Baptist Church, in an East Coast city. As Christmas is nearing, and it seems that he has nothing but problems to deal with. He has teenagers in youth programs that the church can no longer afford to support, he has a dwindling congregation, he has a heating boiler that is on its last legs, and he has an aggressive real estate developer (Gregory Hines) who is itching to take a wrecking ball to the whole church.

In addition, Henry has a lovely wife, Julia (Houston), who is feeling neglected in her marriage, as she watches her husband run himself ragged while trying to solve all the problems. Henry may be frustrated, but he sure knows how to pray. He prays to God to send him someone to help him. What he doesn't realize is that his prayers have been answered. An actual angel has been sent from Heaven to Earth to assist him, in the embodiment of Dudley (Denzel Washington).

Julia assumes that Dudley has been sent by the church board, and warmly accepts him into their lives. He also ingratiates himself to the couple's young son, who also accepts Dudley because of his innocence and honesty. The cast is also full of wonderful character players. Jenifer Lewis is hysterical as Julia's chain-smoking mother, and Loretta Devine play's Henry's overworked and slightly-clueless secretary. In addition, Whitney's mother, Cissy Houston plays Mrs. Havergal, one of the church choir members with a mind of her own. Her inclusion in the film is one of the most delightful aspects of this charming film.

By far, some of Whitney's most important scenes are the ones she has as the choir leader at church. It gives her a lot of screentime to appear totally in her element. When Dudley has the opportunity to take Julia to a jazz club, she runs into an old piano playing friend of hers, Britsloe (Lionel Ritchie). Like all Christmas movies, *The Preacher's Wife* has a warm and happy ending, which in this case is uplifting without being sappy or syrupy.

Playing Julia in *The Preacher's Wife* provided Whitney with her strongest film role to date. She seems very focused and comfortable with her character. And, her rapport and chemistry with both of her leading men is charming. The scenes with her screen mother, Jenifer Lewis, have a wonderfully bantering mother / daughter warmth to them. Director Penny Marshall successfully kept the plot moving, and she drew very believable performances out of Whitney and the rest of the cast.

The reviews for *The Preacher's Wife* were quite good, and they were equally positive for Whitney Houston. According to Kevin Thomas in *The Los Angeles Times*, "*The Preacher's Wife* is one Christmas picture that actually is in the spirit of the season. It's warm, sentimental, amusing yet serious, bringing fantasy to bear upon the painfully real . . . Washington and Houston, who has plenty of opportunities to sing as the leader of St Matthews' gospel choir, are among the most attractive, charismatic actors on the screen today, and they are terrific here."

In *The San Francisco Examiner*, Barbara Shulgasser claimed, "The main appeal of the slight but diverting 1947 . . . *The Bishop's Wife* was its cast of attractive lead actors . . . *The Preacher's Wife* has a nearly identical plot . . . featuring an equally attractive cast . . . Transferring the action to a black church where Houston regularly sings gospel music is the update's major improvement on the original . . . Houston is completely adorable and her voice soars through the movie's musical numbers."

Roger Ebert in *The Chicago Sun Times* loved it by proclaiming, "*The Preacher's Wife* is a sweet and good-hearted comedy about the holiday season . . . I found myself enjoying *The Preacher's Wife* for its simple but real pleasures; For the way Houston sings . . . and also for Denzel Washington, who is able to project love without lust, and goodness without corniness. This movie could have done more, but what it does, it makes you feel good about."

Well, not everyone agreed. Wrote Denis Seguin in *Eye Weekly*, "*The Preacher's Wife* is a lousy update of *The Bishop's Wife* . . . a story of divine inspiration, the film is uninspired, a more than usually cynical exploitation of star power. It's so obviously a platform for the singer there are times when you think you're watching a rerun of the Grammy Awards in the late '80s."

As she had with *The Bodyguard* and *Waiting to Exhale* before it, Whitney Houston put her solo album career aside to put her focus on the soundtrack album. In this instance, she was finally able to delve into her gospel singing roots, to make her musical choices lively, relevant to a 1990s audience, and to create some new music that stood up on its own. It also gave Whitney the opportunity to give her famous mother one of the album tracks, as well as having a duet with gospel legend Shirley Caesar. At Whitney's insistence, even Bobby Brown had a guest appearance on the album. In addition, Robyn Crawford had a hand in the album too, as she is credited as one of the "Associate Album Producers."

To call *The Preacher's Wife* soundtrack album an all-gospel LP is misleading, however it contains a full 80 percent gospel content. It includes two separate versions of the album's biggest solo hits, the pop love ballad "I Believe in You and Me," and the upbeat "Step By Step." It fact it is "Step By Step" that is the most feverously infectious song on the album, which was written by rock star Annie Lennox.

Whitney's subsequent gospel excursions include "Joy," "Hold On Help is On the Way," "I Go to the Rock," and "I Love the Lord." Whitney and Shirley Caesar, backed by The Georgia Mass Choir unleash some exciting gospel fire on "He's All Over Me." And Cissy Houston takes the spotlight as she sings "The Lord is My Shepherd" with the Hazekiah Walker Choir.

Whitney also takes her turn at doing some Christmas oriented songs as well. The new song "Who Would Imagine a King" and the traditional "Joy to the World" are nice reminders that this is a holiday-oriented story.

One of the most interesting, and satisfying cuts on the album is the rap / gospel number "Somebody Bigger Than You and I," which features Bobby Brown, Faith Evans, Johnny Gill, Monica, and Ralph Tresvant. Whitney also gets her own share of ballads too. Diane Warren penned the beautiful ballad of devotion, "You Were Loved," and Babyface wrote the thumping "My Heart is Calling," both of which he produced.

Interestingly enough, one of the versions of the song "I Believe in You and Me," labeled the "single version," was produced by David Foster of "I Will Always Love You" fame" With the exception of the Babyface-produced numbers, one song by Foster, and "Step By Step" by Stephen Lipson, Whitney Houston is listed as the co-producer of this album—along with Mervyn Warren, and she co-produced one cut with Ricky Minor. Apparently, Whitney was now taking more control of her own musical destiny, and this time around, she was hitting all of the right buttons. Although the album contained no Number One pop hits, it did have the distinction of becoming the most successful gospel album of all times—selling over 5 million copies worldwide.

The week of December 28, 1996, *The Preacher's Wife* peaked at Number Three on the *Billboard* album chart. In January of 1997 the song "Step by Step" made it to Number 13 in England. The 24th Annual American Music Awards at the Los Angeles Shrine Auditorium on January 27 found Whitney back in the winner's circle, as she was named the Favorite Female Artist, Adult Contemporary. The song "I Believe in You and Me" hit Number 4 in America in February.

The NAACP Image Awards were handed out on February 8, 1997, with *The Preacher's Wife* soundtrack being named Outstanding Album, and Whitney was named Outstanding Actor / Actress. This was her first—and only—real acting award.

On February 10, Bobby Brown's Atlanta-based record production company, Bosstown Inc. filed for Chapter 11 bankruptcy. The bankruptcy filing came only fifteen minutes before Brown was served with an official court order to pay $194,000 to Stude Editech Inc., for recording equipment which he had purchased and couldn't afford.

On February 26 the Grammy Awards were presented in Madison Square Garden in New York City. Having sold over 3 million copies in America, the *Waiting to Exhale* soundtrack became the most nominated album in Grammy history. That night Whitney, together with Mary J. Blige, CeCe Winans, Chaka Khan, Aretha Franklin, Brandi and Toni Braxton, performed an all-star medley of their songs from the album.

In March the song "Step by Step" peaked at Number 15 in the U.S., and "I Believe in You and Me" hit Number 16 in England. The final single from *The Preacher's Wife* album, "My Heart is Calling" peaked at Number 77 in America in July.

In spite of Bobby's occasional antics, Whitney Houston was riding on the crest of the greatest streak of success ever. Although *The Preacher's Wife* didn't set any box-office records, the critics loved it, and audiences agreed that it was her most relaxed and charming film performance yet. In the span of five years she had starred in three hit films, and was the main star on three incredibly successful soundtrack albums. Whatever sales slump she had experienced with her last solo studio album, she had certainly made up for it with the soundtracks from *The Bodyguard*, *Waiting to Exhale*, and *The Preacher's Wife*. It looked like things were going swimmingly well for her. Next up for Houston: the much-anticipated all-star musical version of *Cinderella*.

CHAPTER ELEVEN

"IT BEGINS TO UNRAVEL"

As Whitney and Bobby were vacationing in Europe during the summer, something very interesting was reported. While floating on a yacht in the Mediterranean Sea off the island of Capri, something happened that was never fully explained. On July 21, 1997, Whitney was brought to Capilupi Hospital where a doctor had to sew up a two-inch cut on her cheek. Two stitches were required to close the wound. When she spoke to the Italian police, Whitney tried to blame it on a swimming accident when she hit a rock. However crew members on the rented yacht insisted that she sustained the wound while on the boat. It was surmised that Whitney and Bobby had simply gotten into one of their trademark physical fights. These had reportedly become a regular occurrence.

On October 5, Whitney Houston was the star of her own massively promoted live concert performance on HBO. Firsthand witnesses claimed that she "appeared stoned" when she hit the stage and started rambling to the audience in some unrehearsed monologue. According to *Entertainment Weekly*, "she strained to sing her tunes, reeled off a random, bewildering medley of tributes to dead celebrities—including the Notorious B.I.G. and Princess Diana—and dripped more flop sweat than Nixon." One of the press reviewers said that watching the concert was like "a tape-delayed near-death experience."

Record producer Andrew Skurow claimed, "I was shocked watching that HBO debacle from Washington D.C. I think it aired only once because it was so bad. She appeared to be wasted during the whole thing." Audience members were reportedly sinking in their seats in sheer discomfort, wanting to escape.

A songwriter of one of Whitney's greatest hits—who was at the concert—confessed that he was "embarrassed" by what he witnessed during that particular concert. "She couldn't hit any of the notes. She has ruined her voice," he sadly proclaimed. "I couldn't wait 'til it was over. She was excruciating to watch."

Whitney received her next bit of unflattering press when she suddenly canceled her appearance on the top-rated daytime TV talk program, *The Rosie O'Donnell Show*. Houston was scheduled to be the main star on the October 30, 1997 episode of the show, when, forty-five minutes before she was supposed to arrive for the taping, she announced that she was backing out of the appearance. Not to be stood up that easily, O'Donnell peppered the episode in question with snotty remarks about Whitney.

Since Houston claimed that she suddenly had a case of stomach flu, Rosie told her audience that day, "I hope she's *very* ill." To fill in the gap in the show, O'Donnell had to stretch the other guest segments to take up the slack. This was an extremely difficult situation, since this was the first day of the traditional November TV "sweeps" week in which advertising sponsors gauge the ratings. To completely rub salt in the wound, that very day that Whitney was too ill to be on Rosie's telecast, she found time to accompany Bobby Brown to his own television appearance on another talk show, *The Late Show with David Letterman*.

The *Cinderella* made-for-TV movie, which five years previous seemed like a great idea and a perfect project for Whitney—since she herself was something of a real-life Cinderella—went through a major concept change. It was originally announced that she was going to be playing the title role. However, she was no longer seen by the public as an innocent young girl. For whatever reason, she wisely bowed out the title role, but she remained as one of the producing partners on the project. Instead of portraying Cinderella herself, she opted to play the Fairy Godmother who has the ability to turn pumpkins into carriages, and mice into horses. As Cinderella, Houston invited Brandy, the star of TV's *Moesha*, to be the star. It was the perfect bit of casting in this mixed racial, color-blind version of the fairy tale classic, since Brandy had the natural innocence that Whitney no longer possessed or radiated.

The rest of the of the cast included Bernadette Peters as the Wicked Stepmother, Whoopi Goldberg as the Queen, Victor Garber as the King, and Jason Alexander as the Courtier. They each turned in delightfully over-the-top performances, and gave the production its proper buoyancy. The songs were all pre-recorded and beautifully produced by Arif Mardin. Also, Whitney's close friend Robyn Crawford worked behind the scenes as the Associate Producer.

However, while the film was in production, troubles were being reported throughout Hollywood According to sources on the set of *Cinderella*, Whitney never showed up on time for the filming. The resulting film showed her off as weak and uncertain in her speaking voice, and she looked buried alive in a costume that was confusingly elaborate and unflattering instead of impressively awesome.

In *Cinderella*, Whitney comes across less Fairy Godmother, than she does Scary Godmother. Her entrance on camera should have been visually exciting, and her attitude should have been charmingly delightful. For some strange reason she performed the part in a pushy, haughty, irritated, and intimidating fashion. Playing the role with the tone of a surly 1990s "fly-girl" was all wrong.

When she recited her dialogue lines, her voice sounded raspy, and in one scene it actually cracks mid-sentence. It sounded like she and Bobby had been up all night partying. She seemed to save nothing for her performance. For all but one scene she was squeezed into a skin-tight gold dress that made her look pudgy and pregnant. She sang the song "Impossible" with Brandy, which has some snappy life to it, but mainly Whitney is "impossible" to believe as the Fairy Godmother. She should have appeared dazzlingly magical, but her performance was aggressively lackadaisical.

The rest of the cast fortunately sparkled throughout. And, Brandy is so charming as Cinderella—she carried the film perfectly. Dancing with her Prince (Paolo Montalban), she absolutely glows. The lavish sets are all fairy-tale-perfect, decorated in a sumptuous Vienna 1900 fashion, borrowing directly from the distinctive artwork of Gustav Klimt.

When *Cinderella* originally aired on November 2, 1997 it was a huge ratings success—drawing over 34 million viewers. It was Whitney's performance that was a disappointment to critics and audiences alike. It is also acknowledged as Houston's weakest film performance. According to Ken Tucker in *Entertainment Weekly*, "Whitney Houston, however—once upon a time slated to play the Cinderella role herself in this production—strikes a wrong note as a sassy, vaguely hostile Fairy Godmother."

In still another Houston disaster, she suddenly pulled out of another concert appearance at the last minute, on November 29, 1997. She was scheduled to perform a forty-five minute set of songs and be paid a cool million dollars at a performance at RFK Stadium in Washington, D.C. She proclaimed that she was struck with a "sudden flu-like illness." The most bizarre twist in the story is the fact that the event was actually a mass wedding ceremony for 2,500 couples, who were from the religious cult of Reverend Moon. Regardless, spacey Houston was a "Moonie" no-show.

Interestingly enough, after marrying Whitney, instead of her mega-star stature buoying Bobby Brown's recording career upward, association with him has only dragged her further downward. His most recent CD, *Forever,* was released in November 1997 on MCA Records—making it to Number 61, and the single from it, "Feelin' Inside," peaked in England at Number 40. Since that time, his actual career has mainly dried up.

In spite of her recent trail of bizarre behavior, Whitney's popularity was still intact. On January 11, 1998, she tied for the "Female Musical Performer" prize at the twenty-fourth annual People's Choice Awards.

However, Bobby was not having the same streak of luck. On January 29, 1998, Brown was convicted of DUI charges in a Fort Lauderdale, Florida court. The presiding Judge Leonard Finer sentenced the "Humpin' Around" star to five days in a jail cell, thirty days of drug and alcohol rehabilitation, a fine of $500, mandatory attendance at a DUI driving school, random drug and alcohol testing, 100 hours of community service, recording a series of public service announcements, and a one-year driver's license suspension. Both Whitney and Bobby were present for the sentencing. He was released from legal custody on a $15,000 appeal bond. Reportedly, the pair were in tears as the verdict was handed down.

On February 27 Houston was presented with The Quincy Jones Outstanding Career Achievement Award at the Soul Train Awards. She was also honored with a serenade from Monica, Ronald Isley, Kenny Lattimore, and Terry Ellis. They sang her a medley of her hits at the event, held at the Shrine Auditorium in Los Angeles.

April 23, Whitney was in Nashville, where she performed her gospel song "I Go to the Rock" at the Dove Awards. And, on June 10, 1998, in an uncharacteristically friendly move, Whitney presented the annual "Hitmaker Award" at the Songwriter's Hall of Fame Dinner—to, of all people—Diana Ross. The event was held at the Sheraton New York Hotel and Towers. On June 20–21, Whitney was amidst a pair of concert dates in Gerry-Weber-Stadiom, at Halle / Westphalia, Germany. This kicked off a ten-date series of concerts throughout Europe.

Meanwhile it was business-as-usual for Bobby. On June 21, 1998, Brown was arrested on suspicion of sexual battery. This followed an incident at the swimming pool of the Beverly Hills Hilton Hotel. The singer was freed on bail.

On August 7, 1998, in a teaming of the decade's top rival divas, Whitney Houston and Mariah Carey went into a sound studio in New York City, and recorded the song "When You Believe" for the soundtrack of the animated film *The Prince of Egypt*. The press was expecting the pair to get into some sort of cat fight, but the session reportedly went well between the two singers. Throughout the decade of the 1990s, it seemed that the pair were constant rivals on record charts. There are so many parallels between Whitney Houston's career and Mariah Carey's. While Houston's singing success was the product of Clive Davis's star-making machinery, Carey was married to the head of CBS Records, Tommy Mottola—who acted as her own Svengali.

Whitney performed on October 11 at the fourth annual International Achievement in Arts Awards, held at the Beverly Hilton Hotel in Beverly Hills. The event raised money for her own charity, The Whitney Houston Foundation for Children, as well as The Starkey Hearing Foundation.

At long last, Whitney's fourth studio album was released on the market on November 28, 1998. Entitled *My Love is Your Love*, upon Whitney's insistence, it had a harder-edged, inner-city rap-inspired sound to it, which was completely different that any album she had released before. Stylistically it is known for being a huge left turn for her. Instead of courting her usual audience, she chose to experiment. Her singing on this album is much more sassy and assertive, and it was actually quite a successful excursion into hip hop. However, was that what her audience wanted to hear from her? Apparently not.

The *My Love is Your Love* album is an often interesting and dramatic departure for Whitney Houston. But, it is also a very inconsistent album. One half of it is comprised of dynamic and somewhat aggressive hip hop music, and the other half of the album is indistinguishably bland and boring.

The album opens with "It's Not Right But It's Okay," which is by far the best and most exciting song on the whole album. Produced by Rodney Jenkins, it features the sassiest and most alive and vital track. In the context of the song Whitney is heard confronting her lover—presumably Bobby—of cheating on her. Lyrically she sings with snappy self-confidence about having the evidence of philandering via incriminating credit card receipts. She scolds, she hoots and hollers, and she sounds great on this dynamic and finger-popping song about love gone wrong.

Further reflecting her new, more aggressive singing style comes on the song "Heartbreak Hotel. This is not to be confused with the Elvis Presley hit of the same name. Joined in song by a pair of up-and-coming Whitney wannabes, Faith Evans and Kelly Price, this is a pulsing soul-fest with this trio of girlfriends tunefully shunning an inconsiderate lover.

Shifting gears to present a song of devoted love, the title cut—"My Love is Your Love"—comes across like a pledge of love to Bobby. Also, there is a voice cameo from Bobbi Kristina, which is meant to be cute, but comes across as irritating.

The beautiful and shimmering "When You Believe" contrasts Mariah Carey's clear multi-range voice with Houston's own steely delivery. Surprisingly, the pair blends well together on this inspirational duet from the *Prince of Egypt* film soundtrack. It is ironic to note that this song was the first and only teaming of the two leading hit-making pop divas of the 1990s. Right after it was released it seems, both of their careers seemed to slow down considerably.

The next song on the album, "If I Told You That" is a curious song in that it finds Whitney singing of bringing "something" else into a sexual love affair. However, it makes one wonder what—or who—she is singing about? Bringing in another man? Another woman? A circus act? It is never explained, but by the growl in her voice, it is strongly implied here that Whitney is up to something controversial and experimental.

The last truly impressive song on this album is "In My Business," which teams Houston with hip hop rapper Missy "Misdemeanor" Elliott. Known for her own catchy and vibrant records, Elliott here inspires Whitney to deliver some real sparks while singing of the "ho's" [slang for "whore's"] who want her man.

All of these harder-edged songs do their best to kill Whitney's own former "good girl" image. This album represented a total persona departure for her, and because of this many of her former fans clearly passed on purchasing it.

The album's subsequent songs, "I Learned From the Best," "Oh Yes," "Get it Back," "Until You Come Back" and You'll Never Stand Alone" all seem to blend together as forgettable filler. Furthermore, Whitney's performance on these songs sounds completely uninspired. Only Babyface's "Until You Come Back" has some vocal sparks—but there are not enough to truly bring it to life. For the most part tracks seven to twelve are a total yawn.

Finally, the album ends on a high note. The thirteenth cut, not included on the track list—or the liner notes—is Houston's percolating cover of Stevie Wonder's "I Was Born to Love Him," reportedly produced by Lauren Hill.

This album represents a new musical stance for Houston, and it truly splintered her fan base. The two best songs on the album, "It's Not Right But It's Okay" and "Heartbreak Hotel" courted hip hop and soul audiences. However, those who were used to looking to Whitney to deliver the kind of "adult contemporary" ballads that she made famous, were turned off by her stylistic switch of directions.

Yet, the musical quality of Whitney's voice was still good on this album, although her range doesn't seem as wide as it has in the past. Executive Produced by Clive Davis and Whitney Houston, *My Love is*

Your Love represented the final studio album of all new-material that Davis and Houston would work on for quite some time. Some stormy times would lie ahead for both of them.

Also, Robyn Crawford is credited here as an "Album Manager"— whatever that job entails. In the liner notes, Whitney wrote to her husband, "You were meant for me. Nothing can come between this love. I know 'cause I'll never let you go. Let's give 'em something to talk about." There was no problem in that department.

Whitney's *My Love is Your Love* album was her most disappointing American and Australian chart album yet—becoming her first one not to hit the Top Ten in those countries. It peaked at Number 13 in the United States, and only hit Number 42 in Australia. However, it made it to Number One in Austria and Switzerland, Number Two in Germany, and Number Four in Great Britain. The big duet song of Houston and Carey's, "If You Believe," only made it to Number 15 in America, yet it hit Number Four in England. However, the CD single "I Learned from the Best" made it to Number One in Germany.

On November 30, 1998, Whitney saluted Clive Davis, at the "Seasons of Hope" dinner to honor him, along with Barbara Walters and Tom Hanks. The event took place at the Winter Garden of the World Financial Center in New York City. December 7 found her onstage with Kelly Price and Faith Evans, at the Billboard Music Awards presentation, at the MGM Grand Garden Hotel, in Las Vegas, Nevada. They performed the cut "Heartbreak Hotel" Houston's new album. And three days later she was a guest on the TV show *Late Show with David Letterman.*

She continued to make the rounds of the TV shows promoting her latest album. Since her contract with Arista Records was due to lapse soon, and she needed to make this album a success. On January 11, 1999 she performed with Babyface and Wyclef Jean at the twenty-sixth annual American Music Awards telecast. Whitney and her producers sang the songs "Until You Come Back" and "My Love is Your Love." Two days later she was on TV's *The Tonight Show with Jay Leno.* February 16 she was in London to sing "It's Not Right But It's Okay" at the eighteenth annual BRIT Awards, presented at The Docklands Arena.

The week of March 2, 1999, Whitney's "Heartbreak Hotel" single peaked in the United States at Number Two. Gone are the days when Houston's name on a song or an album would instantaneously mean "Number One." Whitney was officially on a downward spiral—and her career was headed for trouble.

At the Academy Awards telecast on March 21, Whitney Houston and Mariah Carey performed their duet, "If You Believe," live at the Dorothy Chandler Pavilion in Los Angeles. The song went on to win an Oscar that evening. The award actually went to the songwriters, but Whitney and Mariah had the honor of being the singers who would always be associated with it.

On April 13, 1999, Whitney Houston was one of the female stars to headline the stunning TV special, *VH1 Divas Live '99*, which was broadcast live from The Beacon Theater in New York City. The event was not without its glitches, however.

The show was opened by the indomitable queen rock diva, Tina Turner. She entered the theater singing her hit "The Best." Turner followed it up with "Let's Stay Together." She was joined on stage by Elton John, and they presented a duet of "The Bitch is Back," to be joined by the one and only Cher. The three stars segued into Tina's red-hot classic "Proud Mary." Following Cher's solo segment, several of the "new" divas took the stage to show off their voices, including Faith Hill, Brandy, and LeAnn Rimes.

The last half of the show was dominated by Whitney Houston, who performed a wonderful duet version of "Ain't No Way" with Mary J. Blige. Then Whitney performed a solo version of her biggest hit, "I Will Always Love You." Next she was joined by Chaka Khan to present the ultimate duet version of "I'm Every Woman."

For the big all-star finale, it was expected that all of the divas would be joining together for the last number, a reprise of "I'm Every Woman." Brandy, Faith, LeAnn and Mary all joined Whitney and Chaka. However, conspicuously missing from the proceedings were the two biggest stars— Cher and Tina. Inside sources claim that both mega-star divas wanted no part of sharing the stage with Whitney. Both Tina and Cher are strongly opposed to drugs, and that is the assumed reason neither wanted to be seen in the company of the troubled Ms. Houston.

For the rest of the year Whitney continued to have a strong presence on the music charts. Both "It's Not Right But It's Okay" and "My Love is Your Love" made it to Number Four in America. However "I Learned From the Best" peaked at Number 27. Ultimately, her *My Love Is Your Love* sold 10 million copies worldwide, and tied with *I'm Your Baby Tonight* as her lowest selling studio albums. Only four years ago she had sold 34 million copies of *The Bodyguard*, and she was only on half the album. Clearly, *My Love is Your Love* was not the blockbuster album everyone hoped it would become.

As the twentieth century came to an end, Whitney Houston was still ranked among the most successful singers of the century. By the end of 1999 she had sold over 110 million albums worldwide. She had produced three very popular films, and was the fourth largest Number One hit single producing artist in the history of recorded music. Unfortunately, the only place for her to go from here—was down. And, it seemed that from this point onward, she was doing everything in her power to hasten her own downward slide.

CHAPTER TWELVE

"I FOUGHT THE LAW"

January of the year 2000 ushered in whole new century, and—unfortunately—a whole new existence for Whitney Houston. When her career began in 1985, it seemed that everything she touched turned to gold. However, from January 2000 to 2006, it seemed that everything Whitney touched turned into sheer disaster.

She began the year in the sunny "pineapple paradise" state of Hawaii. On Tuesday, January 11, her stay was over and she went to the Keahole-Kona International Airport in Kailua-Kona. She was a ticketed passenger on a United Airlines flight bound for San Francisco. As she arrived at the security check point prior to her flight, airport security officers inspected her bag, and discovered Whitney was in possession of a Ziploc plastic bag containing 15.2 grams of marijuana with her. The security officers, who were the employees of Wackenhut of Hawaii, accused her of committing a crime. However, they could not legally arrest Whitney for this offense. The only time they were allowed to physically arrest someone by force, is if it involves airport or aircraft security. They did, however, confiscate her floral print carry-on bag, and proceeded to call the local police.

As they waited for an actual police officer to be summoned, slippery Whitney simply turned, and quickly headed for her flight. Before the cops arrived, she had boarded the San Francisco-bound plane. In the state of Hawaii, possessing fifteen grams of pot carries with it a $1,000 fine, and a possible thirty days in jail. Whatever the stakes, paranoid Whitney didn't stick around to pay the consequences. Reportedly, by the time police officers arrived on the scene, Houston was already in the air. For her it was: "Bye-bye Hawaii!"

Whitney was now legally "wanted" by the state of Hawaii. However, since her crime was classified as a "misdemeanor," the state of Hawaii wasn't going to go to the expense of extraditing her to stand trial on this non-felony issue. This was just beginning of "The Whitney and Bobby Follies of 2000."

The press had a field day when news of Whitney's "bust" hit the airwaves. The *National Enquirer* ran a story called "Angry Whitney Blasts Cops Who Seized Her Pot." In the article they quoted "a pal" of Houston's who claimed Whitney complained to them, "It ain't nothing. It was only half an ounce of pot. What's all the fuss about?" Of her narrow escape, the huffy Ms. Houston proclaimed to her friend, "There's no way in hell I was going to hang around and let those 'rent-a-cops' put me in jail over this bullshit."

It was again awards season, and Whitney's *My Love is Your Love* album garnered more attention, especially in light of the "front page news" of the previous month's pot bust. On February 17, 2000, Whitney was named the "Female Artist of the Decade" at the fourteenth annual Soul Train Awards.

Meanwhile, American television comedians like Jay Leno and David Letterman got in their share of jokes about Whitney's marijuana bust on their network programs. On February 23, 2000, at the telecast of the Grammy Awards, broadcast from The Staples Center in Los Angeles, the diva was publicly "roasted" by none other than Rosie O'Donnell. Still holding a grudge for Houston's sudden cancellation in 1997, Rosie was not someone to piss off.

Rosie, knew right where Whitney was seated in the audience when she began her opening monologue that evening. Houston was nominated for an award, and she was slated to perform amidst the program.

On "live" satellite network television Rosie O'Donnell, mentioned the rock group The Doobie Brothers, and snidely said, "Whitney has always been a big supporter of the 'doobies,' what can I say, but 'Maui Wowie!'" At that comment, Houston, who was seated in the audience near the stage, was shown on-camera, extending her middle finger, and "flipping" Rosie "the bird" while millions of her fans watched in shock.

The diva ended up winning the Grammy Award that she was nominated for that evening, crowning "It's Not Right but It's Okay" as the year's "Best R&B Female Vocal Performance." However, the next day the press was more interested in the very public Whitney / Rosie feud, than they were in the additional trophy she had won.

Concurrently, she was also paying the price for a recent streak of missed, or canceled performances. The previous summer she backed out of a show in Concord, California, with only thirty minutes notice. Now, in the new year, the show's producers were suing her for $100,000 in expenses and damages. On March 6, 2000, Whitney was scheduled to perform at the Rock & Roll Hall Fame presentation in New York City. She was slated to present Clive Davis with his induction honors, but she was an unexplained "no-show."

Arista Records was preparing a two disc *Greatest Hits* release of Whitney's most successful songs, and it was decided that she would do a couple of special duets to enhance the package. This was to become another near-disaster amidst Houston's year-long collision course. When the diva postponed several planned recording sessions with George Michael, it caused her close personal assistant, Robyn Crawford to pick a huge fight with Whitney.

According to one insider, "The battle that caused the split happened in March during the Soul Train Awards when Whitney was supposed to record a duet with George Michael for her *Greatest Hits* album. George had made a special trip from London to Los Angeles to be on the album with Whitney. But Whitney kept him waiting for a week, then finally pulled a 'no-show.' When Robyn confronted Whitney about her 'no-show,' a horrible shouting match ensued between the two, which ended with Robyn quitting. Robyn was simply fed up with having to clean up the messes that Whitney left."

Next up on Houston's spring cavalcade of mishaps concerned her scheduled appearance on the March 26, 2000, telecast of the seventy-second annual Academy Awards. She was to be one of several performers who were to sing a production number medley of Oscar-winning songs.

The musical director for the segment of the show, was none other than Burt Bacharach, who had been responsible for the greatest string of her cousin Dionne's hits. Now Whitney was due to work for him for the first time. The other singers who were booked for the song medley segment were Queen Latifah, Isaac Hayes, Garth Brooks, Ray Charles, *and* Dionne Warwick.

Whitney was slated to sing the Judy Garland classic song from *The Wizard of Oz*, "Somewhere Over the Rainbow." She was then supposed to sing a solo segment of "The Way We Were," and a duet version of Dionne's "Alfie," with her famous cousin. However, she showed up for the March 24 rehearsals at The Shrine Auditorium in Los Angeles, as *The New York Post* reported, both mentally "out of it" and completely "discombobulated."

According to someone who was at the rehearsal, "She was pacing the backstage area, getting more and more agitated. She was sweating profusely and her neck muscles were twitching. It almost looked as if Whitney had been using drugs or something had gone into some type of withdrawal. Whitney started singing to herself real soft, but her voice kept cracking and she couldn't remember the lyrics. She looked and behaved like she was high as a kite on drugs or booze."

With Bobby Brown in tow, the minute Whitney arrived at the scheduled full rehearsal, it was clear to everyone present, that she was amidst some sort of substance abuse dilemma. When it came time for her to begin singing "Somewhere Over the Rainbow," on-lookers were shocked when she opened her mouth to sing, and her voice sounded awful. Even more embarrassingly, she couldn't remember all of the lyrics to the song.

Tabloid newspaper *The Globe* reported that one witness claimed, "She couldn't concentrate and lost her way throughout the song. She was slurring her words. Her jaw was quivering as she tried to belt out the song." Then, suddenly, Whitney ran from the stage, into the auditorium and planted a huge kiss on the lips of Bobby Brown.

Bacharach figured that she was just nervous, and he gave her another chance at rehearsing her songs. When it came time for her to sing "The Way We Were," things got even crazier. A *Globe* source claimed, "She got up onstage and started bopping up and down, singing like a little girl. Burt stopped dead. He couldn't believe what he was hearing."

Another eyewitness, quoted in *The Star*, recounted: "Two times she began singing 'Alfie' while the orchestra was correctly playing 'Somewhere

Over the Rainbow.' Finally, Burt got up from his seat at the piano, walked over to center stage where Whitney, Garth Brooks, and her [cousin] Dionne Warwick, where standing, and snapped: 'This just can't go on any further.'" Bacharach reportedly contacted the show's producers, and with their consent Whitney was immediately fired from the show. In her place, Faith Hill was summoned, in the eleventh hour, to replace Houston. Dionne Warwick reportedly left the stage in tears, saddened at the spectacle her cousin Whitney had made of herself. With her tail between her legs, disgraced Whitney left the auditorium, boarded a plane, and headed back home to New Jersey.

The other stars on the show had no idea what to make of what they were witnessing. Garth Brooks reported to *People* magazine, "Um, I can only say this about Whitney: She came in, she rehearsed, she tried her best, but she was so sick, and we'll just leave it at that."

Right after this unfortunate debacle, Burt Bacharach publicly proclaimed, "Whitney's chronic condition is very sad."

According to a television producer, who had worked with Houston, "When this Oscar thing happened, it did not surprise me. She has a reputation for being a flake and no-showing, and it's dangerous to book her because until she walks on that stage, there's no guarantee she's going to show up."

On April 10, 2000, Whitney was slated as one of the headliners for a gala concert to celebrate the twenty-fifth anniversary of Arista Records. This was a huge gala event taped in Los Angeles, with all of the greatest stars of the label's rich history, each invited to perform. The show was then edited into TV special which aired in America on May 15 on NBC-TV. The program starred Barry Manilow, Aretha Franklin, Dionne Warwick, Annie Lennox, Carlos Santana, Brooks & Dunn, Alan Jackson, Sarah McLachlan, Patti Smith, Kenny G., Natalie Cole, Carole King, Melissa Etheridge, and of course—Whitney Houston. Unfortunately, Whitney screwed-up this gig as well, embarrassing herself in front of this all-star cast.

When Whitney and Bobby arrived at the Newark, New Jersey airport, and boarded their flight, they decided that they didn't want their assigned seats. They wanted 1A and 1B, so they simply sat in them. When the ticket holders for those seats arrived, they were not amused, and insisted the Bobby and Whitney go and sit in their own seats. Finally an argument ensued.

According to one of the other passengers, "He finally agreed, five minutes before we were due to depart. But suddenly Bobby Brown stood up, looked a Whitney and said, 'I'm not going.' He grabbed his bag and walked off the plane. Whitney looked shocked and bewildered. And when the flight attendant announced, 'We're closing the doors,' Whitney suddenly picked up her things and followed Bobby off." They reportedly went to nearby Teterboro Airport, and chartered a jet, at the cost of $65,000, instead of being hassled with the rules of a commercial jet.

When they arrived in Los Angeles, they were apparently in full "party" mode. They partied so much that Whitney managed to miss the scheduled rehearsal of her performance. Viewing the footage of this television special reveals that Whitney is either drunk or high for her performance on the *Arista Records' 25th Anniversary Celebration* special. She looked horrible, and only seconds after she took the stage, she tripped on the hem of her own gown, and nearly fell down. It was clear that she was completely out of it, and even before she was finished with her medley, she was drenched in sweat.

After recovering herself from nearly falling down on stage, she danced around erratically, often looking like she was going to lose her balance. And there was clearly something wrong with her sequined gown, which she kept tugging at, screwing up the beading on it in several places—so that it looked like a mess. She kept grabbing it and pulling it up in the front, each time doing further damage to the fabric.

Whitney sang a successful medley of her hits "I Wanna Dance With Somebody (Who Loves Me)," "How Will I Know," "I Believe In You and Me," and "I Will Always Love You." She received a standing ovation. Then came her live version of her most recent hit, "My Love is Your Love." It turned into a muddled fiasco. For this final song she was joined on stage by Monica, Deborah Cox, Angie Stone, and Faith Evans. Off in the wings you could see Bobby Brown dancing like a maniac. He was not supposed to be part of the show at all. When Whitney invited him on stage to join her in the song, he too was dripping sweat from his face, and the brown button-down shirt he wore under his cream colored suit was soaking wet and stuck to his body in spots. The drug-addled pair began to act crazier and crazier on stage, like they were at a high school play and not a professional concert.

Singing the lyrics to "My Love Is Your Love," Whitney handed Bobby her microphone, and he tried to lead the audience on some nonsensical wordless jam. Bobby proceeded to turn the number into a rambling mess, as he whirled about the stage like a dervish, repeating choruses of "eye-yei-yei-yei" over and over again. By the time Whitney took the microphone back, she had lost her place in the song. Fortunately the song ended before Houston could turn it in a worse meandering cacophony than it became. As she left the stage, the bewildered audience trailed off with their response. She should have stopped after she successfully sang "I Will Always Love You." Instead her medley ended on a muddled low note.

As she left the stage, she said in to the microphone, "The record's not over yet, remember. God bless you. I love you." And, that cryptic message would mean what? No one—including Houston seemed to know what she was rambling on about.

The National Enquirer proclaimed, "She added to her humiliation at [Clive Davis's] April 10 party by struggling through . . . speaking rather than singing some of the words."

What a mess Whitney was that night. There is a wonderful Robert Altman film from 1975 called *Nashville*. In the context of this film, actress Ronee Blakley plays a famous country singer who has an onstage nervous breakdown in front of one of her audiences at the Grand Ole Opry. That is what watching Whitney Houston in concert had become. One cannot watch her in performance anymore, and not think, "What is going to go wrong?" Is she going to self-destruct right here and now?

When her performance was finished that evening, it was uncertain what the final applause she received really was for. Was it for her stunning performance? Or was it a resigned vote of confidence from an audience who was relieved that she didn't fall face-first onto the stage—especially in light of the highly-publicized Oscar debacle which had occurred less than two weeks ago?

It seemed that everyone there was relieved that she had simply gotten through the number without collapsing. Clive Davis was quoted as saying after the show, "She proved tonight she still can soar." Pressed to talk about Houston's career disasters, he declined comment by saying, "I'm not going to talk about personal things."

Backstage, *People* magazine prodded Dionne Warwick, to see if the rumor was true that she and Natalie Cole were planning on staging a confrontational "intervention" to help Whitney? Said Dionne, "I support her. I care for her, but no, I don't advise her."

Another of the stars that night was someone who wanted nothing to do with Whitney. It was Aretha Franklin. According to one confidential source, "Aretha has been totally unamused by Whitney's drug antics for years. Aretha has nothing to do with drugs, and in fact has done her best to keep her own sons from going down that self-destructive path. She doesn't want to be associated with Whitney in any way, and is very disappointed in Houston's behavior."

It seemed like even Whitney's most faithful friends were questioning her actions during this period. In early 2000, *The National Enquirer* quoted a source close to the Houston family as saying, "Robyn Crawford, her closest associate and personal assistant, recently quit in frustration. Robyn yelled at her, 'I can't just sit by and watch you kill yourself.' And Robyn can't just let her best friend go. So she joined forces with John and Cissy in an intervention. They've confronted Whitney and told her she's messing up badly."

Reportedly, Clive Davis, Dionne Warwick and Natalie Cole all confronted Whitney with her drug addiction during this trip to Los Angeles. Houston was undeniably high as a kite at the Arista twenty-fifth anniversary show, and her friends could remain silent no more. According to one insider, "Some of Whitney's best buddies confronted her and told her she needs treatment."

Natalie Cole especially felt that Whitney would listen to her. Cole had her own very well publicized drug addiction, which she had confronted and eradicated. She was convinced that Houston would listen to her, because she herself had been down that same road before.

While all of these stories were circulating about Whitney, it made one wonder why her mother and her father didn't just take control of their daughter's life? However, behind-the-scenes sources claim that Cissy and John Houston often verbally clashed with Whitney. They were also most concerned about the welfare of their granddaughter, Bobbi Kristina. On more than one occasion they—together and separately—had huge blowout fights with Whitney about the mess she was making of her life. Still, she wouldn't hear of it. Sources close to her claimed that she was still very deep in denial. She was convinced that she didn't have a problem.

There were stories of Whitney aiming her explosively volatile temper at anyone who tried to tell her what to do. That spring, *The National Enquirer* reported a recent blowout fight between Whitney and Cissy Houston. It came backstage before a concert. Cissy had joined the tour to keep her eye on her daughter, as well as to sing with her onstage. According to one eyewitness, "Whitney's mom fell victim to one of her vicious mood swings one night last July when she joined her on tour. Only moments before going onstage at her concert at University Park, Pennsylvania, Whitney and Cissy got into a horrible argument in the green room. The crew just stood and watched as she lashed out at their mother. Whitney was absolutely vicious, shouting, 'I'm the one making all the fucking money and I'm the one calling all of the fucking shots and you're going to listen to what I say. If you don't like the way things are going, then pack your fucking bags and get your ass out of here!'"

Apparently, by now Cissy was getting quite vocal about what she thought of her daughter's recent behavior. In early 2000, Whitney was facing the united front of Robyn AND her parents.

Now that she had been confronted by Robyn, Cissy and John Houston, Dionne, Clive, and Natalie Cole, what did Whitney do to get herself off of drugs? Nothing. She didn't want to hear about it, and she continued down her self-destructive path.

That spring, Houston was slated to be the cover subject in an upcoming May 2000 issue of the women's publication, *Jane* magazine. When she showed up for the photo shoot, she was apparently stoned on something.

In true Whitney form, she was four hours late for the appointment. Everyone was kept waiting without explanation. Finally, the dazed diva arrived. According to the magazine's editor, Jane Pratt, "She was singing to herself. Then she would pretend to play the piano, like an air piano. Her eyes were very heavy-lidded." When Houston tried to tell her that she had just been to the dentist and had Novocain, Pratt wasn't buying that nonsense excuse. According to Pratt, "Novocain doesn't make you act that way. Everyone there thought she was on something."

However, as Jane Pratt was to concede, they did capture at least one good photo of Whitney. "[She] gave one of the best cover shoots ever. She's a consummate performer." However, when *People* magazine printed news of Houston's "stoned" solid photo shoot, it only further fanned the flames of her fan's growing contempt for her undeniably stupid "melt down" in recent months.

Meanwhile, during the spring of 2000, Arista Records released the two-disc album *Whitney Houston: The Greatest Hits*. In America it made it to Number Five on the *Billboard* charts, and in England it hit Number One. Worldwide, it sold over 8 million copies. The album is essentially divided into two separate modes. The first disc gathers all of her best ballads, and the second disc contained all of the up-tempo songs. It was a great celebration of all of the wonderful music she had made in the past. It also included four newly recorded tracks, including three star duets. With George Michael she recorded a duet version of "If I Told You That." With Enrique Iglesias she sang, "Could I Have This Kiss Forever." And with Deborah Cox, she recorded "Same Script, Different Cast." The new solo recording was the snappy song about relationships called "Fine." The album closed with her rousing version of "The Star Spangled Banner." The whole album package contained one glorious hit after another. It was like a sad reminder of how Whitney Houston *used to sound*.

Furthermore, Arista also released a DVD package of *Whitney Houston: The Greatest Hits* in May of 2000, which contained all of the video performances of her best songs. It debuted on the video chart in *Billboard* at Number One. The *Arista Records' 25th Anniversary Celebration* special was also released as a hit DVD package.

Oddly enough, at the exact same time, there was a power struggle going on at Arista Records. When Arista was purchased by entertainment conglomerate, German based Bertelsmann Music Group (BMG), the parent company began making some internal decisions about the fate of the label. Ultimately, since Clive Davis was concurrently sixty-seven years old, BMG chose to exercise one of its mandates to retire executives above the age of sixty. In an odd and very unpopular power struggle, Clive was forced out of his position as the head of Arista, and L.A. Reid was hired to replace him. The press very much sided with Clive, since Arista was the label which he had carefully personally created. Davis promptly went out and started a new record label all his own, called J Records. What did this mean for the fate of Whitney Houston's career? Since her own contract was about to lapse, would she sign with Arista, or would Clive Davis lure her over to J Records? And, if Clive was forced out of Arista, what would become of the future of the label? Would his successors know what to do with Whitney? Or, was Davis fed up with her drug-induced drama? What was to happen, and how it was to effect Whitney's recording career, was to remain a mystery for several more months.

In the May 2000 issue of *Out* magazine, Whitney gave one of her most taste-free interviews. Speaking to the gay monthly publication, Houston was again burning to tell the world that she was not a lesbian. The article quoted her as saying, "I ain't 'HO'in.' I ain't suckin' no dick! I ain't gettin' on my knees. Something must be wrong: I can't really just sing. I can't be just a really talented, gifted person. 'She's got to be gay!'"

Meanwhile, the spotlight next shifted to Bobby Brown. He and Whitney had flown down to the Bahamas to hang out and vacation. However, on May 10, 2000, when the couple returned to the mainland, customs agents at the Newark, New Jersey, International Airport arrested him, and transported him to Ft. Lauderdale. He was then turned over to the custody of the Florida police, who ushered him into a jail cell. It seemed that he had been wanted by the state of Florida since June of 1999, for violating the terms of his parole, stemming from his infamous 1996 barroom brawl in Orlando. It seems that Bobby's urine sample, taken at that time, tested positive for cocaine content. When Brown refused to come back and be tested again, the warrant was issued.

On May 22, the possibility of bond was denied by Judge Leonard Feiner. The judge deemed Bobby as "a flight risk," and they didn't want to let him out of police custody. Brown spent a month cooling his heels in a Ft. Lauderdale jail cell where he awaited his June 19 court date.

Apparently, Whitney ran down to Ft. Lauderdale, expecting to use her checkbook to spring Bobby from jail. She was amazed to find that bail was denied. According to a close source, "She was absolutely devastated when he wasn't released. Then when she got home, she had to battle with her parents over her daughter."

This latest scandal caused members of Whitney's inner circle to choose up sides—when it came time to discuss the custody of little Bobby Kristina. Apparently, her parents threatened to legally take the child away from drug addicted Whitney and Bobby at this time.

In June of 2000, *The Globe* quoted a source as saying, "John and Cissy have told Whitney that her drug use could cost her custody of Bobbi. They've made it clear that if she continues on a downward spiral, they will seek custody of their granddaughter. It's the one warning that frightens Whitney because she loves that little girl more than her own life."

Another source claimed, "The family is talking intervention if she doesn't shape up. They're delighted Bobby is out of the picture. In fact, a family member tipped off the police when Bobby and Whitney's plane would be landing so the cops could pick him up. They didn't want him anywhere near Whitney again. They even moved the headquarters of Whitney's company Nippy [Inc.] from Fort Lee, New Jersey, to Newark without telling him."

Meanwhile, in Florida, Bobby Brown was serving his seventy-five day sentence in a seven foot wide by twelve foot long jail cell. As inmate number 500014529, his daily chores included doing the other prisoners' laundry, and mopping floors. It was a far cry from a suite at The Peninsula Hotel.

While Bobby was behind bars in "The Sunshine State," Robyn Crawford came back to Whitney's life, trying to patch up their friendship, and to try to talk Houston into divorcing Brown.

According to a source quoted in *The National Enquirer*, "Whitney's drug use was out in the open and Bobby was in jail. Robyn could sense that Whitney was in a lot of trouble." In a desperate phone call from Houston, Robyn was called to her side. "Whitney was crying so hard over the telephone that Robyn could barely understand what she was saying. Whitney explained that she really wanted to clean up her life. She promised Robyn that she was trying desperately to stay away from drugs, but that it was difficult without having someone there to offer her support. Whitney begged Robyn to come back to be with her during this difficult time and asked her to stay until Bobby was released from jail. After listening to Whitney's painful cries for help, Robyn agreed to come back—but only temporarily. Robyn told Whitney she would do everything she could to help her walk the straight and narrow, as long as Whitney vowed to stay strong and help stay clean." Robyn reportedly came back to Houston's side for a while.

Even without Bobby around, Whitney's life and her career were a disaster. She was booked at Caesar's Palace casino in Atlantic City for the three-day Fourth of July weekend. However, the concerts were a typical calamity for the diva. According to one witness, "She stopped in the middle of eight or nine songs, forgot words, and her voice cracked."

Once it was announced that Bobby was being released from jail—because of good behavior—she ran down to Florida to be by his side. From there, the partying lifestyle began all over again.

The on-camera reunion of Whitney Houston and Bobby Brown, on July 7, 2000, was absolutely lunatic to watch. Dressed in jeans, a white sleeveless top, and a sweaty headband around her forehead, Whitney looked more like a sweat-covered groupie than an international superstar. While TV cameras rolled, and Bobby exited the North Broward County Detention Center in Pompano Beach Florida, Whitney threw herself at Bobby, wrapping her skinny arms around his neck, and her legs around his back. She looked totally stoned as she clung to Brown, refusing to let the TV cameras look into her eyes.

Even comedian Chris Rock was present with his own camera crew. Brown hugged Rock and said to the cameras, "It's beautiful out here."

Cissy Houston went to far as to claim in *The Star*, that in her eyes, Bobby Brown was "the devil incarnate." According to one source, "Cissy told me: 'Whitney never had these problems until she married that man. I've warned her about him until I'm blue in the face but she doesn't listen to me. She says she loves him, so what can I do? I just pray to the Lord that she can regain her old self and be a happier, more together person."

Instead of repenting for their problems, Whitney and Bobby continued the partying, full throttle. On July 25, 2000, the collision course duo checked in at The Grandover Resort and Conference Center in Greensboro, North Carolina, at ten in the morning. According to the staff of the hotel, they rarely came out of Suite 1114. Across the hall, in Suite 1113, Bobbi Kristina, and Brown's three illegitimate children, were looked after by family friend Ellen White.

A staff member claimed, "You think they'd know better. The smell of marijuana from their suite was drifting into the hallway. It was sickening—their daughter was staying right across the hall in another suite." The couple seemed to be awake the entire night long, calling room service at all hours. The debris the bewildering Browns left behind included a plastic bag with marijuana crumbs in it, a wadded up pack of cigarette rolling papers, a cigar tube, tobacco cigar leaves, a grass 'roach' in the ashtray, 16 empty Budweiser beer bottles, and an empty half gallon bottle of Jack Daniel's Punch.

According to *The National Enquirer*, what the cleaning staff found in the suite once Whitney and Bobby checked out was horrifying. One staff member revealed to the tabloid, "There was also evidence that cocaine was used in the suite. On the bathroom counter lay an empty package of baking soda and a spoon with burn marks on the bottom, necessary items to freebase cocaine—Whitney's preferred method of using the drug, according to insiders. The baking soda and cocaine are mixed with water and heated in a spoon to form hard chunks, known as 'crack.' To smoke it, users sometime[s] split open a cigar and fill it with the drug. At the resort Bobby bought a cigar—and tobacco leaves torn from the stogie where left next to the baking soda."

The couple checked out of the resort at 11:00 PM on July 26, 2000. Witnesses saw Whitney yelling at the four children in the lobby. Exasperated, she headed for the bar and ordered a Jack Daniel's whiskey, while Bobby tried to calm her down. According to one witness in the hotel, "Whitney got angry and sat three tables away from Bobby. She looks very thin, much thinner than she looks on TV. And, her eyes look tired."

On July 28, 2000, the battling Browns were back home in Mendham, New Jersey. It seemed that the New Jersey Division of Youth and Family Services had received an anonymous phone call from someone fearing for the safety of Bobbi Kristina, and they paid the couple a visit, to investigate. The couple was cooperative, and no legal action was made to remove their daughter from their custody.

In an article in *The Star*, it was disclosed that, "Other neighbors in the exclusive town of Mendham report that the superstar singer and her hubby are regulars at the Black Horse Pub and MacKenzie's Restaurant, where one source says they often look 'totally wasted.'" Apparently, "wasted" Bobby and Whitney sightings were quite common. Furthermore, Whitney's mansion, which sits on five acres of prime real estate, was often the site of loud and boisterous parties which never seemed to come to an end.

In July of 2000, *The National Enquirer* received a huge scoop when a man claiming to be Whitney and Bobby's drug dealer, granted an exclusive interview with the publication. Identified in the article as "Uncle Rob," the man reported in great detail, the degree of drug abuse that the pair had been indulging themselves in—to the tune of $750,000 in the past decade. In the article, "Uncle Rob" revealed, "Whitney is doing a lot of cocaine—too much. Ten years ago, she was spending about $1,000 a week on cocaine and marijuana. Now it's about $2,500. She can't stop and she'll destroy herself. I've even told her, 'You're doing too much. You've got to slow down.' . . . One day a few months ago, I delivered cocaine to her home in the afternoon, then in the evening, and then at 6:00 AM she called for another $400 worth. I told her, 'Hey, don't you people ever go to sleep?' . . . She'd call at night, in the afternoon, or at 6:00 AM, waking me up, sounding zonked out and desperate, begging for cocaine." Now, that is a bad sign, when even your own drug dealer tells you to knock it off!

Friends close to Whitney and Bobby were concerned for Houston's health. According to one, "It's so sad when you see her. Sometimes her conversations make no sense. Whitney's off on her own planet."

Another one lamented at the time, "The people who really love her are terrified that her constant drug use could trigger a fatal heart attack. They pray they don't find Whitney dead."

Also in July, one of the people who helped keep Whitney's voice in shape, Dr. Julian Groff of North Miami Beach, suddenly died. He had occasionally traveled with her as her personal physician. In the past he also cared for Cher, Frank Sinatra, Michael Jackson, Tom Jones, and other major stars. Now, without Groff in her life to advise her, Whitney would continue to increasingly do more and more damage to her singing voice.

In August 2000 *The Enquirer* had another scoop on their hands when they found that: "Whitney Houston and Bobby Brown launched into a terrifying days-long drug marathon that climaxed in a near-fatal crack overdose for Bobby . . . On August 7, after Bobby returned home [from Los Angeles], Whitney and her husband ordered up a supply of coke . . . Whitney and Bobby began their drug spree on August 7 and kept going until Bobby literally hit the floor unconscious shortly after 3:00 AM on August 8." According to one witness, the episode happened in the kitchen of the couple's house. His heart started beating at an accelerated pace, and he collapsed onto the floor unable to breathe.

Paramedics had to be called in, claimed the article, "A frantic Whitney called 911. Rescuers had to revive Bobby with oxygen—and even hooked him up to heart paddles!" It was just another night of partying with Whitney and Bobby.

MCA Records released the album *Bobby Brown's Greatest Hits* in September of 2000. It did not become a hit album. This also signified the end of his recording career with the label, and in general. From this point forward, his main claim to fame was to be as "Whitney Houston's husband."

In September of 2000, the state of Hawaii issued a statement in which prosecutors requested that Whitney turn herself in to their custody, prior to an October 26 arraignment date. The charge carried a $1,000 fine, as well as thirty days in jail. Furthermore, if she set foot in Hawaii, she faced being arrested. It was getting to the point where they must have had to keep a map of the United States handy to keep track of which states currently wanted to arrest which one of them, for what charge!

Basically, her lawyers managed to negotiate their way out of a prosecution from the state of Hawaii. According to *The Globe*, "The pop diva agreed to contribute $4,025 to local causes after her lawyers negotiated her plea on charges she was carrying pot in her tote bag . . . the plea means Whitney does not admit guilt. And sources say she decided to go the 'no contest' route to avoid a public spectacle, after learning that *Court TV* intended to cover her trial if she went to court."

That fall, John Houston celebrated his eightieth birthday with a lavish party at Justin's, a posh Manhattan supper club, which is owned by

Sean "Puffy" Combs. However, Whitney was a conspicuous "no-show" at her own father's party. According to one source, "She's still angry at what she sees as her family's meddling. She thinks they believed she has a drug problem, tried to get her into rehab and tried to break her and Bobby up when he was in jail."

When the two-layer red velvet cake was brought out, the inscribed icing read "To the best of fathers. Happy Birthday, Dad, Love, Whitney." Usually it was Whitney who sang her dad "Happy Birthday," but this year her brother, Gary, did the honors.

Although Whitney did not attend the party, at 1:00 AM—obviously sensing an open bar—Bobby Brown showed up. According to eyewitnesses, "When Bobby entered the room a hush fell over the crowd. You could cut the tension with a knife."

It wasn't long before people began to seriously fear for Whitney's health. On October 16, 2000, Whitney and Bobby were in Washington D.C. for the religious rally known as The Million Family March. Over 400,000 people were present to make a stand for family values, and religious unity. People were startled when they saw Houston at the event. According to one source, "She seems to be fading away. The bones in her arms and legs stand out and her face looks as though the flesh is stretched too tight."

According to another friend, "One look at her and it's painfully clear that something is taking a terrible toll on her health. She looks like somebody who doesn't eat or can't hold their food down. Can anyone close to her still be in denial? Are they all going to wait until something tragic happens and say, 'Drugs? Who knew?'"

In a shocking *National Enquirer* report, entitled "Whitney in Drug Overdose," the publication was able to site two recent near-death experiences for the diva. Furthermore, it revealed that on several occasions, Bobby Brown had been brought from the depths of death's door.

There was one incident in an unnamed Los Angeles luxury hotel. Apparently Bobby had left the hotel, and Whitney was three hours late to meet him. Brown calmly sent one of his buddies up to the hotel room to check on her. He knocked on the door, and didn't receive any answer. Using a duplicate key, he let himself into the suite, only to find Whitney unconscious and sprawled across the bed. According to one source, "There was also a rolled-up [dollar] bill and a water pipe." These are clear signs of cocaine use.

Fearing a scandal, instead of summoning an ambulance, Brown's assistant called a doctor to come to the hotel and revive Houston. According to the same source, "The doctor ended up saving Whitney's life. Whitney later admitted she'd been doing cocaine." No kidding?!

The same article claimed that it was a repeat of a similar incident in Denver, Colorado. According to a family friend who was there, "They were both doing coke and crack in a hotel suite. Suddenly Whitney's body reacted violently—the rush of drugs to her heart sent her into shock. She went into convulsions. Bodyguards grabbed her and began putting ice on her head, neck and chest to keep her awake and breathing. They rushed her out of the hotel to a van and threw her inside. Whitney was wearing just gray sweatpants and a T-shirt. The van driver raced through Denver to get her to a medical facility before it was too late." Again, she was narrowly saved.

The unnamed friend revealed that Bobby was often in such life-threatening situations as well: "When Bobby overdoses, his bodyguards strip him and throw him into the bathtub. Then they hold him down in the bath and fill it with ice. They do it to revive Bobby and keep him breathing. Then they get him up and make him walk around for a couple of hours, working off the effects of the overdose. They know that if they let Bobby go to sleep, he'll stop breathing and die." This is what Whitney and Bobby's lives had become, a harrowing and senseless avalanche of cocaine use, and desperate living.

During this era *The National Enquirer* reported that Houston's bills to one of her drug dealers for her supply of cocaine averaged $175,000 per year.

Booked in Vegas in late 2000, Whitney headlined four days at the Aladdin Resort on the Strip. Every night of her performance, Bobby would arrive with his "posse" of drinking buddies, and slam down Courvoisier cognac. The first night Brown grabbed the microphone from the band, and shouted obscenities. He reportedly announced over the microphone, "I hope you all are spending lots of money here because this lousy place has to pay us on Friday!" That's a great way to warm up the crowd for your wife!

During the Christmas season, Whitney and Bobby were in the Bahamas at a star studded holiday event held at the exclusive Ocean Club. According to an insider quoted in *The National Enquirer*, "Baby Spice of The Spice Girls was a guest at the party, and Whitney thought Bobby was getting too friendly with her. Whitney told me she and Bobby got into a big argument in their room. Bobby, who was drunk, grabbed Whitney around the neck from behind in a chokehold. Whitney was screaming for him to let her go—that she couldn't breathe. But Bobby kept choking her. Whitney said she felt like she was going to suffocate to death. She managed to grab a heavy ashtray and slammed it over Bobby's head to break his hold on her. Whitney hit him so hard the ashtray broke into pieces. Blood was pouring from Bobby's head, and he staggered out of the room. Whitney slammed the door behind him. She was afraid he would come at her again. Bobby was lying in a bloody heap when hotel help came by with towels to put over his wound."

Bobby was rushed to the local hospital. Doctors wanted him to spend the night there, but he refused. Meanwhile, Whitney chartered a jet and returned to New Jersey. Concluded the inside source, "She was truly afraid for her life. She could easily [have] had him arrested for assault or even attempted murder." So, that's what it's like to spend the holidays with the battling Browns!

After what had been an astronomically blunder-filled year for Whitney Houston, she was still nowhere near ready to face her demons. What else could one say, except: "Houston, we have a problem."

CHAPTER THIRTEEN

"WHATCHULOOKINAT?"

In the year 2001, Whitney Houston sunk to newfound depths. Concert promoters were becoming increasingly leery of booking her for performances, because she had such a spotty track record for actually showing up for the engagements. Now she was faced with new problems— even if she did arrive for a gig, there were now legitimate concerns that she might not be able to remember the lyrics to her songs once she was on stage.

Even as guests, she and Bobby were becoming increasingly un- desirable in show business circles. At a party that was thrown for Magic Johnson's birthday, at Los Angeles' House of Blues, the Browns were actually asked to leave. The party, arranged for by Johnson's wife, Cookie, drew such celebrities as Angela Bassett, Halle Berry, Vivica Fox, and Marla Maples. At the event, without warning, Bobby jumped up on stage and began singing. Whitney very loudly screamed at him to get off of the stage.

According to *The National Enquirer*, "Bobby finally realized he was bombing and leaped offstage. Whitney stormed outside, still screaming. Magic, in a fury, caught up and told them to split immediately—or he'd THROW them out! Whitney and Bobby beat it—and Magic told pals he'd never invite them again, adding: 'Whatever Bobby's on, Whitney's on too.'"

On March 4, 2001, it was Bobbi Kristina's eighth birthday. To mark the occasion, Whitney and Bobby threw a party at a roller skating rink. The Florham Park Skating Rink was only fifteen minutes from their Mendham mansion. Reportedly, the duo arrived a half-hour late, and came accompanied by a phalanx of a dozen burly security guards. According to people at the party, Whitney and Bobby were quite rude to the other skaters who were there, and were aggressive towards anyone who got in their way on the roller rink floor.

Said one on-looker, "Her hair was limp, she had no make-up on and she looked like she hadn't slept in days. I was worried seeing her look so unhealthy."

Whitney tried on one pair of roller skates in her size, but decided that she didn't like them. "These are no good. Get me another pair," she snapped at one of her bodyguards as she threw the skates onto the floor like she was a spoiled child.

After that, Whitney hit the skating floor in a frenzy. "Whitney looked like she was trying to burn off a lot of nervous energy," said one source. "She was waving her hands around furiously and weaving in and out. She even pushed other skaters out of the way when she had to."

When Houston wanted to get frozen blueberry drinks at the refreshment counter, she wasn't in the mood to wait for them. Said an on-looker, "The poor woman behind the counter didn't know what hit her. The skating rink is a very low-key place and the staff isn't used to dealing with moody celebrities."

Yet, the crazy behavior came to a crescendo when Whitney took a hold of a carving knife to cut the cake, and instead raised it over her head in an alarming fashion.

Reported *The Globe*, "But the most bizarre behavior came after she gathered the guests around and sang a solo version of 'Happy Birthday' to Bobbi. She picked up the knife and started to perform some sort of strange ritual, eyewitnesses say, holding it and waving it with both hands above her head, before the cake was cut." According someone there, "It was really odd behavior."

Ebony magazine in early 2001 announced that they were going to salute Cissy Houston at a planned "Mothers & Daughters" banquet. She was thrilled by the honor, and naturally wanted Whitney to accompany her there. The diva turned down her mother's request. An insider claimed,

"Cissy was upset, but she called Whitney to change her mind because the evening was so important to her. She even asked Whitney to attend as a Mother's Day gift, thinking that a special plea like that would persuade her to attend. But it didn't work. Whitney didn't surprise her by showing up."

In June of 2001 it was announced in *The Star* and *The Globe* that Robyn Crawford was once again back in Whitney's life, as a very influential force. *The Star* headlined their cover story with "She's Back With Galpal & Bobby's Furious . . . WHITNEY GAY LOVE TRIANGLE SCANDAL!"

According to one family friend, "Bobby's freaking out. Whitney leaves him with a telltale sparkle in her eye and a spring in her step each time she's meeting Robyn. Whitney has made it perfectly clear over the years that she and Robyn have something special and it has nothing to do with Bobby."

In Europe and Asia, a second Houston "greatest hits" package was released. Entitled *Love, Whitney*, it is a single disc, gathering together all of her greatest ballad hits. It made it to Number 22 in the United Kingdom, and sold over 500,000 copies.

Finally, late in the summer of 2001 the terms of Whitney's negotiations with Arista Records were made public. She ended up resigning her contract with Arista. There were never any press announcements about Clive Davis making an offer to Whitney Houston at his new J Records label. One must suspect that at this point in time she had become one of the greatest disappointments in his life. He had constructed one of the most brilliant and glittering careers of the twentieth century for her, and she had in turn done everything in her power to ruin her health, her popularity, and her voice.

Instead, Clive courted several other former stars, including Luther Vandross, Liza Minnelli, and Rod Stewart. He invited Monica and Angie Stone to come to his new label, but—very conspicuously—no immediate offer was made to troubled Whitney. Davis obviously knew that Whitney had to sort out her personal problems first. For a new hot female singer for his label, instead he chose to create a new pop diva, with his latest talented discovery, Alicia Keyes. Instantly, Clive added his magic touch, and her first album, *Songs in A Minor* became a huge Grammy-winning hit.

However, Arista Records, now under the control of L.A. Reid, was already facing a lot of skepticism from the industry. Arista was the custom-created dream of Clive Davis. Could someone half his age, with a lot less experience, successfully keep the label afloat? Time would tell.

Since it was Whitney Houston who had by far sold the most records for Arista, it seemed like a natural move to induce her to stay with the label. It was an era in which huge and ludicrous amounts of money were thrown around to sign up some of the biggest money-makers of the 1990s. The offer that L.A. Reid made to Houston was possibly the most unwise of all.

In August of 2001, it was officially announced that Arista would be resigning Whitney Houston to the label for a whopping $100 million. Instantly upon signing, she would receive the astronomical advance sum of $25 million. The additional $75 million would be contingent on the sales of her albums, and fulfillment of the terms of her contract. The deal called for six new albums, and two compilations.

L.A. Reid told *The Hollywood Reporter*, "There has never ever been a question of her leaving Arista. The day it was announced that I would even potentially be coming in, Whitney Houston was the first Arista artist to reach out to me and be supportive. Even when the gossipmongers were saying the label was doomed [without Clive], there was never discussions of her leaving. Not between myself and her, or her lawyers, or her representatives or her husband or anyone."

It was soon to be revealed as one of the most foolish and obscenely financially wasteful business decisions ever made in the record business. It would only be a wise decision if Whitney were to produce another album of the magnitude of *The Bodyguard* soundtrack album. Was Houston's career strictly the product of Clive Davis's star-making machinery, or was it based on her image and talent? Only time would tell.

In the next sixty days, Whitney would brilliantly demonstrate just how foolish this deal was—on Arista's part. She instantly proceeded to run through massive amounts of cash to celebrate this profitable new recording contract. And, in September she was about to ruin her public image in the most irreparable way one could imagine.

With an instant "advance" of over $25 million in her pocket, Whitney and Bobby decided to stage a real rip-roaring celebration. *The Hollywood*

Reporter had announced the new deal in its August 3–5, 2001 issue. And on August 8, Bobby Brown was admitted to a local hospital emergency room, near death—by overdose of cocaine.

In *The Star*, an "insider" sadly reported, "Arista wired $32 million into her account and before the ink was even dry on the contract, Whitney bought a kilogram of cocaine over several days and spent $150,000. Whitney turned daughter Bobbi Kristina over to the nanny, and she and Bobby headed for their private 'drug den.'"

According to eyewitnesses, the Browns not only partied, they also had a huge argument. It seemed that Whitney had video evidence that Bobby was cheating on her, with another woman. Houston screamed at Bobby, "I'll fucking divorce you over this! Don't think I won't!" In their own well-traveled fashion, the couple continued to argue and to do drugs at all hours of the day and night.

The source revealed, "Days blended into nights and with each passing hour, Whitney and Bobby and their partying pals became more blasted. They smoked and snorted huge quantities of the white powder and they were really fired up. In the early hours of August 8, Bobby's eyes rolled back in his head, and he started foaming at the mouth. He looked like an epileptic having a seizure. In reality, he was overdosing on massive quantities of the cocaine. Whitney became hysterical. She was already amped up on the effects of the drug. She was yelling, 'Baby, don't die!'"

Someone placed a frantic call to "911" emergency services, and at 2:48 AM two Mendham Township, New Jersey, police officers responded.

Naturally, the staff at Whitney and Bobby's house had been trained in how and where to stash all signs of illegal drug use. As the police were phoned, all evidence of paraphernalia and drug residue was swept clean. And, the recording studio now reeked with the masquerading scent of air freshener.

According to *The Globe*, "Patrolmen John Santucci and Steven Crawford kept Brown alive until the medical technicians arrived."

Next, a squad of paramedics arrived at Houston's *"casa de cocaine"* of a mansion. The medical technicians administered oxygen to Bobby, and Whitney rode with him in the ambulance, to Morristown Memorial Hospital.

Another eyewitness was quoted as saying, "She was barely coherent herself. Bobby refused to take a urine or blood tests at the hospital because he can't afford to have another drug bust on his rap sheet. Plus, Whitney's whole livelihood is riding on this new contract."

Revealed one source, "[Whitney] was sweating, distressed and agitated. Everyone could see Whitney was coked out of her head and there was a real fear she too was at the point of overdosing—just like Bobby." Somehow they stabilized Bobby in a relatively short period of time. At the beginning there was a fear that his heart might stop beating, and they hooked him up to a defibrillator in case they needed to shock his heart back into action.

Against the advice of the hospital staff, only ninety minutes from the time he arrived on a stretcher, Bobby Brown left the hospital. He also refused to submit to several tests that the doctors wanted to run. They wanted to do several tests to diagnose the reason for his condition. A source quoted in *The Globe* explained, "Bobby was anxious to get out of that hospital as fast as he could. He knew the tests would show positive for everything he'd been taking for three or four days—namely cocaine and marijuana washed down with cognac!"

According to Dr. James Whitlock, a prestigious neurologist from Salem, New Hampshire, "It's entirely possible for someone to have a cocaine-based seizure and appear to be at death's door, then walk out of the hospital an hour later. Some seizures have very little aftermath."

Right after that episode—the very next night—it was Whitney who collapsed into unconsciousness at the mansion. Reported *The National Enquirer*, "She and her husband Bobby Brown smoked crack and entertained guests. One female guest thought Whitney was dying and picked up the phone to call '911,' but Whitney suddenly came around."

Well, after signing her new Arista recording contract, and partying their way to the hospital, it was now time for the public to get a good, undeniable look at what Whitney was doing to herself. Without a doubt, her shocking performance at Madison Square Garden on September 7, 2001, was the horror show to end them all.

The reason for the performance, was a gala concert celebration to mark Michael Jackson's thirtieth year as a solo recording star. In addition to being a star with Jermaine and his other brothers, Michael also released his own solo albums and hit singles on Motown Records—beginning with "Got to Be There" in 1971. Produced by Jackson and his promoter friend David Gest, the event turned into a huge three-ring circus of an event. The stars on this concert included Monica, Liza Minnelli, Gloria Estefan, NSYNC, Mya, 98°, Usher, Luther Vandross, and the reunion of all six of the Jackson brothers (Michael, Jermaine, Tito, Marlon, Jackie, and Randy). In the middle of it, Whitney Houston was to make a performance with Mya and Usher.

However, what eyewitnesses saw that evening was horrifying. Whitney Houston hit the stage in a revealingly short dress, hanging off one shoulder. The flesh-exposing outfit showed off the fact that she had wasted away to mere skin and bones. Her arms and her legs were painfully thin, and her collar bone looked like it had only a wafer-thin bit of flesh on it. Her face wrinkled at the eyes from the weight loss, and her fingers were frighteningly bony. Website *www.ABCNews.com* called her "scarily skinny," and commentator Matt Drudge noted that she had "wasted away into skeletonism."

Singing the Jackson song "Wanna Be Startin' Something," Whitney revealed that her once incredible voice, was a now a gruff and raspy whisper. And, she was thin as a reed of bamboo. Whitney was also expected to perform in concert on Monday, September 10, 2001, but reportedly she was talked out of it by her mother and other family members—her sisters-in-law—Donna and Pat Houston. They were embarrassed by her appearance, and convinced her that she should quit appearing in public until she got her act together.

Witnessing the horrifying photos of Houston at Madison Square Garden, Clive Davis reportedly wrote her a letter, pleading with her to get help. According to a source quoted in *The National Enquirer*, "Clive Davis saw the pictures of Whitney, too, and he was shocked. His letter helped convince Whitney she needed to get her life together."

When the press ran photos of the shocking new "Whitney lite," there was no hiding the fact that she was slowly killing herself. On September 13, a rumor circulated through the press that Houston had just killed herself with an overdose. The rumor was quickly dispelled. However, according to the *New York Post*, TV network MTV had already assembled an extensive bunch of film clips of Whitney Houston for her obituary, just in case she suddenly dropped dead.

The story became even more bizarre, as the tapes of the *Michael Jackson: 30th Anniversary Celebration* TV show were prepared for broadcast, as a CBS-TV special on November 13, 2001. Whitney looked so horrific that it was revealed that video technicians had to use a computer technique of blurring the image of Whitney, so that the TV audience couldn't see so many of her bones showing through her nearly transparent skin. However, when the show aired, there was no question that she was in serious danger of accidentally killing herself. The blurred body shots of Houston shell revealed that she was a skinny as a chopstick. She was described in *The Star* as "a walking skeleton."

Worse yet, the famous singer she was now most closely compared to was the equally-talented Karen Carpenter. Karen had one of the most glorious voices of the 1970s and 1980s. However, she was anorexic, and she died in 1983—basically of starvation. At the time of her death, Karen had wasted away to almost nothing. Now it was Whitney who looked like she was going to expire any moment. Reportedly, her weight in pounds was now in the low nineties.

There were all kinds of rumors in September of 2001, that Whitney had finally realized her life was in danger. There was talk about Whitney and Bobby going to the Koh-Samui Detox Center which is located on an island in the Gulf of Thailand. However, the twenty-one-day detox program was nixed by the duo at the last minute.

Only half-heartedly wanting to quit her steady diet of cocaine, two times in September of 2001 Whitney had made plans with her mother to go to the posh health spa, Miraval, just outside of Tucson, Arizona. It isn't a "dry out" clinic per se, but a health resort. It seemed less intimidating to her than a hospital atmosphere. Finally, she made firm plans to check into Miraval on October 4.

However, reported *The National Enquirer*, "Two days before she went to a spa, Whitney and Bobby had one of their drivers deliver a supply of cocaine to their home in Mendham, New Jersey, according to the close source. 'It was supposed to be one last binge. That's what all drug addicts say.'"

While she was at Miraval, on Sunday, October 7, health guru and writer, Dick Gregory came by to give her some words of encouragement. Whitney was touched by his gesture, and seemed to listen to his advice. However, her actions proved that she still wasn't serious about drying out from drug use. She checked herself out in days, and returned to her old ways.

Continued *The Enquirer*, "After the Arizona trip Whitney spent another week with Bobby at the famous Canyon Ranch Health Resort in Lenox, Massachusetts. But once again her attempts at rehab were pitifully insincere: Before the limo ride from New Jersey to the Lenox health resort, Whitney and Bobby had their driver pick up a supply of drugs, a close source revealed."

On a more amusing note, in 2001, Houston's rival Mariah Carey was bought out of her multi-million dollar contract with Virgin Records—after producing a colossal "bomb" of an album and a film—both called *Glitter*. Suddenly, in January of 2002, it was reported that Carey was considering signing a recording contract with Arista. According to an item in *The New York Post* entitled "Whitney Seethes Over Mariah," the story claimed that Houston "went ballistic" when she heard that her arch rival on the record charts might try and eclipse her at Arista. Ultimately, Mariah signed with another label, but for a moment it looked like Carey was muscling in on Houston's territory.

Meanwhile, Whitney and Bobby were working on producing the first album of her new $100 million deal with Arista Records. In the beginning of 2002, rumors were already being circulated that the songs they had recorded so far, were substandard tracks, on which Whitney sounded absolutely horrible.

In a scandalous report in the February 12, 2002 issue of *The Globe*, entitled "Whitney Collapses! Drug-Dazed Diva Drifts In & Out of Stupor," harrowing reports of her recording progress came to light. According to the article, Whitney and Bobby would be up for days on end, partying and doing coke and attempting to nail down tracks for her new album. Then they would "crash" for days at a time as well. According to one source, "She was out cold for two days. When she finally came around, she buried herself under her quilt and sobbed her heart out."

Then there were the ill-fated attempts of continuing her recording career. She was no longer singing, it was like she was talking the lyrics to her songs. "A family friend" confided, "Her voice was raspy and raw and at least an octave lower than before. The more it kept cracking, the more she blamed Bobby and the studio equipment. When it was obvious she couldn't hit a note, Bobby suggested a 'little pick me up.' He may have wanted to make her feel better, but more cocaine was the worst thing she could have done."

Reportedly, a few days later, when Whitney wanted to hear the resulting tapes, Bobby made some lame excuse about the tape equipment being on the blink. In reality, he didn't want her to hear how awful she sounded. According to one eyewitness, "She knew Bobby was lying and she'd sounded terrible. As she disappeared into her room where she keeps her onyx 'stash box,' she hollered at Bobby, 'You are one miserable low-life!'"

Finally grasping what a mess she was making of her life, over the next couple of months she successfully gained twenty pounds, and was looking better. She was anxious to show of her new and healthier look on the 2002 VH1 special, *Diva Las Vegas*. Also on the bill were Mary J. Blige, Cher, Celine Dion, Stevie Nicks, Shakira, Cyndi Lauper, and The Dixie Chicks.

Houston was slated to sing one song, a duet with Mary J. Blige. In the past, Blige had her own drug problems, and she had made a well-publicized recovery. Since that time, Blige has taken an anti-drug stance. So, when Whitney arrived in Vegas for the rehearsals and the show, Mary wasn't about to put up with Houston's nonsense.

According to one source, "On Wednesday, Mary called Whitney to coordinate their schedules so they could make it to their 1:30 PM rehearsal on time that day. But when Whitney tried to explain that she simply wasn't in any physical condition to rehearse, Mary went ballistic."

Blige said to Houston, "What? Are you serious? You won't rehearse with me? I can't believe this! How could you do this to me?" Mary was so mad that members of Whitney's entourage had to go to Blige's room to calm her down and assure her that Houston would be at the rehearsal.

When Blige called producers at VH1 and told them that she didn't want Whitney to be part of her act, they informed her that Houston was a much bigger star, and that they wouldn't hear of Mary nixing the duet. Fortunately a compromise was worked out. Said an insider, "The rehearsal went off without a hitch, and Mary and Whitney even hugged when it was over. Then during the live performance, they hugged again, and it was obvious they'd put their feud behind them." This was however, just the beginning of people wanting to distance themselves farther and farther away from Whitney, for fear that she her latest melt-down would reflect on them.

In July of 2002, the first single from her forthcoming *Just Whitney* album, was released. According to *Entertainment Weekly*, "'Whatchulookinat,' a bitter taste from her forthcoming follow-up, is a stumble in the wrong direction. The dated funkless groove isn't worthy of a second-stringer like Deborah Cox. And the paranoid, Jacko-like lyrics about press persecution highlight her recent troubles, which she should be helping us to forget." The song was released onto the marketplace "dead on arrival." In the United States, it only made it to Number 96. It peaked in England at Number 13. Word on the street was that recordings for the new album were all a complete disaster.

One of the most devastating blows came in late August of 2002, when her own father filed a lawsuit against her. Filed in New Jersey Superior Court, it claimed that John Houston and his business partner, Kevin Skinner, worked for Whitney, to obtain for her legal representation, and to subsequently help her negotiate her new Arista contract. She turned to her father and begged him for help when she had her marijuana troubles in Hawaii. He successfully came to her rescue. Then when it came time to negotiate the $100 million record contract, again John Houston was there, asking for a mere 7 percent cut for his time and effort. Again she "stiffed" him for the money.

Furthermore, when he saw first hand what a mess she and Bobby were making of her life, he was determined—as her father—to make sure she didn't put all $100 million "up her nose" by buying cocaine. To do this, he sued her for the full $100 million, and the suit called for an injunction requiring her to put 20 percent of all her earnings in trust, so that she would have something left over once her career hit bottom, and no one would hire her to sing.

A friend of the Houston family was quoted in *The Star*. Shockingly they revealed, "John saved Whitney from destroying her career. But she's never paid him—nothing! It's ridiculous. He's eighty-one years old, and she won't give him what she owes him. He's ashamed of her and really, really angry with both her and Bobby."

Continued the family friend, "She was cash-broke at the time. John and Kevin had to get her a $3 million advance from Arista just to save her New Jersey home. But when it came time to pay for all his work, she didn't pay. She refuses to pay."

For Whitney Houston, things were rapidly going "from bad to *worse*." In September of 2002 *The Globe* reported, "Whitney's new album is already overdue, unfinished and unnamed, even though she signed on with Arista honcho L.A. Reid more than a year ago—and her new single 'Whatchulookinat' is a big flop. Whitney's arguing with Arista over song selection."

Whitney and Bobby had taken up residence in the Swissotel in the Buckhead neighborhood of Atlanta, Georgia, so they could record at nearby Silent Sounds Studio. The same publication claimed, "One source says that at 6:00 AM, the singer and her husband dialed room service and ordered a box of baking soda, which . . . is used in the processing of cocaine powder to make crack."

Said an eyewitness, "She's painfully thin. She may not even weight a hundred pounds and she has brown splotches all over her face. When she goes out in public she is usually made up and wearing clothes that cover her shoulders and arms."

In October of 2002, Whitney and Bobby were riding in his brand new Porsche convertible in Alpharetta, Georgia. When they pulled into the driveway of a moderately-priced motel, the La Quinta Inn, people in the parking lot recognized the troublesome duo. A couple of passers-by loudly said to each other, "Is that REALLY her?" Foul-mouthed and paranoid Houston snarled back at them "Dammit—what's your problem? Motherfucker! Everywhere I go, it's the same thing—everybody looking at me!"

On November 7, 2002, at 2:30 AM, Bobby Brown was arrested—again. A traffic cop with a speed-detecting radar gun stopped Brown while he was driving his Cadillac Escalade. He was doing fifty-two mph in a thirty-five speed limit zone, in the exclusive neighborhood of Buckhead. Riding with him were several pals, not including Whitney. And, in his possession was just under an ounce of marijuana.

He was put in jail in Buckhead for that evening's fresh speeding and pot possession charges. At 9:00 AM he was released on that charge, after paying $1,300 bail money. However, while he had been cooling his heels in his cell, the Buckhead officers checked out Bobby's ever-growing police record they found that he was "wanted" by the county of DeKalb—conveniently nearby. It seemed that there was a warrant out for his arrest for failing to appear in court on a set date, as part of his current probation—stemming from his 1996 DUI charge.

So, at 9:00 AM he was taken into custody, from the Buckhead police station to the DeKalb County Jail. After paying another $10,000 in bail for the parole charge, finally at noon, Bobby was again a free man.

And so went the scenario of "just another night" in the crazy life of bad boy Brown. By now he had no real career—except that which he etched out on Whitney's coattails. He was officially Co-Executive Producing his wife's new Arista album, but in reality real producers—like Babyface—were actually creating the tracks. Bobby no longer had a record deal of his own. And, the only times he was seen on stage, was making impromptu appearances at Whitney concerts, or if he got drunk and jumped up on stage.

Speaking of Whitney concerts—here she was about to release a new album, and was she booking a promotional tour? Absolutely not. First of all, it was now doubtful in the mind of the public that she was capable of mounting an hour-long stage show. Then there was the fact that concert promoters no longer wanted to book her. Based on her last couple of public appearances, she was a complete financial risk. Would she show up? Would she forget the lyrics? Would she die on stage? Everyone seemed to be asking these questions.

In November of 2002, *The Star* revealed that her father's business partner, Kevin Skinner, had received "death threats" from Whitney Houston and Bobby Brown. Attempting to try "gangsta" scare tactics to induce John Houston and his partner to drop his $100 million lawsuit, they only succeeded in making themselves look even more foolish.

According to Kevin, "They are afraid of what I might reveal about Whitney's personal life. They don't want her father John and I to sue, and they sure don't want me testifying in court in the lawsuit. That's what the death threats are all about! I believe anything is possible with them."

A source quoted Whitney as screaming, "I hate Kevin—I could KILL the bastard! This is all his doing. My father would never dream of suing me on charging me for his help!"

Kevin added, "They told John that they were going to 'do me in.' And when they came to kill me, he might get 'done' too, if he was in the car with me." What a charming duo Bobby and Whitney were turning out to be!

On November 20, 2002, John Houston was admitted to Columbia Presbyterian Hospital in Manhattan. Reported *The New York Post,* "The multi-million dollar lawsuit Whitney Houston's father lodged against her has given him so much stress, he's been admitted to a hospital, his business partner said."

Kevin Skinner told TV's *Inside Edition,* "He was sick before the lawsuit, but it definitely amplified his condition."

Finally the long-awaited first album of the new $100 million Arista deal had a release date: December 10, 2002. And, to promote her dramatic "comeback" album, Whitney agreed to be interviewed on ABC-TV's news program, *Dateline,* by Diane Sawyer. It was Whitney and Bobby's intention to let the viewing public know that everything was normal and on the up-and-up with them. Instead, the hour-long December 4, 2002 telecast brilliantly demonstrated that both Houston and Brown were full-blown self-destructive substance abusers. As if the visual evidence of both of them on-camera that night wasn't enough evidence, both of them freely and shamelessly bragged about their drug abuse. Across America, jaws spent a good hour agape, as Whitney and Bobby presented the slow-motion at-home train wreck to end them all.

It was an interview that Clive Davis would NEVER allow her to give, had he still been in the picture. It was clear that Davis—or anyone in her life with any power or influence—would have talked her out of making this misguided appearance.

First of all, she looked like hell. She had put on some weight since the Michael Jackson show "skeleton" appearance. However, she still appeared emaciated. And, the quality of her once-incredible voice was terrible. She sounded raspy, and her voice literally cracked several times as she spoke.

Seated in the living room of her Atlanta home, Whitney Houston fielded frank questions from Sawyer.

"Is it alcohol? Is it marijuana? Is it cocaine? Is it pills?" Diane asked point-blank.

"It has been at times," replied Whitney.

"All?" Sawyer prodded.

"At times, uh-hmmm," said an unflinching Houston.

With regard to her status as a "drug addict," Whitney claimed, "I don't like to think of myself as addicted. I like to think . . . I had a bad habit . . . which can be broken."

According to the diva, she was done partying. "That was a moment in time that happened to me, that I was going through, that I'm over. I'm beyond it. It's past. It's done." By the look on her face, it was clear that she was not telling the truth about herself.

When Sawyer asked her what the biggest "devil" was in her life, she proclaimed that it was herself. Her horrified fans all wished that someone would please call in an exorcist!

And then there was the lawsuit her father had filed against her. "My father is eighty-one, very sick. His health is failing. Somebody who my father's associated with has put him up to some . . . has put fear in his heart as if he's not my father." She was obviously missing the point that her father was suing her partially for her own good—so she would have some money left after he was gone.

Speaking about her skeletal appearance, Whitney defensively replied to Sawyer, "Let's get that straight. I am not sick. OK? I've always been a thin girl. I am not going to be fat, ever . . . I'm five-foot-seven and thin."

The evening's most quoted "sound byte" came when Diane gingerly asked her if she smoked crack cocaine, and Houston—in her best snappy "fly girl" voice replied, "Crack is cheap! I make too much [money] for me to ever smoke crack. Let's get that straight, OK? I don't do crack. I don't do that. Crack is whack!"

As though he was there for either comic relief, or just a desire to get in some "air time" on TV, Bobby made a sudden impromptu appearance in front of the TV cameras. First of all, he looked like he was so sweat-covered it was as though he had just come in from completing a five-mile jog. He then laughably told Sawyer that he was a daily pot smoker, because he used it to treat his "bipolar" metabolism.

Next, little Bobby Kristina made a brief appearance on the show. The innocent, and obviously sweet child, smiled on camera to reveal a mouthful of jagged teeth begging for dental care. Whitney just signed a $100 million contract, and she couldn't take her beloved daughter to the dentist? Who did they think was going to watch this debacle on national television and walk away thinking they were just everyday parents and role models? Obviously, no one from this planet.

It was a three ring circus, and Whitney and Bobby were barely capable of jumping through the hoops. If the viewing public had thought the duo was a pair of drugged-out idiots before—this was all the confirming evidence that was needed. The press fall-out after the telecast wasn't just negative, it was hellishly bad.

According to reports published in *The Star*, an insider is quoted as saying of Houston and Brown, "I don't think they realized that baring so much in front of the camera would turn out this way. I think they believed that a lot of people would rally to their side, saying: 'They've finally come clean about the drugs. Maybe now they can get their lives together.'"

In *The Miami Herald*, Evelyn McDowell wrote, "Houston said she doesn't like to think of herself as a drug addict, while appearing frail and strung out. She has lost touch with reality."

Social commentator Bill O'Reilly went on TV calling Houston "a degenerate." According to his damning editorial—having witnessed the *Dateline* interview, "You've got a little daughter in the house, you're taking drugs, there's no denial. You're a degenerate. From the interview we got from Ms. Houston that she used or uses alcohol, marijuana, cocaine and pills and that her husband uses marijuana every day, so he says. Isn't it impossible to have a child living in the home [and] not see these individuals 'high?' I mean, this woman is a drug addict. They use drugs. She isn't off drugs. [It] isn't possible for the girl not to know the parents are high."

And on the subject of questioning the Browns' qualifications as parents, O'Reilly blasted, "Whitney Houston is a scarecrow, a skeleton, and the other guy [Bobby] is in and out of courts every other week. I say flat out it is 'child abuse,' because I can't imagine a nine-year-old watching her parents in that condition—constantly in trouble with the law, constantly seeing their physical appearance falling apart—and not being affected by it. It's impossible."

With regard to Bobbi Kristina's safety, *The Star* revealed that Whitney's New Jersey house was under constant surveillance by the authorities. The publication claimed in December of 2002, "Whitney is furious at Cissy. She is convinced she's the one who keeps calling the youth authority people complaining and turning her in."

According to a specific source quoted in *The Star*, Whitney and Bobby had formulated a strategy in case there were threats to remove Bobbi Kristina from their care. The source claimed, "They're planning on leaving the country if the cops try to take Krissy. What's why they've been staying in their house in Atlanta and avoiding New Jersey. They know the heat is on up there. Bobby has said to me, 'Despite all the troubles we had, it's being a mother that has kept Whitney going.' Bobby is really afraid that Whitney might go off the deep end if the authorities take Bobbi Kris away from them."

In December of 2002 comedy TV show *Saturday Night Live* presented their own lampooning skit about the drug-addicted Browns. In the context of the skit, a disoriented Houston (Maya Rudolph) inquires as to where she left her own daughter. When Bobby Brown (Tracey Morgan) began to drip water from his bad wig, Whitney led him off camera for his marijuana therapy. *Mad TV* had also recently raked them over the coals. In the *Mad TV* skit, Whitney (Debra Wilson) had her hair in curlers, and was wandering around the house in her bathrobe, looking for Bobbi Kristina. Then an equally out-of-it Bobby proceeded to sing an off-key duet with Whitney on a colorful plastic children's toy tape recorder. The skit presented them as foolish drug addicts. On December 10, 2002, when the *Just Whitney* album was released in the stores, this comic scenario didn't seem like such a far fetched concept.

Critics and the public agreed that *Just Whitney* is positively the most plodding, boring, and pointless album of Houston's entire career. In the lyrics of five different songs of the ten, she is heard trying to justify her crazy lifestyle and her erratic mood swings.

On "One of These Days" she complains about the week she has just had. On "Tell Me 'No'" she proclaims that she never takes anyone else's advice. "Try It on My Own" sounds like a defiant song about her split with Clive Davis. "My Love" is a "they told us it would never last" kinda salute to her dysfunctional marriage to Bobby. "Whatchulookinat" sadly speaks of the self-destructive spectacle she had made of herself since the year 2000. And, on the song "Unashamed" she vows to live with her own mistakes. Judging by the sound of this dreadful album, this was truly one of the biggest mistakes of her career.

Totally divorced from Clive Davis's instinctive ability to pick hit songs, it was Whitney and Bobby Brown who are credited as the Executive Producers of this album. *Just Whitney* simply lacks any songs of real distinction. The only track which has any remote interest is the paranoid and defensive "Whatchulookinat," and its distinction is merely that of a sad curiosity.

The Whitney / Bobby duet "My Love" was clearly recorded for the pair's own vanity. Beginning with a Brown monologue about the couple's ten-year anniversary, the song is neither inspiring, romantic, nor convincing. They should have just recorded "Jailhouse Rock" as a duet. That would have made much more sense, since Bobby spent more time in jail cells than he did on record charts.

Furthermore, there was no question that her singing voice was in bad shape. What was once one of the most beautiful and expressive voices of the 1980s and 1990s was now raspy, deeper and less agile than ever before. The only high notes that are hit on this album are performed by the background singers, because Houston had totally lost her once-glorious vocal range. Her singing on this album sounded like a bad "demo" instead of a finished recording.

The songs included on *Just Whitney* are all new compositions, with the exception of a completely awful cover of "You Light Up My Life." Houston sounds especially horrible here, especially when she tries to sustain notes she can no longer hit. Where is Debby Boone when you need her?

The song "Unashamed" is even more paranoid than "Whatchulookinat." The song finds Houston vocally standing up for the many bad decisions she has made in her life. She might have been "unashamed," but it didn't eradicate the downward spiral of shame she had created.

What she should have been ashamed about is what she had done to her once crystal clear voice. This is a highly unpleasant album to listen to, and even talented producers like Babyface and Missy "Misdemeanor" Elliott couldn't save this Titanic-scaled disaster.

One of the most fascinating and telling aspects of this album came on the photos of Houston on the cover and interior of the CD package. On the front cover, and three out of five interior photos, Whitney's eyes are completely closed. Once considered a ravishing beauty, it seemed that she could no longer look her fans in the eye, for fear they will see what is really going on in her life.

The critics absolutely assassinated the record—from the boring material, to the joyless and energy-free way that the "new" Whitney now sang her songs. Most of all, no one seemed to be able to believe how Houston had completely destroyed her vocal cords. According to New York record producer Andrew Skurow, "The drugs have obviously had an affect. Whitney's voice hardly sounds like her own anymore. It's so sad, I hope she gets her life together because she's incredibly talented."

The first week that *Just Whitney* was in the stores, it debuted at Number Nine in America on the *Billboard* charts. It sold over 200,000 copies that first week in the US, then—thanks to negative word on the street—sales figures plummeted instantly. Ultimately—by mid-2003—it slowly went *Gold* in the US, for sales of just over 700,000 copies, then it swiftly dropped off the chart. This made it the poorest selling new album of her entire career. It was officially written off as a complete and total "bomb." Furthermore, in her second biggest sales market, England, it only peaked at Number 76.

In a bold but misguided attempt to deflect all of the degrading press, the first single from the *Just Whitney* album was the song "Whatchulookinat" which Whitney and Bobby had hoped would reverse the tide of negative criticism. "Whatchulookinat," proved to be a dead-on-arrival release on the charts. It only made it to Number 96 on the *Billboard* Pop Music chart in America. After eleven Number One hits, this signaled the end of an era for Ms. Houston. In publications around the world, reviewers not only attacked the album, they turned on Whitney herself—with a vengeance.

England's *The Guardian* claimed, "Few artists' careers have been so afflicted by adverse publicity as that of Whitney Houston." Regarding the album, writer Alexis Petridis pointed out, 'Like [Michael] Jackson's *Invincible, Just Whitney* does everything in its power to suggest all is normal with the artist behind it . . . *Just Whitney* takes a musical step backwards."

Der Tagesspiegel, in Germany announced, "Nowadays her career is not safe anymore. Her comeback might even be the end of her career."

In America the results were equally as dismal. *People* magazine harpooned this whale of a Whitney project by proclaiming, "On only the fifth studio album in her seventeen-year career, Whitney Houston proves that less is sometimes just less."

Tom Moon in *The Philadelphia Inquirer* sited the song "My Love" from *Just Whitney* to snipe, "in a duet with her husband, Bobby 'Pass Me That Doobie, I'm Bipolar' Brown, the two lovebirds talk a good game, but demonstrate little spark."

In *The Atlanta Journal-Constitution*, reviewer Craig Seymour claimed, "The biggest misstep on the album is the defensive 'Whatchulookinat.' If the jittery, bone-thin Houston still needs to ask what we're looking at, she obviously hasn't gazed into the mirror lately."

It also caused *San Francisco Chronicle* writer Neva Chonin to publicly point out that "*Just Whitney* . . . has been hyped as a righteous slap in the faces of naysayers who claim that la Houston is a real-life Neely O'Hara." Unfortunately, Whitney was becoming the twenty-first century incarnation of Neely, the tragic booze-and-pills star who ruined her own career in Jacqueline Susann's best-selling show business fable, *Valley of the Dolls*.

Even in her own home state, New Jersey's *Newark Star Ledger* reported, "Whitney defenders insisted her music would erase all concerns. Well, here's her new album at last; now it's time to really worry." Insisted writer Dan Leroy, "Can anyone explain how the world's savviest R&B executives could relaunch a purported drug addict with 'Whatchulookinat?,' a single pulsing with a dope fiend's paranoia?"

On December 13, 2002, Whitney was in Manhattan to have lunch with her brother, Michael Houston, at expensive Chinese eatery Mr. Chow's. Over a table of prawns and a beef appetizer, the siblings had a fiery and obscenity-filled conversation in front of a restaurant full of horrified on-lookers.

The argument was over the concurrent lawsuit between their father and Whitney. "Lay a chunk of change [on Dad]", Michael was heard insisting to his wealthy sister.

"Say's who? His messenger boy?" Whitney snapped back at him, according to a startled on-looker.

According to another witness, "The dining room was crowded and everyone was watching in shock. Harsh words and some profanities were exchanged. The argument ended with her saying, 'Forget about it!' and him saying, 'No way' Then Michael stormed off, cursing about Whitney not doing the right thing and how she'd be sorry for not seeing things his way. He was so steamed, a glass panel on the restaurant door broke on his way out."

After his hasty exit, a source quoted in *The Globe* claimed, "Whitney stayed calm and made a point of paying for the damages. She was clearly in control and took responsibility herself. Her friends were proud of the way she handled it." But were they also "proud" of the glowingly toxic disaster she had made of her career and her life?

In a year-end wrap-up of hot gossip subjects in *USA Today*, writer Ann Oldenburg wrote about the five worst celebrity disasters of 2002, called "For Five Stars It Was A Very Bad Year." Along with Michael Jackson dangling his baby out of a German hotel window, Winona Ryder's "guilty" shoplifting conviction, Britney Spears career cool-down, and Rosie O'Donnell's defiant "coming out," was Whitney's ill-fated *Dateline* experience. According to the article, **"DEFINING MOMENT:** 'Crack is wack.' RECAP: When Whitney Houston said those words to Diane Sawyer on national television, it became one of the next day's most repeated phrases . . . she and her husband Bobby Brown [admitted they] did use alcohol, cocaine and marijuana. THE CONSEQUENCES: Web sites, radio deejays, talk show hosts and fans were buzzing about her—and not in a good way."

If Houston were a vaudeville star, the next words she heard from the theater's "wings" would have been, "Get the hook!"

As the year 2002 ended, Whitney Houston had successfully turned herself into a global laughing stock, via her horrifying *Dateline* appearance. She and Bobby successfully Executive Produced the singularly "worst" album of her entire career. Her scalding critical "Whatchulookinat" single was a resounding "bust." Her singing voice was "shot." Cissy Houston was furious with her. Child protective services were reportedly investigating taking her daughter away from she and her husband. Bobby was still routinely getting into trouble with the law. Her brother was disgusted by her behavior. And, her loving father—who was suing her for her own good—was gravely ill and under hospital care. Could things get any worse in the shattered nightmare world of Whitney? The answer: "Yes."

CHAPTER FOURTEEN

"WHITNEY: HER DRAMATIC FALL"

The year 2003 was only three weeks old, and already there was trouble for Whitney Houston and Bobby Brown. Her family was totally divided against her, as her father—John Houston—lay dying in a hospital bed. It was no secret that her entire family hated Bobby Brown, and that they directly blamed him for ruining Whitney's life. But, for whatever deluded reason, she insisted on staying by Bobby's side.

On January 13, 2003, Bobby was in Los Angeles, where he was a "surprise" guest on the TV telecast *The American Music Awards*. He had made a cameo appearance during the performance of a young rapper on the awards telecast. Bobby's appearance consisted mainly of dancing around the stage like a drunken maniac. The audience seemed totally bewildered that he was there at all, since it had been a good ten years since he had released a recording of any significance.

However, by being in Los Angeles, he was also obviously breaking the terms of his latest parole hearing—stemming from his 1996 drunk driving charge. By leaving the state of Georgia, he violated the terms of his $11,000 bond. Because of his television appearance in California, the Georgia State Court issued an immediate warrant for his arrest.

On the advice of his lawyer, on Friday, January 17, Bobby Brown turned himself in at the DeKalb County Jail. After serving three days of his eight day sentence at the DeKalb County Jail, Bobby Brown was admitted to nearby Grady Memorial Hospital. He had complained of an ailment that was undisclosed to the press. He was released early for good behavior. However, as part of his release, he was required to pay $2,600 in fines, and to perform 240 hours of Community Service.

He was also required to remain on probation for another two years. He was forbidden from driving an automobile for a year, and he was required to undergo substance abuse counseling. Brown still faced various other charges, emanating from his November 2002 arrest, involving speeding, marijuana possession and for driving with neither automotive insurance nor a driver's license. It seemed like Bobby's trouble with the law was simply an ongoing thing with him. No matter how many times he was humiliatingly thrown into a jail cell, he seemed to repeat the same parole violations time and time again.

Meanwhile, major adjustments were being made in Whitney Houston's life. When word officially came down that her new *Just Whitney* album was being declared a sales failure, all hopes of receiving a cent of royalty money from it vanished too. Furthermore, she seemed to be supporting her entire family. As 2003 began, so did some sweeping financial changes. She announced to her family members—who were on her payroll—that their salaries were all going to be cut in half. According to a report in *The Globe*, "Sources say the multimillionaire songbird has already chopped her mom Cissy's salary by more than half—from a tidy $1,600 a week to a mere $550. And she's doing the same to brothers Michael and Gary, and sister [in-law] Donna, who run her company Nippy Inc." And, regarding her father, Whitney was defiantly quoted in *The National Enquirer* as saying, "[He will] never get $100 million out of me.

Arista Records kept releasing singles from the *Just Whitney* album, hoping that the unsuccessful fate of "Whatchulookinat?" was just a fluke. It was not. Subsequent singles, "One of These Days" and "Make It On My Own" didn't make it anywhere near the Top 40. The whole album was deemed a very expensive mistake.

While John Houston spent his last days in a hospital bed, Whitney received the jarring news that no matter what happened to her dad—even if he died—the lawsuit he filed, would remain in effect. Confirmed John's lawyer, Philip Levitan, "It's an action of his estate and the estate could continue it. There are other people who could easily testify to the facts."

It was revealed in the press that on at least one occasion Whitney had indeed visited her father in the hospital. From his hospital bed, dying of diabetes, John claimed, "I'm not well at all. But the doctors are trying to fix me up."

The Star had the last official press interview that John Houston gave. At the time he claimed, "Whitney will always be my daughter and I will always love her . . . The lawsuit is a business situation, and I think Whitney would have paid the debt by now if it wasn't for that Bobby Brown. He's nothing but a low-life skunk and he's driven a wedge between me and my daughter. I never trusted him."

On February 2, 2003, when the end finally came for John Houston, his only daughter, Whitney, was nowhere to be found. A close friend quoted in *The Star* claimed, "John would have liked Whitney to be there. He wanted to tell her he still loved her. He knew the end was near and wanted to say 'goodbye.'" Reportedly, his last words were, "Tell Whitney I forgive her."

According to sources, while Whitney was badly shaken by the death of her father, Bobby Brown was actually relieved. A family friend confirmed, "John hated Bobby with a passion. He thought Bobby was the source of all Whitney's troubles." It seems like an accurate assessment.

A source quoted in *The Star* claimed, "John's death has shaken Whitney badly. You can't say the same about Bobby, who's glad the old man is gone."

Whitney attended John's wake at Whigham funeral Home on February 6. However, she was conspicuously missing at his funeral service when it was held the next day at St. James A.M.E. Church. Another source claimed, "Whitney was too shaken to attend the actual service. She was an absolute mess. Very distraught, not making sense. Whitney was babbling."

With her father's death—and for that matter her career's death as well—Whitney's only work now came from making guest appearances on TV specials, and showing up at awards shows. With no tour planned to support the disastrous *Just Whitney* album, her cash flow was in danger. To earn more money from her recording deal, she has to record more material. That's where the idea for recording a Christmas album came from. For her, it would be a "safe" way of releasing an album, without the pressure of making it a sales hit. Since Christmas albums usually only sell in the vicinity of 500,000 copies, the expectations on this album were already seriously low.

In April of 2003, Whitney and Bobby went to Miami, Florida to attend the Haitian Music Awards. They stayed at the Hyatt Regency Hotel in downtown Miami. For them, it erupted into still another public embarrassment.

According to a hotel staff member, "They came in at 4:30 PM. [In the bar] Bobby did shots of Absolut vodka chased by beer. Whitney was sipping a White Russian. They went to the awards show, then came back at 1:30 AM." Then a group of heavily drinking firemen started to heckle Bobby by saying, "Hey Bobby, buy us some drinks. You're a millionaire!" When Brown yelled back that he would buy them water, the six firefighters ordered cocktails, and billed Bobby's tab. After that, it all escalated into a drunken shouting match between Brown and the firemen. Said the source, "The louder he got, the more the firemen waved and jumped up and down. They were just delighted to have wound him up. One guy was imitating Whitney, holding two glasses to his ears like oversized earrings. Another was yelling, 'You're has-beens!' Things escalated. Bobby wanted to 'take it outside.' I was just about to call the cops when the firemen left." With that, Brown paid the couple's staggering $500 bar bill, and left as well.

Said one eyewitness in the bar, "It was pathetic. People are now making fun of them openly."

The press continued to have a field day covering the troubled diva. In a scalding 2003 article about Houston, Ernest Hardy in *LA Weekly*, claimed that during this era West Coast drag queens were delivering more entertaining Whitney performances than Houston did herself. Reviewing the act of one such "faux Whitney," Hardy found the performer "pressing her eyelids tightly together as though it pained her to think, wobbling slightly in her heels and wearing a glazed look in her eyes—all while intentionally flubbing her lip-syncing." This was the way the public was beginning to think about the real Whitney. It was an unflattering image which the real Ms. Houston continued to perpetuate.

On May 22, 2003, Whitney was booked to be one of the stars on the latest incarnation of VH1's *Divas* series of TV specials. This particular edition was called *Divas Duets*. It starred Queen Latifah, Chaka Khan, Mary J. Blige, Celine Dion, Shania Twain, Lisa Marie Presley, Pat Benatar, Beyoncé, Jewel, Ashanti, and Whitney Houston. Sharon Osbourne was the on-camera commentator and co-hostess with Latifah. On the show, Whitney sang a duet with Bobby Brown, and then a solo on the *Divas* program.

When Whitney and Bobby arrived in Las Vegas, the day before the show, they were both in prime party mode. They checked into the ritzy Bellagio Hotel on May 21, and they hit the gambling rooms. According to a report from FOX-TV gossip reporter, "Bobby was in the casino of the Bellagio, in the high-stakes area. A gambler at one blackjack table— thinking Bobby would pay him back—gave him $5,000 to play. Bobby lost it all and then ducked his own security guards and just walked off. Whitney wound up paying out the five grand [$5,000] to defuse the situation. Other reports from the hotel confirm that it was all-night party time in the Brown suite at the Bellagio. Whatever it was they were up to, by 8:00 AM they had partied to the point where Whitney's nose was uncontrollably bleeding."

The Star quoted a source as saying, "She got really scared. Her security people took her in a private limo to a clinic. She was holding all these bloody tissues to her nose at the time."

When she left the AAA Ear Nose and Throat Medical Group, she had a completely bizarre contraption of gauze and cotton strapped to her face. *The Star* published photos of Whitney with this device on her face, designed to ease the pressure in her nostrils. She looked ridiculous.

Another source claims, "Years ago, doctors were telling Whitney that she was ruining her nasal passages. But she's been ignoring the warnings. And her nose problem is only getting worse."

While all of the divas got a chance to be paired with interesting partners—Jewel and Beyoncé, Lisa Marie and Pat Benatar—Whitney performed only with Bobby Brown in the "duet" format. It was Mary J. Blige who sang a duet with Chaka Khan. It seemed that no one else on the bill wanted to be seen on camera with her.

Finally it came time for the Whitney and Bobby spot in the show. They lumbered around the stage in an un-choreographed fashion while singing a duet version of their two recordings together: "Something in Common" and "My Love." All the while, the audience seemed to hold their collective breath, wondering if Whitney was going to successfully get through the number or not. Mid-song she now has the annoying habit of jumping up and down like a six-year-old whenever she wanted it to appear that she was doing an impromptu dance step.

Their performance was pathetically disturbing to watch. Here was whittled down Whitney on national television professing her undying devotion to the man who was helping her ruin her life and her career.

However, later in the show, came the evening's all-time low point. When Whitney returned to the stage to sing "Try It on My Own" as a solo, she gave the most awesomely awful performance of her entire television career. Her singing was incredibly strained throughout the song, as though she knew she couldn't push herself too hard, for fear that her nose might start bleeding again.

On more than one occasion, her voice painfully cracked, and her hand went up to her throat as if it hurt her to croak out whatever notes she could find. At one point she even called out for the sound man to turn up the auditorium house volume, so that there would be an echo effect to masquerade the fact that she couldn't hit the notes. It was sad and pathetic, to see that the once-great Whitney Houston was now incapable of getting through just one song without losing her voice. Didn't she used to have it all?

The evening ended with all of the "divas" singing along with Stevie Wonder. Whitney sang a couple lines of "I Was Born to Love Him." She sounded dreadful, and it was perfectly fitting that she would sing a song about loving a man whom her mother hates. In a production number that was supposed to carry a divaesque tone of sisterly love, it came across as being distinctively disjointed. None of the other singers—including Mary J. Blige—seemed to want to stand anywhere near Houston. Obviously not one of them wanted to be associated with her and her disastrous lifestyle.

Not to let any grass grow under their feet, less than a week after the *Diva Duets* live telecast, the Browns turned up in—of all places—Israel. The story was that Whitney and Bobby were going to Israel to be the guests of a group calling themselves the Black Hebrews. The Black

Hebrews live in the southern city of Dimona. According to this sect of American ex-patriots, they claim to be descendants of a lost tribe of Israel. However, the Israeli's don't officially recognize the group as either Jews or citizens of their country. They also believe in polygamy, and of having children by many wives. This obviously would be a good selling point for Bobby. There was also talk of the pair starring in a Christmas special for HBO, and that they would seek help from the Black Hebrews, in cleaning up their drug act.

While in Israel, the story became even more bizarre by the moment. Whitney and Bobby actually met with Israeli Prime Minister Ariel Sharon, at his official residence. As though the often-arrested duo would be suitable emissaries to represent America? "Welcome to Jerusalem," Sharon said to the Browns. *The National Enquirer* ran photographs of the duo, spiritually dunking themselves in the River Jordan, looking like a pair of wet cats.

On Monday, May 26, 2003, Houston told press reporters in the Israeli resort town of Eilat that she was currently amidst a "spiritual retreat." However, it is even easier to suspect that the duo was just "scoping out" a possible location to run to, in case American authorities try to take their daughter away from them. Things were not exactly going well for them in the United States. Perhaps it was time to flee the country?

This was underscored when the couple came back to America. On August 22, 2003, Bobby Brown was again arrested in the Atlanta area. This time around, he was having dinner with Whitney in a restaurant in Alpharetta, Georgia. The charge—again—was for parole violation in DeKalb County. He was put behind bars in a place he was now very familiar with—the DeKalb County Jail.

By now the press was getting weary of Whitney, and they clearly hated Bobby. Britain's *Night and Day* magazine went so far as to bluntly point out, "Several years her junior and coarsely nicknamed 'Sperm Bank' for his capacity to father illegitimate offspring, Bobby Brown was and is a professional bad boy . . . [who is] in and out of the music charts, [and] the Betty Ford Clinic."

On November 18, 2003, Whitney's *One Wish: The Holiday Album* was released. Instead of drawing her music to a whole new audience of fans, it proved to be an even bigger sales disaster than *Just Whitney* the year before. By now it was common knowledge that Houston was in the middle of her "substance abuse" era. It wasn't just gossip anymore, it was a matter of common knowledge by now. In a way, this album was a great idea: to present Whitney in a pristine holiday light for a change. However, photographing her in snowy yuletide white on the cover wasn't going to disguise the damage that had been done. In the end, no one but her most devoted fans were buying it.

One of the biggest problems that the album suffers from, is the diva's new, deeper, raspier voice. "Oh, Holy Night" and "I'll Be Home For Christmas" really reveal all of the damage that Whitney had done to her vocal chords since 1996. At one point in the song "Oh, Holy Night," instead of hitting what should have been a "signature Whitney Houston" high note, instead finds her reaching down towards a low baritone. It made for a painful Christmas experience.

To make matters worse, two songs from *The Preacher's Wife* soundtrack album were included as the album's final pair of tracks: "Who Would Imagine a King" and "Joy to the World." While they are beautiful to listen to, they conclusively offer the stark contrast between her voice of "then" and her voice of "now." What a difference seven years had made. In spite of some fine musical arrangements, what should have been a "great" album—*One Wish: The Holiday Album*— is merely an "O.K." album.

The music critics were less-than-enthusiastic. *Rolling Stone* gave it "Zero" Stars out of a possible "Five." Sal Cinquemani in *The Slant* wrote, "One can't help but think that *One Wish: The Holiday Album* is nothing more than damage control. The singer hasn't had a bona fide hit since 1999 . . . Houston's voice just isn't what it used to be—she warbles her way through an otherwise understated version of the contemporary classic 'I'll Be Home For Christmas' . . . Just compare these performances to the crystalline voice on the album's final two tracks . . . which were taken from the soundtrack to 1996's *The Preacher's Wife* . . . sung by one of our greatest vocalists—even if she's no longer at the top of her game."

Jon Pareles in *The New York Times* saw the album's strong and weak points. He observed, "Momentarily freed from the pressure to choose the right pop pose, Whitney Houston can simply bestow her vocal gifts on the familiar songs . . . The ballads are impressive, though they can verge on soupy; turning ecumenical, she adds Hanukkah and Kwanzaa to Mel Tormé's 'Christmas Song.' A medley of 'Deck the Halls' and 'Silent Night' shows a frisky side, and 'O Come O Come Emmanuel' is the tour de force . . . enough to make a listener forgive Ms. Houston for pushing her daughter forward on "Little Drummer Boy.'"

One Wish: The Holiday Album only charted in the United States, and hit a peak of Number 44. One single from the album, the song "One Wish (For Christmas)," made it into the Top 20 on the American "Adult Contemporary" chart. However, by August of 2009, it had still only sold 433,000 copies, according to *Billboard* magazine. In contrast to her glittering past, she had established a new low point for sales.

In 2003 Whitney and Bobby sent out press releases about how they were going to star together in a film called *Beffy & Charlie*. That may have been their intention, however, there wasn't a film studio in Hollywood willing to bankroll such a nonsensical project. No one was crazy enough to attempt to make a movie with a leading man who is often "wanted" by the police in several states, and a leading lady who was now more known around Hollywood as someone who routinely cancelled as many appearances as she made. The *Beffy & Charlie* project had the same kiss-of-death curse that Madonna and Sean Penn had with *Shanghai Surprise*—and the cameras never rolled.

At this point it seemed that things were bound to get a lot worse for Houston and Brown, before they get any better. How many times could Bobby be arrested before he finally got the message, and started to obey the law? And how many more times could Whitney afford to bail him out? His performing career was all but finished. Other than a few "cameo" roles in films, he was not an actor. And, without a label deal, he was no longer considered a recording star.

Whitney had her own career mess to contend with. Already acknowledged as the bread-winner in this dysfunctional family, her income was in serious trouble. Yes, she did sign a contract with Arista Records for a guarantee of $100 million, however she had to produce more hits before any more cash was to flow into her bank account. *Just Whitney* was such a horrendous "bomb" of an album, that it ultimately lost money for Arista.

And, her film career is over as well. She looked horrible, and was clearly unstable.

Whitney continued to wage her own private war against the press. During this era, Houston was quoted as saying, "It's really strange. Michael Jackson said it best: 'You become this personality instead of a person.' That's what's strange about this 'image' business—the more popular you become, the weirder they want to make you. I read some stuff about myself in the last year—it's like 'Who the fuck are they talking about?' I mean, they talk about my husband . . . They don't even know him. They have no idea who he is. They don't know what we're like when we're in the house. But the media always distorts shit. It's never, never what I said. It's never how I said it; it's never how I thought that person perceived me. It's always some other crazy shit—which is why I don't like doing interviews. Because they lie. They just outright lie." Whitney Houston clearly was totally out of touch with reality. She wanted to blame her troubles on anyone but herself.

On May 5, 2004 Bobby appeared in court in Fulton County, Georgia where he was facing "misdemeanor battery charges." Apparently he and Whitney got into one of their notorious fights in their home near Alpharetta, in the Georgia suburbs. Amidst the fight Bobby hit her in the face, bruising her cheek and leaving her with a cut lip. When the police were summoned Brown was officially charged with beating the woman he claimed be madly in love with.

Unfortunately, things were to get a lot worse for Whitney Houston before they improved. As though she could sink any lower than the spectacle she made of herself during Diane Sawyer's interview with her, Mr. and Mrs. Brown were about to make even bigger fools of themselves. In 2005 television audiences were shocked by Whitney's most self-destructive project yet: her role on the television reality show *Being Bobby Brown*. The very idea that Bobby Brown should end up the star of his own television program was astonishing in itself. The press confirmed that the deal with the Bravo television network could only proceed if Whitney Houston agreed to be seen in every episode. Oddly enough, she agreed. The curiosity factor of seeing Whitney and Bobby together on camera—unedited and unscripted—was the only reason for viewers to tune in at all.

The first episode of the program aired on June 30, 2005. In the July 7, 2005 issue of *The Hollywood Reporter*, Barry Garron called the show, "the most disgusting and execrable series ever to ooze its way onto television." Pondering the reason for the shocking program's existence, Garron wrote, "Is it the lionizing of a lowlife convicted of failing to pay child support for his out-of-wedlock kids, drunk driving and a cocaine-related parole violation? . . . Is it his insufferable ego? . . . Is it his constant crude comments? . . . Or is it just his disgusting persona?"

The public wondered if things were really as bad as the critics and the gossip columns had been claiming? *Being Bobby Brown* offered conclusive evidence that things were far worse than anyone could have possibly imagined. And, as outrageous as it seemed, Bobby actually came across much more favorably than Whitney.

The eleven episodes of the series *Being Bobby Brown* were filmed the year before—from January to June of 2004. Actually there were ten original episodes, and the eleventh one was comprised of clips from the original ten. Obviously much more footage was shot of Bobby and Whitney than was used, and it was edited in a fashion which used as much screen time of the troubled diva as humanly possible. As it was, there were far too many long segments of Bobby preening himself like the boastful jailbird he was. One internet critic suggested that the program would have been better if it were re-titled: *"Being Mr. Whitney Houston."*

As it was, *Being Bobby Brown* was a slow-motion train wreck. It drew viewers merely for the "shock value" of watching it in awe. Bobby and Whitney did not disappoint. Speaking of his son Bobby Brown Jr. in one episode, Bobby egocentrically claimed that the boy was only "special to me because he carries my name." At one point he summoned Whitney by commanding, "Bring that ass in quick. I'm going to show you what I'm going to do with it!"

The cameras followed the shocking duo around 24/7 to show them off at their most dysfunctional. Whitney often had her face covered in large dark sunglasses which she used to hide behind. In one sequence the duo is seen in a restaurant being rude to other patrons who recognized them. It wasn't long before the Browns became so comfortable at ignoring the camera crews, that they really "let their hair down." In the most notoriously disgusting interlude captured on camera Whitney complained to Bobby about being constipated. Shockingly, Bobby verbally offers to remove the offending matter for her manually. It couldn't get much worse. Thankfully, the cameras did not follow her into the bathroom.

No shy butterfly, Whitney came across as being haughty, obnoxious, spoiled, crude, and obviously "high" on something for the entire show. Whitney was not about to let Bobby get all of the best quotes on the show. Often she told him, "Kiss my ass." When asked to do something she did not want to do, she blasted back: "Hell to the 'no!'" It became the catchphrase of the whole series. It became such a joke that there were even "Hell to the 'no!'" tee shirts printed up and sold. To poke fun at her, the satiric TV show, *The Soup*, repeated showed the clip of Houston shouting "Kiss my ass." Whitney had officially become the laughing stock of the entertainment industry. If *Being Bobby Brown* did not end both of their careers, nothing would.

To the producer's credits, the individual episodes all had some sort of cohesive theme to them. Episodes included "At Home With the Browns," "Happy Mother's Day," and "Bobby Does London." In the later episode the pair is seen in the British capitol shopping at famed Harrod's department store, where they even met up with the store's owner Mohamed Al-Fayed. In another episode the duo was depicted vacationing in the Bahamas. For both of the Browns, it appeared that their individual musical careers were finished. They were both reduced to caricatures of themselves: both famous merely for being infamous, and lost within the confines of their own notorious fame.

Unfortunately, Whitney—who had looked so beautiful and innocent in *The Bodyguard*—often came across as a jaded witch or a screeching bird of prey. And the pair's parenting skills seemed to parallel that of a pair of alligators—a species notorious for devouring their young. Watching this series, one could not help but have extreme sympathy for little Bobbi Kristina Brown. To have this pair of crazies as one's parents seemed to be a horrifying concept.

Being Bobby Brown ran from June 30 to August 2005, each week offering another scandalous episode. It became the "guilty pleasure" viewing of the summer. Finally on December 22, 2005 a last episode, entitled

"Christmas With the Browns," was aired. In 2008 it was announced that the series was going to be released on DVD for home viewing. However, Whitney reportedly refused to sign a "release" to allow her segments to be included. That was the end of the matter.

In the book *Bobby Brown: The Truth, The Whole Truth and Nothing But . . . ,* Brown is quoted as saying, "I have a serious problem with this because this affects my income. There is a lot of money to be made off the DVD, but because she won't cooperate, we'll never see it. First of all, I never asked her to show up on one of the sets. She would take it upon herself to show up anyway. I even went as far as telling her that she could leave. I made sure she knew she did NOT have to be there, but she always found a way to end up on the set. Now she regrets being part of it."

Now the show only exists on the homemade videotapes of Houston fans and other shocked viewers. The evidence is shameful at best. *People* magazine labeled this televised spectacle as being nothing short of "bizarre." *The Hollywood Reporter* best summed it up by pointing out, "Not only does it reveal Brown to be even more vulgar as the tabloids suggest, but it manages at the same time to rob Houston of any last shreds of dignity."

On one episode of *Being Bobby Brown*, Whitney is heard asking the camera crew, "What are we supposed to be doing here?" That was one of the most telling moments of the entire series. What was she doing with Bobby Brown? What was she doing with her career? And, what was she doing with her life in general? At this point, even she seemed clueless.

CHAPTER FIFTEEN

"LIKE I NEVER LEFT"

By 2006 the fate of Whitney Houston was in the hands of the two most important men in her life: Bobby Brown and Clive Davis. It seemed that either Bobby would destroy her once and for all, or she would leave him and Clive would save her. Fortunately for her millions of fans around the world, the second scenario was the one that eventually prevailed.

Apparently, Bobby thought that Whitney was bluffing when their marriage was rumored to be in trouble in January of that year. Brown was seen in public partying and carousing with several woman in a casino. When asked about his wife he told the press, "She's my friend. She's the better half of me. They say opposites attract, but we're not opposites. We're one person. We're loving life, and we're just trying to be as good to each other as possible." He was obviously in denial.

In April of 2006, *The National Enquirer* published photos of a bathroom which Whitney and Bobby had "trashed." The damning photographs undeniably showed drug paraphernalia, and evidence of a party of mega-proportions. The photos were taken by Tina Brown, Bobby's sister and sold to the publication. She also reported in the accompanying tabloid article that Whitney was engaging in lesbian affairs, and was so paranoid that she had holes drilled in the walls of her residence to see if the police were outside.

Even though Bobby reportedly cheated on Whitney with other women, he somehow harbored the idea that she would never actually leave him. He told *People* magazine in May of 2006, "We are happily married . . . We are going to stand for each other for as long as we life. I adore that woman. She helps me see God. I look in her eyes and I see God." Obviously, Whitney was beginning to see something much different in Brown's eyes.

In August of 2006 the press was reporting that Bobby was having an affair with a woman by the name of Karrine Steffans. Although Bobby never publicly confirmed nor denied it, apparently all was not well in the Houston / Brown household.

Clearly, Whitney Houston was no angel. She had already shown herself to be a hard, determined, strong-willed woman, who was in control of her own destiny. If she was ever going to escape from the influence of her self-destructive husband, the decision was ultimately going to have to be hers and hers alone. Somehow she finally saw Bobby for what he was: her worst enemy. Her only salvation was to get him out of her life, and to seek help. That is exactly what she did.

Finally, after fourteen years of marriage, Whitney Houston officially began proceedings for a "legal separation" from Bobby. In the court papers, filed in Orange County, California on September 8, 2006, the singer also asked for full custody of thirteen-year-old Bobbi Kristina. According to the documents, Bobby Brown would only be granted "visitation" rights to see his daughter, and no financial settlement. Official "divorce" papers were expected to be filed in court in October of that year.

The same week, Whitney was seen on the arm of Clive Davis at the fifteenth annual Ella Awards ceremony. The event, which was held at The Beverly Hilton Hotel, was hosted by The Society of Singers, and that year's recipient was Johnny Mathis. In addition to being with Clive, Whitney was also in the company of her famous cousin, Dionne Warwick—who performed as part of the show. According to *Access Hollywood*, "Whitney looked every bit the picture of health and happiness, the likes of which the public hasn't seen from her in quite some time."

The press immediately responded to seeing Davis and Houston reunited. The pair of former business associates were officially back together. It was Clive who had originally seen the potential in Houston's talent in the 1980s. It was Clive who created, crafted and orchestrated her singing career. And now it was to be Clive who was going to save the shambles she had made of her career, and of her life.

That evening at The Beverly Hilton Hotel, Davis officially announced that he and Houston were already in the process of planning her "comeback" album. Clive told MTV, "Whitney is Whitney, and there ain't nobody like her. It'll be Whitney. It won't be something reaching for a current trend, that's for sure."

The times had changed drastically since Davis and Houston had originally united to select and record their first two mega-successful albums together: *Whitney Houston* and *Whitney*. When Sony Music had subsequently merged with BMG / RCA Music, Clive was again back at the reigns of Arista Records, which was the label Whitney was still signed to record with. It was as if fate had seen a way to reunite them.

As early as 2006, it was obvious that the only person in the music business that Whitney would listen to for career guidance and direction, was Clive. Also, it was clear that Houston's entire career was Davis's creation. He was the only man who could bring her back to the stature in the business that she had once attained. Now her resurrection was officially in his hands.

This was not to say that it was all smooth sailing from this point forward. There were still several more mistakes for Whitney to make on her road to recovery.

In 2007, Whitney's divorce proceedings from Bobby were underway. In April of that year a judge awarded custody of Bobbi Kristina to Whitney. In court Whitney was asked about Brown's reliability as a father, and replied, "If he says he's going to come [visit his daughter], sometimes he does. Usually he doesn't." Although Bobby would have limited visitation rights with his fourteen-year-old daughter, he would not be legally entitled to another cent of Whitney's money. According to Judge Franz Miller, the divorce would become final on April 24, 2007. And so ended the marriage of the battling Browns.

In January of 2008 it was revealed that Bobby had attempted to overturn the terms of the divorce, in a play to receive alimony payments from Whitney. He was flatly turned down. Apparently, "being Bobby Brown" was not as easy it had once seemed.

Whitney's initial attempts at a comeback were not that easy either. On April 27, 2008, she had the opportunity to prove her critics and doubters wrong. Instead, she clearly demonstrated that her troubles were far from over. She was paid a reported $3 million for her appearance on the final night of the all-star Plymouth Jazz Festival, which was being presented in Tobago. The islands of Trinidad and Tobago are located next to each other, and are both famous as tropical resort destinations. Both islands are in the Caribbean Sea, close to South America, off the shore of Venezuela.

Houston was booked to perform her set of music prior to the evening's final superstar act: Rod Stewart. Before the show began the press was horrified to find that Whitney would not allow photographers to be present for her set, with the exception of one cameraman who granted Whitney "veto" rights over the resulting images.

For the $3 million she was paid, Whitney managed to disappoint both the press and her fans who were hoping that the diva would prove that she was not only "back," but was also in great physical and vocal shape. She was reportedly a disaster from the moment she took the stage.

She opened her show with the song "It's Not Right, But It's Okay," but she quickly demonstrated that she was anything but "okay." By the time she reached her third song, "Saving All My Love For You," she was already losing her voice. According to reporter Jawn Murray of the internet press site *Black Voices*, "the once-soprano's newfound tenor voice was in full rasp."

Dressed in a white gown, Whitney skipped around the stage shouting repeatedly to the crowd: "I love you Trinidad!" However, she was not in Trinidad at all. When members of the audience repeatedly shouted at her, "This is Tobago!" she ignored them and obliviously repeated, "I love you Trinidad!" Not only was she not in Trinidad, she acted like she was on Mars.

Realizing that she could not successfully sing through her entire act, she began to ramble to her audience about the festival. "Hearing so many of the greats that have performed this weekend bring back so many memories," she claimed. "My daughter and I have listened from our porch each night and I have enjoyed Diana Ross, Smokey Robinson, and En Vogue."

After that she attempted to sing her biggest hit, "I Will Always Love You." However, in the middle of the song she realized that she was vocal trouble. As the song began to build, she began to lose ground—and voice. Instead of even attempting to finish the song, she quickly segued into the song "I'm Every Woman," which she could more easily shout into the microphone. When she finished the song she bowed to the audience and the half-hearted applause she received, and then she squatted down on the stage. She was acting so strangely that the crowd worried if she would be able to stand up from her unattractive and very un-ladylike squatting position.

According to amazed on-lookers, the once-glorious star's career problems were far from over. The reviewer from *Black Voices* wrote of the evening: "R&B diva Whitney Houston disappointed a sold-out crowd who came to see a rare performance by the trouble-prone singer." She might have been on her career trail, but there were apparently several more bumps in the road that lie ahead. Whitney may have thought that she was a huge success in Trinidad, but she was in reality bombing-out in Tobago!

Likewise, the year 2008 wasn't a good one for her personal life either. She might have gotten rid of Bobby Brown, and was now romantically linked with R&B singer Ray J., but things were not at all well at home. Bobbi Kristina Brown, who was now a teenager, was feeling some extreme growing pains of her own. As many people had predicted, being Whitney and Bobby Brown's daughter was no picnic.

In May of 2008, *The National Enquirer* reported that Bobbi Kristina was had not only adopted her parents "partying" lifestyle, she was also dealing with some extreme depression issues as well. According to the article, Bobbi Kristina was heavily drinking alcohol with her friends, and had shockingly attempted suicide. Press reports claimed that she spent three days at the Peachford Psychiatric Hospital in February of 2008 for observation and was apparently "suffering a breakdown." Whitney never made an official statement about her daughter's health.

In the world of show business, planning a career "comeback" is a tricky business. Sometimes it works, sometimes it does not. As 2009 began, it was set to be a year which would witness the "return" of two of the biggest superstars of the 1980s. Each of these stars was known to have formerly been the most successful recording and touring acts in their fields: Michael Jackson and Whitney Houston. Like Whitney, since the massive success of *Off the Wall*, *Thriller*, and *Bad*, Michael's life and career had completely fallen apart. While Whitney had watched her popularity and health disintegrate through an ill-fated marriage and reported illegal drug use, Michael had been dogged with legal allegations of child molestation and a deep dependence on prescription drugs. When Jackson suddenly died of an apparent drug overdose on June 25, 2009, he was in the middle of preparing for an upcoming series of concerts in London, England which he hoped would revitalize his flagging popularity.

Sadly, the strain of preparing for his concerts put so much pressure on his life, that the stress seemingly consumed him. Happily, Whitney chose a more low-impact path, and ultimately it has spelled "success" for her. Instead of relying on the strain of concert engagements, the Houston comeback was to depend on the one element that original brought her fame: a carefully planned and exquisitely assembled record album.

Fortunately for Whitney, she had the man who created her debut album at her side, guiding her through the process. With the destructive influence of Bobby Brown no longer in the mix, and with Clive Davis masterminding the recording and marketing of her new album, she was on her way back to the top.

Like her debut release, *Whitney*, a full two years was taken to assure that the success of the new album—*I Look to You*—would be carefully planned. Just as he had assembled a top-notch team of writers and producers to work with her twenty-five years before, Davis again hand-selected the people who were to bring Houston's voice back to prominence. This time around the production team would include Sean Garret, will.i.am, Akon, Alicia Keys, David Foster, Diane Warren, and R. Kelly.

As early as 2007, the album was in progress. At the time singer and producer Akon told *Billboard* magazine, "The voice is there; I don't think anyone could ever take that from her. As long as we apply that voice to hit records, she'll be right back where she left off." Already plans were in place for Akon to record a duet with Whitney, appropriately entitled "Like I Never Left."

On February 6, 2009, Whitney Houston made her first high-profile public appearance at Clive Davis's gala in Los Angeles, the week of The Grammy Awards. At the pre-Grammy party she sang four songs including,

"I Will Always Love You," "I Believe in You and Me" and "I'm Every Woman," just to prove to the industry and the press that her voice and self-confidence had returned.

Clive told the press, "You wait for the great songs to be written. The great hits Whitney has given to the public for so many years—you keep encouraging and setting the bar. R. Kelly and Whitney just went into the studio with a great song called 'I Look to You.'"

In July of 2009 it was announced that the wait for Whitney's first new non-holiday album in seven years would be released on August 31 in Europe, and on September 1 in America. The album, entitled *I Look to You* was so anticipated that months before its release, the website www. WhitneyHouston.com was actually carrying a ticking clock to signify how many days, hours and minutes it would be before the album hit the stores. It was being treated like the blast-off of a highly anticipated rocket ship.

Using David Foster as one of the album's producers seemed like the perfect way to link her past successes with her new beginning. Foster had worked on the song "I Will Always Love You" from the soundtrack of *The Bodyguard*, and he co-produced her 1998 album *My Love is Your Love*.

With pride Clive spoke of the care that was taken in planning this album. According to him, "The same way her debut album took a while to put together, you just don't do it by going into a computer. You wait for the material to justify a new album."

There were three very high-profile listening parties held in London, New York City, and in Los Angeles, to try and build press and public anticipation of the new album, *I Look to You*. In London it was held on July 14 at The Mandarin Oriental Hotel, in New York City it took place on July 21 at Jazz at Lincoln Center venue in Columbus Circle, and in Los Angeles it was staged on July 23 at The Beverly Wilshire Hotel.

Dean Piper of London's *Sunday Mirror* attended the first event. According to him, "I managed to bag an invite to one of the biggest and most exciting events of the year so far—the exclusive playback of Whitney Houston's eagerly awaited new album *I Look To You*. Each track was introduced by legendary producer Clive Davis at the swanky bash at the Mandarin Oriental."

Weighing in on the tracks, Piper claimed, "'Million Dollar Bill' reminds me of a summer track . . . it was pure smile factor and a real feel good anthem. Vocals were ace . . . 'Call You Tonight'—This track is huge—very catchy chorus and produced by the award winning Stargate. I liked this one more than most . . . 'Like I Never Left' (featuring Akon)—This track was described as a pure island track. It's fine if you like Akon—but personally he makes me want to poke needles in my head. It's a good song for radio though. But not her finest hour . . . 'A Song For You'—This is pure pop and a total GAY style gay anthem. It made the entire room want to jump up and remember the days when 'I'm Every Woman' was in the charts. It'll be a fans favorite and she sounds awesome . . . It's exceedingly good to have Miss Houston back—and she's more then ready for action."

Gossip columnist Roger Friedman was at the Jazz at Lincoln Center event, and reported that when "Houston walked out and got a standing ovation and cheers . . . She deserved it, too . . . Whitney brought along mom Cissy Houston, cousin Dionne Warwick, and daughter Bobbi Kristina, who's blossomed into a beautiful young woman."

New York fashion photographer Domani Moyd was also present, and he was most curious to see how Whitney appeared. He reported, "She looks healthy and clean. Bobby Brown and crack-be-damned, she's back. She's a Princess." But he added, "She looks 'real'—in her eyes you can see the pain."

Explaining the whole star-studded listening party atmosphere, Moyd explained, "It was very surreal. It's a small room and we were only a couple of rows back from Diane Sawyer and Martha Stewart."

With regard to the music he heard that evening, Moyd claimed, "I think it's well done. They're not gonna make people forget what has happened." The one song that he loved the most, was "Million Dollar Bill." According to him, Whitney got on stage and explained, "Alicia Keys called and said, 'I'd really like to write a song for her.' Whitney said, 'Alicia was the only one who was "getting" me.'"

Domani added, "People have been humbled by the death of Michael Jackson, so people are clinging to what is dear to them . . . At the end of the day, Whitney Houston is a superstar and there aren't that many superstars around."

As the "buzz" surrounding the upcoming release of the album grew, there seemed to be an overwhelming amount of international anticipation. Whether the album was good or bad, it was the superstar "comeback" of a legend.

In August of 2009 the first songs began to leak out on the internet: "I Look to You" and "I Didn't Know My Own Strength." No one was really blown away by them. By mid-month it was announced that the first American single was going to be "Million Dollar Bill." Reviewer Brian McCollum of *The Detroit Free Press* was one of the first people to predict its success. According to him, "The first thing you notice about Whitney Houston's new single is that you've never noticed a Whitney Houston single like this before. With a bright, organic vive lifted straight from late '70s R&B, 'Million Dollar Bill' promptly makes its point: After seven tumultuous years off the recording scene, Houston intends to return with a fiery grace. The upbeat, feel-good cut . . . follows a pair of leaded ballads . . . that flummoxed fans who were craving a more rousing comeback. 'Million Dollar Bill' is the answer they needed . . . Houston provides a blast of hope simply by sounding good."

As the first American single, "Million Dollar Bill," was released, Tom Corson from RCA / Arista Records claimed, "That's a great indicator there's an audience just dying to get Whitney back. She's happy, healthy, motivated and singing well. It's a cultural event."

On Monday, August 31, 2009, at long last the new album by Whitney Houston, *I Look to You*, was released. The press coverage about the diva making a dramatic return, made this the most anticipated album of the year. In fact, internet CD seller Amazon.com, proclaimed that the album went to Number One based on one day sales, which was a great sign.

On first sight, the cover photo of Whitney is very striking to behold. She is looking straight at the camera, and she has a very serious look on her face. There is a minimal amount of make-up on her face, and her expression seems to say, "Alright, you know what I have been up to, but I am cleaned-up AND I am back."

In fact, that is the theme of the songs on the album. Several of the tailor-made lyrics of these songs are clearly platforms for Houston to explain what she has been through in the last seven years. Even some of the titles are defensive in nature: "Like I Never Left" and "I Didn't Know My Own Strength." In the song "Nothin' But Love" she is heard singing that she "ain't gonna regret anything I've done."

In the booklet that is included in the CD, there are two especially beautiful photos of Whitney by Patrick Demarchelier. The first one, which appears on page two is truly stunning, and for the first time in years, Whitney has her eyes wide open, and is looking straight at the camera with a look of contentment on her face. The other memorable one is a full-body shot towards the back of the booklet where she is backlit, and looks like a strong middle-aged woman whose life has been full of experiences.

Musically, the album is beautifully produced throughout. Sometimes Whitney comes up to everyone's vocal expectations, yet on other songs she falls short. There are no bad songs, but there are some definite lackluster ones.

There are four main highpoints to the *I Look to You* album. They are the songs "Million Dollar Bill," "Nothin' But Love," "A Song for You," and "I Didn't Know My Own Strength." They are by far the strongest tracks on the album, and they all succeed for different reasons.

"Million Dollar Bill" wisely opens the album, and it has all of the excitement that everyone is looking for from Whitney, complete with a catchy chorus line. Written by Alicia Keys, it succeeds because it is such a dynamic sounding track, that it sets Houston soaring, and never looking down. Thematically, it has nothing to do with her position in life. A strong, upbeat, and very catchy song, "Million Dollar Bill" was the perfect choice for her first single, and it is worth the price of the CD for this track alone.

The title track, "I Look to You," while poignant, clearly shows that Whitney's voice isn't what it used to be. Lyrically, this is such a finely crafted song, which Houston would have sung the hell out of twenty years ago. However, her 2009 voice is in a much lower key. What makes the song succeed is the conviction in Whitney's performance.

The next extremely strong track on the album is "A Song For You," which is a classic ballad written by Leon Russell. Produced here by Scandinavian team, Stargate, it is the album's one "get up and dance" number. Starting as a slow ballad, a minute into the song it kicks into high gear, and really catches fire and causes a disco inferno.

The other really perfect song here is Diane Warren's "I Didn't Know My Own Strength," which was produced by David Foster. It is the album's major "And I Tell You I'm Not Going" moment, where Whitney's vocal pleas really come through effectively.

There have been other singers in the past who have gone through traumatic circumstances, and emerged from them with their souls intact, but their voices altered. Billie Holiday comes to mind. She was a sweet-voiced big band singer in the 1930s. However, by the 1950s, drug abuse had ravaged her voice. Still, the recordings she made in the '50s, with the top jazz musicians in the business backing her, were effective in a new way. Although her voice was rougher, when this lady sang the blues, her darker voice had more expression to it. The same can be said for Rosemary Clooney. A popular singer in the '50s who became a movie star—*White Christmas*—she became addicted to tranquilizers and sleeping pills. By the '90s, although the youthful sweetness in Rosemary's voice was gone, she was still able to record some of the most effective music of her career. Perhaps this is what is to become of Whitney Houston's recording and performing career. She will never be able to effortlessly hit the light and effervescent notes that she did in her twenties, but perhaps some of her most expressively performances are still yet to come.

The press reviews began pouring in days before the new CD was in the stores, or available for download in its most finished format. One of the most fascinating articles about *I Look to You*, appeared in *The Chicago Tribune*. Writer Greg Kot gave the LP "two stars out of four." He also pointed out how the music business had drastically changed since the time when Whitney Houston was last considered a fully-functioning singing star. According to Kot, "More famous lately for tabloid misadventure and an ill-fated marriage to singer Bobby Brown, Whitney Houston is back doing what she does best: Singing . . . As the music industry entered its most lucrative era, becoming a $15 billion machine by the end of the '90s, Houston was at the forefront, a booming voice with an immaculate."

He also claimed, "Houston has never made a truly great album, the soul sucked out of her gospel-trained voice by shallow songs and sterile production. Her career was guided every step of the way by the heavy hand of Davis, a record executive whose reputation as a pop Svengali

is founded on his ability to mold talent into a marketable commodity
. . . but it's a different era: sales of recorded music are in a free fall, and
Houston has become an afterthought or a punch line. She can still sing—
but how well?"

With regard to the music itself, Kot wrote, "On 'Million Dollar Bill,'
she sounds almost frisky. The tune, coproduced by Swizz Beatz and Alicia
Keys, almost swings . . . It's all downhill from that peak moment, with a
couple of key exceptions . . . nothing else feels quite as elegantly ebullient.
Nor does she ever cut loose; at times it feels as though Houston is just a
pretty ornament on her producers' tracks. In the past, her voice was big
enough to tower over lackluster material, but no more . . . this is Houston
on auto-pilot . . . The Swedish [they are actually Norwegian] Stargate team
turns Leon Russell's ballad "A Song for You" into a disco stomp. It's not
completely successful, but at least it tries to shake up the formula."

The most succinct thing that Kot pointed out was the fact that, as far
as Whitney Houston was concerned, "Her voice isn't what it used to be.
But then neither is the music industry that she once ruled."

In *The Los Angeles Times*, Ann Powers was quick to point out, "The
classic voice isn't there anymore—how could it be?—But the album is an
effective set . . . Certain voices stand like monuments upon the landscape of
twentieth century pop, defining the architecture of their times, sheltering
the dreams of millions and inspiring the climbing careers of countless
imitators. Whitney Houston owns one of those voices . . . Like a Trump
skyscraper, Houston the singer was as showily dominant as corporate
capitalism itself. Then, like many a glorious edifice, Houston's voice fell
into disrepair. Drug abuse and a rocky marriage to New Jack jerk Bobby
Brown made her a tabloid staple. More tragically (for listeners, at least),
her excesses trashed her instrument . . . The pain and, frankly, disgust
that so many pop fans felt during Houston's decline was caused not so
much by her personal distress as by her seemingly careless treatment of the
national treasure that happened to reside within her." She made some very
valid points, the main one referring to Bobby Brown as a "New Jack jerk."

Powers was not overly impressed by the songs Whitney recorded. "*I
Look to You*, the singer's comeback after nearly a decade of ignominy, is
a costly renovation," she claimed. "There's a limit to what Houston can

accomplish, and operating within limits becomes the album's overriding theme . . . Houston's songwriters and producers provide her with top-notch tools; she wields them cautiously and almost humbly, never falling because she never reaches too high . . . What's hard to give up is the dream of painless perfection that the young Houston represented, back in the yuppie era, when her voice sounded like the easy money that was flowing everywhere. Of course, that didn't turn out so well for anyone else, either. Though *I Look to You* doesn't soar like the old days, it's fine to hear Houston working on her own recovery plan."

Jody Rosen in *Rolling Stone* pointed out, "There is a whole Beyoncé generation that knows Houston not as a vocal virtuoso with a multi-octave range but as a tabloid fixture whose dissolution has been unfolding in public for years . . . *I Look to You* spends little time looking back . . . At forty-six, Houston is not the singer she once was. Time and hard living have shaved some notes off that amazing range."

In *Soul Tracks* on the internet, reviewer Chris Rizik wrote of Whitney, "With a decade of personal, physical and chemical dependency problems behind her, this is a different woman who comes to the microphone . . . So it is almost unfair, if predictable, that critics will look at *I Look to You* in the context of the *Ghosts of Whitney Past*, and through that lens there is no way that the middle-aged Whitney can match up. With a vocal rasp that became first apparent in her 2003 holiday album and which is noticeably more pronounced now, and a voice that is a bit lower and certainly weaker than at her peak, Whitney Houston is no longer a singular singer. She is now a mere vocal mortal."

It was clear that the times had changed, and so had Houston. Claimed Rizik, "Whitney simply doesn't have the pipes anymore to hide a songwriter's flaws . . . the Whitney Houston I remember at her peak simply doesn't exist anymore . . . With *I Look to You*, the new Whitney Houston shows that she still has great musical value. Putting aside the cynicism, there is a certain amount of grace that resulted in *I Look to You* even happening. And there is real pleasure in saying that it is a worthwhile return for one of the seminal artists of our time."

On September 1, 2009, Whitney Houston gave a four song mini concert in Central Park in New York City. It was a taped performance that was broadcast the next day on the TV program *Good Morning America*. The appearance was her first major television date since her break-up and divorce from Bobby Brown. She also was interviewed on *The Oprah Winfrey Show*, which was telecast on September 14 and 15.

The *Good Morning America* date was the most telling one, since she was appearing on camera with Diane Sawyer, who conducted the disastrous 2002 interview that marked one of the diva's lowest career points. It was obvious from the very start that Whitney was quite guarded about her appearance in front of the cameras. Instead of getting up early in the morning to appear on the 8:00 AM segment of the show, like the show's guests usually do, Houston insisted that her performance be pre-taped after 11:00 AM the day before the telecast.

Over 5,000 fans gathered to see Whitney that warm Tuesday in September. In fact, people began staking themselves out the night before to get prime spots near the stage at the Rumsey Playfield in Central Park. Once the cameras started to roll it was clear from the very beginning that the *Good Morning America* performance was not perfect. Amidst her Central Park four-song concert, her voice cracked several times mid-song.

Opening with the new single, "Million Dollar Bill," Houston entered the stage in a short beige jacket on top of black leather pants and boots. From the very first notes she sang it was evident that her voice was not in top shape, in fact it was unclear how much that she was actually singing, and how much was being handled by the team of background singers on the stage behind her.

"I love you New York. I love *Good Morning America*. I love everybody," Whitney proclaimed to the crowd. "You're making me feel so good."

Joined on stage by the TV show's hostesses, Diane Sawyer and Robin Roberts, Houston admitted, "I'm so overwhelmed . . . your support, your prayers mean so much to me . . . I never left." Several of the audience members were provided with fans on sticks, some of which read "GMA" to advertise the TV program, and other ones were square cardboard fans depicting the new album cover. The crowd waved them throughout the concert.

Once Whitney removed the short beige jacket, she revealed that she was wearing a gray top with a short knee-length train of gauze which flowed behind it over her black leather pants. Throughout the appearance Houston seemed to be in good spirits. In spite of whatever pressure and vocal difficulties she was having, she adhered to the fabled performer's creed: "the show must go on."

While singing "My Love is Your Love," she was joined on stage by her fifteen-year-old daughter. Giving a nod to slimmed down Bobbi Kristina, Whitney proudly sang, "See I got my baby; me and Bobby's baby."

She next presented the title track to the album, where she vocally opened up and sang the heartfelt "I Look to You," with minimal background voice. Amidst the song she introduced a teary eyed Cissy Houston in the audience. As she sang to the adoring crowd, Whitney pointed to individual members of the audience, and repeated the words "I look to you." Without the sheltered benefits of the recording studio, her voice sounded a bit thin, but she appeared genuinely grateful for the support of the cheering audience.

Although it was edited out of the TV telecast, right before she sang the song "I'm Every Woman," the diva acknowledged the weak shape her voice was in. "I'm so sorry. I did *[The] Oprah [Winfrey Show]*. I've been talking for so long . . . I talked so much, my voice . . . I shouldn't be talking. I should be singing,"

Could she still perform live? Could she still sing and carry a tune? These were the two main questions that everyone had on their mind that day. As members of the gathered Central Park crowd sang and danced to her music, it was clear that there was still a place in their hearts for the once-troubled singer.

Whitney's interview with *Oprah Winfrey*—which was broadcast two weeks later—was quite frank and emotional. Houston looked strong, but a bit weary as the interview began, as though she had no idea which of her demons she would have to face. When she spoke, her voice was raspy and rough. Throughout the first hour segment, Houston fielded questions from Winfrey about her decision to leave Bobby Brown, what all Bobbi Kristina witnessed, her strong mother—Cissy, her nights of doing drugs and staring mindlessly at the television screen, and finding her direction again in life. Whitney revealed that her favorite drug experience had been lacing marijuana cigarettes with crack cocaine. She also spoke of

Bobby Brown's temper, especially when alcohol was involved. According to Houston, she finally knew that her marriage was over when Bobby actually spit in her face. She claimed she was even more horrified when she realized that their daughter had witnessed this display of sheer disrespect.

As the second day of the two-part *Oprah* show the interview continued, and the program was capped off by a strong performance of her song "I Didn't Know My Own Strength." Clive Davis and Bobbi Kristina were in the studio audience, and Oprah showed prerecorded greetings and well wishes from Dionne Warwick, Celine Dion, Christina Aguilera, and Jennifer Hudson. Since the show aired the week that Whitney's *I Turn To You* album entered the charts at Number One in America and Germany, it was indeed a triumphant moment for Houston.

Was this indeed a new era for Whitney Houston, and her world of fans? The fact that her *I Look to You* immediately hit to Number One in several countries was a testament to her star stature. However, she was a different diva than the charming Whitney circa the late '80s, when she one who was once perceived to be "America's Sweetheart." Her innocence was gone, but she still appeared to have a strong future ahead of her in the world of show business.

CHAPTER SIXTEEN

"HEARTBREAK HOTEL"

Since the *I Look to You* album was an instant success on a worldwide basis, it seemed like a natural move for Whitney to launch a concert tour so that she could show her fans that she was "back in action," and that she truly meant to reclaim her star stature. On October 12, 2009, Whitney posted a statement on her official website which read: "This is my first full tour since the *My Love Is Your Love* tour and I am so excited to be performing for my fans around the world after all this time. I am putting together a great show and cannot wait to perform the songs from my new album *I Look To You,* along with some of your favorites." The statement made it sound like her heart was truly into completing the tour with newfound vigor.

However it wasn't long before she proved that she was completely unprepared for the rigors of a concert tour. Ultimately, she also proved that she didn't have the strength or stamina to put on a full show, and she also demonstrated just how badly her years of abuse had ruined her once-glorious singing voice.

The *Nothing But Love* tour ran from December 9, 2009, and continued through June 17, 2010. There were four legs to the tour, which encompassed seven dates in Asia, six concerts in Australia, and thirty-seven in Europe, for a total of fifty. From the very beginning it looked like she was purposely avoiding the harsh and fickle American critics. If this was the plan, it was indeed a wise idea.

The first dates on the tour took place in Russia. On December 9, 2009 she debuted the show in Moscow at Olimpiyskiy, and on December 12, she performed in Saint Petersburg at The Ice Palace. From February 6 to 18, Whitney's *Nothing But Love* tour moved to Asia where she played seven dates in Korea and Japan.

From February 22 to March 6, 2010, Whitney headlined six shows in Australia, and the press reports of a disaster-in-the-making started to hit the internet. In *The Daily Telegraph*, reviewing the Sydney show, Kathy McCabe wrote, "Her acoustic set of old favourites unfortunately could not hide the very obvious problems with her voice, the strain and those coughs that punctuated the Brisbane show were back. By the time she got to the gospel section of the show a steady stream of disappointed, saddened and angry fans started streaming out the doors."

Reportedly Houston was covered with sweat for much of her time on stage during the shows, she took many breaks from the stage, and instead of just singing she had adopted the habit of rambling on-and-on to the audience in an obvious plan to actually sing as little as possible. Another irritating ploy she used was to encourage the audience to sing the songs to her. Several times during her show she allowed her background singers or her brother Gary to take over the bulk of the singing. When she did sing, she proved that she was no longer the adept vocalist whom the world fell in love with. Instead she sounded raspy, and could clearly no longer hit the high notes that made her famous. This was especially obvious during her painful attempts at singing her greatest hit: "I Will Always Love You."

She cancelled two planned dates in Australia, and another one in New Zealand. Her so-called triumphant "return" tour was already off to a bumpy state when she moved the show to Europe. She began by cancelling and / or postponing performances in France, England, Scotland, and Spain. Instead she was booked into a Paris hospital where it was reported that she had a respiratory infection. The press was quick to speculate that she had been using drugs again.

The drug rumors were so rampant that Whitney openly spoke about it to the press. She told *People* magazine the drug allegations were "ridiculous." When the reporter from *People* asked what she did when gossip columnists wrote such things about her, the diva replied, "I just don't respond. I don't even read it."

Finally, on April 13, 2010 the European shows finally began, with a date at LG Arena in Birmingham, England. Ultimately she was to perform concerts in Ireland, Scotland, France, Italy, Switzerland, Germany, Austria, Belgium, Sweden, Norway, Denmark, and Finland.

The press reports were mainly terrible. In *The Independent*, John Meagher wrote of Whitney's Dublin show at The O2, "She spends more time chatting to the audience than singing in the early stages, although her conversation rarely strays beyond the 'I love you, Dublin' type . . . [she] eventually becomes tedious. Even the more tolerable songs—'My Love is Your Love,' for instance—are carried by the strength of her backing vocalists and the enthusiastic singing of the crowd. There are slivers of the super-talented young Whitney—a high note here, a spine-tingling pause there on 'I Will Always Love You'—but they arrive so infrequently it hardly matters. Instead, you are left with the memory of her botched attempts to wring some magic from 'I Wanna Dance with Somebody' and 'How Will I Know?'"

With regard to her concert at London's O2 Arena, John Aizlewood wrote in *The Evening Standard*, "Where once she soared, now she wheezes and croaks, bludgeoning her perfect pop single 'I Wanna Dance (With Somebody Who Loves Me)' into karaoke submission; stripping the moving 'My Love Is Your Love' of all emotion and inflicting grisly carnage on 'I Will Always Love You' (if she is late-period Judy Garland, this is her 'Over The Rainbow')."

Fiona Shepherd reviewed Houston's concert at The Scottish Exhibition and Conference Centre in *The Scotsman* and proclaimed, "It was obvious from this performance that she has lost her vocal agility, her stamina, her poise and her wits—or so it seemed from her nervous laughter, repetitive 'thank you's' and rambling personal tributes. Her band were practiced at covering for her while she took time out to pat away the sweat, re-apply her make-up, impart another nugget of eccentric insight and generally procrastinate."

When Whitney got to Copenhagen, she found something truly rotten in Denmark. Reviewing the show, *MSN Entertainment* headlined their story: "Hundreds Walk Out as Whitney Houston Falters Again." The story reported, "According to *The Copenhagen Post*, critics from 'all of the major media outlets' in the country slammed the concert, insisting Houston's vocals were weak and tuneless . . . Critic Thomas Soie Hansen, of the *Berlingske Tidende* newspaper, writes: 'She looked and sounded like a person who doesn't have many years left to live. At the end of the show she looked like she was ready to explode.'"

The press coverage in Europe was scathing, and reporters and reviewers were not shy about discussing the rumors of Whitney's drug use. What should have been a triumphant return to concert performing, was shaping up to be the very last major tour she would ever attempt.

Although the tour was somewhat of a financial success on some level, it was a critical disaster. All totaled, Whitney's tour grossed a reported $36 million. However, the cancelled Australian dates ended up losing the promoter $2 million.

In terms of artistic success, her *Nothing But Love* world tour was a complete train wreck. Countless thousands of fans walked out on her concerts, bitterly disappointed by what they witnessed. This was supposed to be the big "Whitney Houston comeback" tour. Whatever promise that the temporary success of the *I Look to You* album suggested, her 2010 concerts instantly eroded.

In 2011 Whitney Houston was back in the news, and cocaine was the topic. According to *The National Enquirer*, seventeen-year-old Bobbi Kristina was photographed imbibing in cocaine. Protective mother Whitney reportedly pulled the plug on her daughter's eighteenth birthday party at The Atlantis resort in the Bahamas, and she claimed she was taking back the girl's new Lexus. Furthermore, Whitney reportedly ordered Bobbi Kristina to check herself into a drug rehabilitation facility. Throughout the year Whitney and her daughter continued to feud about the subject of drugs and rehab.

Although it appeared that Whitney Houston had reduced her career to a tabloid soap opera, all of a sudden it was announced that she had been offered a film role in a remake of the 1976 film *Sparkle*. The plot of *Sparkle* tells the story of three sisters who form a singing group, in hopes of achieving Supremes-like success. In the new production of the film, *American Idol* winner Jordan Sparks was signed to star in the title role, and Whitney was signed to portray Sparkle's pragmatic mother, Emma.

After all the troubles that Whitney had on her 2010 concert tour, there was a lot of speculation as to whether or not she would physically be up to the rigors of showing up on a movie set day after day. Much to everyone's delight, when she arrived in Detroit to film her part, Whitney proved that she was not only up to the task, she was heralded as a sparkling presence on the set and on camera.

In the film Whitney will be seen and heard singing the gospel song "Eyes on the Sparrow" and she sings a duet with Jordan Sparks on the song "Celebrate," which was written by R. Kelly. According to producer Howard Rosenman, "It's a great, great gospel song where she's just genius." With regard to working with her on the film Rosenman claimed, "She was fabulous on the set, she was beloved by the crew, she was a total professional."

In January of 2012, Whitney was back in the headlines, and again the news was bad. According to several sources, Houston was broke, and that she had totally gone through all of the money that was once her fortune. One source quoted in *Radar Online* claimed, "Whitney's fortune is gone. Music industry heavy hitters are supporting her and her label is fronting her cash against her next album, but no one knows when that will be released . . . She might be homeless if not for people saving her. She is broke as a joke. She called someone to ask for $100 . . . It is so sad."

Even with all of the bad news that seemed to swirl around her wherever she went, Whitney Houston continued to optimistically make plans for the future. It was as though in her mind she was invincible, and that she had unlimited time. When she began to make plans to attend The Grammy Awards in February of 2012, all that she had on her mind was the fun she was going to have with all of the friends that she would have a chance to see in Los Angeles.

On February 11, 2012, when Whitney went up to her suite at The Beverly Hilton Hotel, she was looking forward to that evening's party. Whether her career was up or down, Clive always treated her like she was the belle of the ball. We may never know exactly what happened in Whitney Houston's suite that afternoon. All we are certain of is that at 3:55 PM she was pronounced dead. One of the most brilliant show business careers of the last 100 years had come to a tragic end.

Around-the-clock Whitney coverage began almost immediately on television news networks like CNN and Fox. Who discovered her body? Was there foul play? Where was Bobby Brown? Was Clive Davis's party going to get called off? What was going to happen at The Grammys? How could she possibly be dead at the young age of forty-eight? Every angle was discussed, including the most important question of all: What was the exact cause of her death?

Whitney had withstood so many life threatening situations in the past that at first, the news didn't seem to be real. Even newscasters confessed to being completely shocked by the tragic news. In spite of everything that was publicly known about Whitney's addictions and demons, it didn't seem possible that she could so suddenly and unexpectedly die.

Clive Davis's Grammy party was held as expected. According to the old show business motto: the show had to go on one way or another. Immediately wheels were set in motion for both the party and The Grammy Awards to—in one way or another—dedicate part of their respective programs as a tribute to the tragically departed Houston.

Whitney had wanted to be at The Beverly Hilton Hotel for Clive's party, and she was, even in death. While the Grammy party was going on downstairs, Whitney's lifeless body was still on the Fourth Floor of the hotel, while an ongoing police investigation was taking place. Her body didn't leave her suite until after midnight.

The following night at *The Grammy Awards*, which were held at The Staples Center, the tragic death of Whitney Houston was very much on everyone's minds. It was as though the shadow of her memory, or maybe even her spirit, somehow hovered over the proceedings.

The show kicked off with a prayer and a moment of silence for Whitney, delivered by the show's host, LL Cool J. Showing up on stage to deliver a mid-show introduction, Stevie Wonder took a moment to publicly say "goodbye" to Whitney. Following a somber segment of the show that was devoted to all of the music stars who had died in the last year, Jennifer Hudson sang a beautiful version of "I Will Always Love You" as a wonderfully fitting tribute to Whitney Houston. It became the most touching part of the entire Grammy show.

The day following *The Grammy Awards*, finally more details of Whitney's last hours began to be released to the public. According to a Beverly Hills police report, Whitney Houston was found "underwater" in her hotel suite bathtub. She had been discovered there by "a member of her personal staff" at 3:25 PM.

The police statement claimed, "She was underwater and apparently unconscious . . . Ms. Houston was pulled from the tub by members of her staff and hotel security was promptly notified."

When the Fire Department personnel and the hotel security members responded to the emergency call, they found Whitney "to still be unconscious and unresponsive . . . They initiated CPR, but were unable to revive her . . . At approximately 3:55 PM Whitney Houston, age forty-eight, was pronounced dead at the scene."

Her autopsy was performed on Sunday, the day of *The Grammy Awards* telecast. Her body was then released by the coroner Monday, for her family to make the funeral arrangements. The police chose not to make the findings of the autopsy public yet, and they also refused to give a probable "cause of death."

The official police report claimed, "As can be expected in a high-profile incident such as this, there have been many rumors circulating and much speculation by the media and the public . . . In order to minimize such speculation, the Beverly Hills Police Department has asked the coroner's office to place a security hold on their findings until they have a complete and final report prepared."

TMZ.com reported on February 13 that members of Whitney's family were informed by Los Angeles County Coroner officials that she did not die from drowning. Instead, they suspected that she had a fatal dose of a combination of Xanax and other prescription drugs mixed together with alcohol. According to the same report, the Coroner officials also informed the family that there was not enough water in Whitney's lungs for her to have drowned.

Slowly tales of Whitney having been on a drinking and partying binge began to emerge as well. Several people described her actions and behavior as being "erratic" during her last days in Los Angeles. She kept interrupting one of Clive Davis's on-camera pre-Grammy press interviews on Thursday, and in the footage from the shooting she acts like she is drunk. When she showed up at Kelly Price's event, videos showed that she appeared to be "disheveled" and sweaty.

The Daily Mail in England later reported, "On Thursday she is said to have gone on a 'wild binge' where she clashed with security guards. The next evening she 'partied heavily, drank and chatted loudly' with friends at the hotel bar . . . Bottles of Lorazepam, Valium, Xanax and a sleeping medication were found in the hotel room, it has been claimed . . . The drugs were believed to have acted as sedatives, causing her to fall asleep in the bathtub once they had been mixed with alcohol from the previous evenings."

While all of this was going on, three of the biggest questions on everyone's minds concerned Bobby Brown, Cissy Houston, and Bobbi Kristina Brown. How were they bearing up in the face of this great personal tragedy?

Cissy was the most grounded, and centered. She issued a statement to the press which read: "We are devastated by the loss of our beloved Whitney. This is an unimaginable tragedy and we will miss her terribly."

Reportedly, Bobby Brown took the news very hard. He was in Mississippi at the time, where he was on the road with the reunion tour of his old group: New Edition. He was able to take the stage at their concert that evening, but he reportedly had an onstage "breakdown" in front of the highly sympathetic audience. At one point during his performance, Bobby pointed to the sky and proclaimed, "I love you, Whitney!"

Unsurprisingly, it was eighteen-year-old Bobbi Kristina who took Whitney's death the hardest. The day of Whitney's death, Bobbi Kristina clashed with the police when she tried to regain entry to her mother's room on Saturday. Since the room was being investigated by the Beverly Hills police to ascertain whether or not it was "crime scene," no one was allowed admittance. That night, Bobbi Kristina had to be taken to Cedar's Sinai Hospital in an ambulance, as she was suffering from stress and a possible anxiety attack. She was released, and on Sunday she was again admitted to the same hospital with the same symptoms.

According to TMZ.com, Bobbi Kristina was "hysterical, exhausted and inconsolable." They also reported that the girl's family members were frightened that fear she is suicidal and are considering getting her help. At Cedar's Sinai she was again stabilized and then released.

Concerned for the well-being of his daughter, on Monday Bobby Brown left his New Edition tour, and he flew to Los Angeles to be with her. According to Bobby in a statement to *Extra*, "Obviously, the death of her mother is affecting her, however, we will get through this tragedy as a family. Again, I ask for privacy during this time."

On Monday, February 13, 2012, Whitney's body was loaded into a private plane, and sent to her home state of New Jersey, for the pending funeral. According to press reports, the funeral arrangements were being handled by Whigham Funeral Home in Newark. It was the same funeral home that handled the final arrangements for Whitney's father, John Houston, in 2003.

In the days after Whitney's death, the thoughts, prayers and condolences of several of Whitney's contemporaries were being sympathetically expressed either verbally, or posted on websites, or via Twitter. They included the following well wishes:

Barry Manilow: "We spent more than twenty great years together at Arista Records with our friend and mentor, Clive Davis. My heart goes out to her family, to Clive, and to everyone who knew and loved this amazingly talented and beautiful artist. I will always love her."

Aretha Franklin: "I just can't talk about it now. It's so stunning and unbelievable . . . My heart goes out to Cissy, her daughter Bobbi Kris, her family and Bobby."

Usher: "R.I.P Whitney Houston . . . A true icon of our time. Gone too soon. My heart goes out to the family in their time of distress."

Queen Latifah: "Oh Dear Lord! Hurting so Bad!!! MY Sister Whitney!!!!!!! Newark please Pray!!! World Please Pray!" (via Twitter)

Tony Bennett: "It's a tragedy. Whitney Houston was the greatest singer I've ever heard and she will be truly missed." (via Twitter)

Oprah Winfrey: "To me Whitney was THE VOICE. We got to hear a part of God every time she sang. Heart is heavy, spirit grateful for the GIFT of her." (via Twitter)

Dolly Parton: "I will always be grateful and in awe of the wonderful performance she did on my song and I can truly say from the bottom of my heart, 'Whitney, I will always love you. You will be missed.'"

Toni Braxton: "My heart is weeping . . . RIP to the Legendary Diva & Icon Whitney Houston!!!!! Such an incredible influence over music as a whole!" (via Twitter)

Celine Dion: "When I started my career, I wanted to be like her. I loved her so much. My prayers go out to her daughter and to all of her family."

Smokey Robinson: "I've known Whitney since she was a little girl and I have always loved her. She was like family to me and I will miss her dearly." (via Twitter)

The list of condolences was endless. Whitney and her music had touched and inspired so many people during her life, and had left behind her such an incredibly body of work.

What will the legacy of Whitney Houston be? Thanks to her films *The Bodyguard, Waiting to Exhale*, and *The Preacher's Wife*; and her amazing recordings like "I Wanna Dance With Somebody (Who Loves Me)," "How Will I Know," and "I Will Always Love You," Whitney's voice and image will always be an indelible part of pop culture. These films and recordings stand as a lasting monument to her talent at its height. They are captured forever on DVD and CD, and we get to enjoy them time and time again.

It is funny how time changes people's memories of their heroes. When we think of Elvis Presley, we now remember the young and exciting rock & roller from the 1950s first and foremost. When we think of Marilyn Monroe, we instantly have the vision of her in that white dress, standing over a subway grating. When we think of Billie Holiday, we think of her with a gardenia pinned to her hair, singing in smoky nightclub. When we think of Michael Jackson, we tend to think of him in the "Billie Jean" video first. Now we are faced with confronting how we will most remember Whitney Houston.

Undoubtedly, in time the Whitney we will always remember will be the gorgeous sophisticated star of *The Bodyguard*, or her emotional vocal performance of "I Will Always Love You," or the fresh-faced singer we first fell in love with in her video for "You Give Good Love." The music she recorded, the film roles she brought to life, and the excitement that she created at the height of her career will always be with us. There will only be one Whitney Houston.

QUOTE SOURCES

INTERVIEWS

The author has drawn upon his own personal observations, as well as having interviewed several people including: Francis Grill, Bashiri Johnson, Charles Moniz, Kenneth Reynolds, Barbara Shelley, Andrew Skurow, and Marsha Stern.

PUBLICATIONS AND WEBSITES

Access Hollywood
Associated Press
Billboard
Black Voices
Cash Box
The Chicago Tribune
Cosmopolitan
Ebony
Fresh!
Globe
The Hollywood Reporter
www.IMDB.com
Jet
The Los Angeles Times
Luce Press Clippings
National Enquirer
The Newark Star Ledger
New Jersey Monthly
The New York Daily News
The New York Post

The New York Times
People
The Post Chronicle
Rolling Stone
The Salt Lake City Desert News (Utah)
Song Hits
Star
Time
US
USA Today
Vogue
The Village Voice
The Washington Post

BOOKS

Bobby Brown: The Truth, the Whole Truth and Nothing But . . . An Un(Authorized) Biography by Derrick Handspike, 2008, Down South Books, Atlanta, Georgia

Diva: The Totally Unauthorized Biography of Whitney Houston, by Jeffrey Bowman, 1995, Harper Mass Market Paperbacks, New York City

Good Girl, Bad Girl, by Kevin Ammons with Nancy Bacon, 1996, Birch Lane Press, New York City

Leonard Maltin's 1998 Movie & Video Guide, 1997, Signet Books, New York City

Rock Stars Encyclopedia, by Dafydd Rees and Luke Crampton, 1996, 1999, DK Publishing, Inc. New York City

Whitney! (C) 1996, by Mark Bego, PaperJacks Books, New York City, and Toronto, Canada

WHITNEY HOUSTON: DISCOGRAPHY

THE ALBUMS

US (United States), UK (United Kingdom), Austl (Australia), Ger (Germany), Aus (Austria), Sw (Switzerland) / Sales = Global Sales in Millions

Title	US	UK	Austl	Ger	Aus	Sw	Sales
Whitney Houston (1985)	1	2	1	1	9	1	22 M
Whitney (1987)	1	1	1	1	1	1	19 M
I'm Your Baby Tonight (1990)	3	4	10	3	2	3	10 M
The Bodyguard [soundtrack] (1992)	1	1	1	1	1	1	34 M
Waiting To Exhale [soundtrack] (1995)	1	8	9	—	—	—	10 M
The Preacher's Wife [soundtrack] (1996)	3	35	34	5	8	16	5 M
My Love Is Your Love (1998)	13	4	42	2	1	7	10 M
Whitney Houston: The Greatest Hits (2000)	5	1	8	2	3	4	8 M
Love, Whitney (2001)	—	22	—	2	1	7	1 M
Just Whitney . . . (2002)	9	76	16	—	42	12	3 M
One Wish: The Holiday Album (2003)	49	—	—	—	—	—	½ M
The Ultimate Collection (2007)	—	3	31	—	38	10	
I Look to You (2009)	1	—	16	1	2	3	
The Essential Whitney Houston (2011)	—	—	—	—	—	—	

WHITNEY HOUSTON Appearances on Other Albums

One Down by Material (1982)
"Memories" by Whitney Houston

Paul Jabara & Friends by Paul Jabara (1983)
"Eternal Love" by Whitney Houston

Love Language by Teddy Pendergrass (1984)
"Hold Me" by Teddy Pendergrass and Whitney Houston

Jermaine Jackson by Jermaine Jackson (1984)
"Take Good Care of My Heart" by Jermaine Jackson
and Whitney Houston

Perfect movie soundtrack album by Various Artists (1985)
"Shock Me" by Jermaine Jackson and Whitney Houston

Precious Moments by Jermaine Jackson (1986)
"If You Say My Eyes Are Beautiful" by Jermaine Jackson
and Whitney Houston

One Moment in Time by Various Artists (1988)
"One Moment in Time" by Whitney Houston

WHITNEY HOUSTON Discography
The Singles

US (United States), UK (United Kingdom), Ger (Germany) / [#] =
Number of weeks at Number One. (US and UK positions According to
Billboard Magazine's Hot 100 and British Chart)

	US	UK	Ger
"Hold Me" (with Teddy Pendergrass)	46	45	—
"You Give Good Love"	3	—	—
"Saving All My Love For You"	1[1]	1[2]	18
"How Will I Know"	1[2]	5	26
"Greatest Love of All"	1[3]	8	22
"I Wanna Dance With Somebody"	1[2]	1[2]	1
"Didn't We Almost Have It All"	1[2]	14	20
"So Emotional"	1[1]	5	—
"Where Do Broken Hearts Go"	1[2]	14	—

	US	UK	Ger
"Love Will Save The Day"	9	10	37
"I Know Him So Well" (with Cissy Houston)	—	—	46
"One Moment in Time"	5	1[2]	1
"It Isn't It Wasn't, It Ain't Never Gonna Be" (with Aretha Franklin)	41	29	—
"I'm Your Baby Tonight"	1[1]	5	5
"All The Man That I Need"	1[2]	13	37
"The Star Spangled Banner"	20	—	—
"Miracle"	9	—	—
"My Name Is Not Susan"	20	29	52
"I Will Always Love You"	1[14]	1[10]	1
"I'm Every Woman"	4	4	13
"I Have Nothing"	4	3	39
"Run To You"	31	15	—
"Queen of the Night"	—	14	—
"Something in Common" (with Bobby Brown)	—	16	—
"Exhale (Shoop Shoop)"	1[1]	11	26
"Count On Me"	8	12	75
"Why Does It Hurt So Bad"	26	—	—
"I Believe In You and Me"	4	16	—
"Step By Step"	15	13	8
"My Heart Is Calling"	77	—	—
"When You Believe" (with Mariah Carey)	15	4	8
"Heartbreak Hotel" (with Kelly Price and Faith Evans)	2	25	61
"It's Not Right But It's Okay"	4	3	14
"My Love Is Your Love"	4	2	2
"I Learned From the Best"	27	—	48
"Same Script, Different Cast" (with Deborah Cox)	70	—	—
"Could I Have This Kiss Forever" (with Enrique Iglesias)	52	—	5
"The Star Spangled Banner" (Re-Issue)	6	—	—
"Whatchulookinat"	96	13	47
"One of Those Days"	72	—	—
"Try It on My Own"	84	—	—
"I Look to You"	70	85	41
"Million Dollar Bill"	100	5	41

AWARDS

Whitney's list of awards is extensive, including six Grammys, a record twenty-one American Music Awards, fifteen *Billboard* Music Awards and two Emmy Awards. Here is a comprehensive list of Whitney's awards:

1985:
Billboard Music Awards:
- "Top New Pop Artist"
- "Top New Black Artist"

1986:
American Music Awards:
- "Favorite Soul / R&B Single" for "You Give Good Love"
- "Favorite Soul / R&B Video" for "Saving All My Love For You"

Grammy Award:
- "Best Female Pop Vocal Performance" for "Saving All My Love for You"

Billboard Music Awards:
- "Top Black Album" for *Whitney Houston*
- "Top Pop Album" *Whitney Houston*
- "Top Black Album Artist"
- "Top Pop Album Artist"
- "Top Pop Female Album Artist"
- "Top Pop Album and Singles Artist"

Rolling Stone Music Award:
- "Best Album of the Year: *Whitney Houston*

MTV Music Video Award:
- "Best Female Video of the Year:" for "How Will I Know"

Emmy Award:
- "Outstanding Individual Performance in a Variety or Music Program"

1987:
American Music Awards:
- "Favorite Pop / Rock Female Vocalist"
- "Favorite Pop / Rock Female LP" for *Whitney Houston*
- "Favorite Soul / R&B Female LP" for *Whitney Houston*
- "Favorite Soul / R&B Female Vocalist"
- "Favorite Soul / R&B Female Video"

Billboard Music Award:
- "Top Female Album Artist"

People's Choice Award:
- "Favorite Female Musical Performer"

1988:
American Music Awards:
- "Favorite Pop / Rock Female Vocalist"
- "Favorite R&B / Soul Female Vocalist"

Grammy Award:
- "Best Female Pop Vocal Performance" for "I Wanna Dance With Somebody (Who Loves Me)"

Billboard Music Award:
- "Top Pop Female Singles Artist"

Soul Train Music Award:
- "Female Album of the Year" for *Whitney*

Emmy Award:
- "Outstanding Individual Performance in a Variety or Music Program"

People's Choice Award:
- "Favorite Female Musical Performer"

1989:
American Music Awards:
- "Favorite Pop / Rock Female Artist"
- "Favorite Pop / Rock Single," "I Wanna Dance with Somebody (Who Loves Me)"

People's Choice Award:
- "Favorite Female Musical Performer"

1990:
American Music Awards:
- "Favorite Pop / Rock Female Artist"
- "Favorite Pop / Rock Single," "I Wanna Dance with Somebody (Who Loves Me)"

Essence Magazine:
- The 1990 *Essence* Award for the Performing Arts

1991:
American Music Awards:
- "Favorite Pop / Rock Female Vocalist"
- "Favorite R&B / Soul Female Vocalist"

Billboard Music Awards:
- Top R&B Album: "I'm Your Baby Tonight"
- Top R&B Album Artist
- Top R&B Singles Artist
- Top R&B Album and Singles Artist

The American Cinema Performer of the Year Award:
- Whitney Houston for *The Bodyguard*

1993:
Billboard Music Awards:
- "Top Hot 100 Sales Single" for "I Will Always Love You"
- "Top Pop Single" for "I Will Always Love You"
- "Top R&B Sales Single" for "I Will Always Love You"
- "Top R&B Single" for "I Will Always Love You"
- "Top Pop Singles Artist"
- "Top Pop Female Singles Artist"
- "Top Pop Album" for *The Bodyguard* soundtrack
- "Top R&B Album" for *The Bodyguard* soundtrack
- "Top R&B Singles Artist"

World Music Awards:
- "Song of 1993" for "I Will Always Love You"
- "Album of 1993" for *The Bodyguard* soundtrack
- "Entertainer of the Year 1993"

MTV Movie Award:
- "Best Song" for "I Will Always Love You"

People's Choice Award:
- "Favorite Female Musical Performer"
- "Favorite Music Video" for "I Will Always Love You"

Soul Train Music Award:
- "Best Female R&B Single" for "I Will Always Love You"

1994:
Grammy Awards:
- "Record of the Year" for "I Will Always Love You' from *The Bodyguard* soundtrack album
- "Album of the Year" for *The Bodyguard* soundtrack
- "Best Female Pop Vocal Performance" for "I Will Always Love You"

American Music Awards:
- "Favorite Pop / Rock Female Vocalist"
- "Favorite Pop / Rock Female Single" for "I Will Always Love You"
- "Favorite Soul / R&B Female Vocalist"
- "Favorite Soul / R&B Female Single" for "I Will Always Love You"
- "Favorite Pop / Rock Female Album" for *The Bodyguard* soundtrack
- "Favorite R&B / Soul Female Album" for *The Bodyguard* soundtrack
- "Favorite Adult Contemporary Album" for *The Bodyguard* soundtrack
- "American Music Award of Merit"

Soul Train Music Award:
- "R&B Song of the Year" for "I Will Always Love You"

- THE 1994 SAMMY DAVIS JR. AWARD As "Entertainer of the Year" for outstanding achievements in the field of entertainment during 1993

Brit Award:
- "Best Soundtrack Album" for *The Bodyguard*

Juno Music Award:
- "Best-Selling Foreign or Domestic Album in Canada" for *The Bodyguard*

1995:
Soul Train Award:
- Hall of Fame

VH1 Honors:
- For her work with Charities

1996:
NAACP Image Award:
- Outstanding Female Artist with "Exhale (Shoop Shoop)"

Soul Train Award:
- Best Female R&B / Soul Single: "Exhale (Shoop Shoop)"

Nickelodeon Kid's Choice Award:
- Hall of Fame

Black Entertainment Television (BET) Award:
- Walk of Fame

1997:
American Music Awards:
- Favorite Adult Contemporary Artist
- Favorite Soundtrack Album: *Waiting to Exhale*

NAACP Image Awards:
- "Outstanding Motion Picture Actress" for her role in *The Preacher's Wife*
- "Outstanding Gospel Artist" for her work on *The Preacher's Wife* soundtrack album
- "Outstanding Album" for *The Preacher's Wife* soundtrack

Blockbuster Entertainment Award:
- Best Female Pop Artist

Essence Award (from *Essence* magazine):
- "1998 Essence Award"

People's Choice Award:
- "Favorite Female Musical Performer"

Trumpet Pinnacle Award:
- "For inspiring others in her chosen profession or career"

Soul Train Award:
- "Quincy Jones Award" for "Outstanding Career Achievements in the Field of Entertainment"

Dove Award:
- "Best Traditional Recorded Gospel Performance" for "I Go To the Rock"

1999:
NAACP Image Award:
- "Outstanding Duo / Group Collaboration" for "When You Believe" by Whitney Houston and Mariah Carey

MTV Europe Music Awards 1999:
- "Best R&B Performance"

Bambi Awards, Germany:
- "Best International Pop Artist 2000"

NAACP Image Awards:
- "Best Female Vocal Performance" for "Heartbreak Hotel"

Forty-second Annual Grammy Awards:
- "Best R&B Female Vocal Performance" for "It's Not Right But It's Okay"

Fourteenth Annual Soul Train Awards:
- Whitney Houston: "Artist of the Decade"

2001:
First Annual BET Awards:
- Whitney Houston: "Lifetime Achievement Award"

ABOUT THE AUTHOR

MARK BEGO is a professional writer who is called "The Number One Best-Selling Pop Biographer" in *Publisher's Weekly* and has been referred to in the press as "The Prince of Pop Music Bio's." He has authored over fifty-eight published books involving rock & roll and show business. He has penned two *New York Times* bestsellers, a *Los Angeles Times* bestseller, and the *Chicago Tribune* bestseller *Dancing in the Street: Confessions of a Motown Diva* written with its subject, Martha Reeves of the beloved recording group: Martha & The Vandellas.

In 1984 he released his biography of Michael Jackson, entitled: *Michael!* It was released the week that Jackson caught his hair on fire filming a Pepsi-Cola commercial, and Bego ended up selling 3 million copies of his book in the United States alone. It spent six weeks on *The New York Times* best-seller list, and was published in six foreign language editions. It was so popular that Bego spent three months following The Jacksons' "Victory Tour" from city-to-city to write the million-selling *On the Road with Michael!*

The following year, in 1985, Bego wrote the million-selling *Madonna!* About the pop icon. It was so popular that he has twice expanded the book as *Madonna: Blonde Ambition* (1992 and 2001). In 1986 Mark Bego became the first author to write a book about Whitney Houston. It was entitled *Whitney!*

From 1978 to 1980 he was the Nightlife Editor for Manhattan's *Cue* magazine, covering everything from Studio 54 to all of the jazz and cabaret clubs in the city. From 1983 to 1985 he was Editor-In-Chief of *Modern Screen* magazine. His writing has also appeared in *People*, *US*, *Billboard*, *Record World*, *Cosmopolitan*, *The Star*, and *The National Enquier*.

He has also written books with Micky Dolenz of The Monkees (*I'm a Believer*), Debbie Gibson (*Between the Lines*), and Jimmy Greenspoon of Three Dog Night (*One is the Loneliest Number*). Bego's book subjects have ranged from Elvis Presley, Bonnie Raitt, Julia Roberts, Joni Mitchell, Billy Joel, and Jackson Browne to Cher and Bette Midler. In 1994, his more general books published included *Country Gals* (life stories of Reba McEntire, Dolly Parton, Tanya Tucker, and other famed women in country music), and *Country Hunks* (spotlighting Vince Gill, Billy Ray Cyrus, George Strait and others). Bego also authored the reference books *TV Rock* [The History of Rock & Roll on Television] and *The Rock & Roll Almanac*. He has also written books about Hollywood in its heyday: *The Best of "Modern Screen,"* and *Rock Hudson: Public and Private*.

At the height of the box-office success of the film *Titanic*, Bego wrote the biography of the movie's star: *Leonardo DiCaprio: Romantic Hero*. It spent six weeks on *The New York Times* best-seller list in 1998. He frequently is seen on television speaking about show business, on such shows as *Entertainment Tonight, Biography*, and *True Hollywood Story*.

In 2008 he published his pop culture book, written with Randy Jones of The Village People, entitled: *Macho Man*. In 2009 three of Bego's books were published in the German language: *Elton John: Die Story, Tina Turner: Die Biografie*, and *Whitney Houston: Die Biografie*. Recently he penned his own show business memoir, *Paperback Writer* (2010), and in 2011 he assisted Freddy Cannon with his autobiography *Where the Action Is!* with an Introduction by Dick Clark.

In March of 2012 Bego releases his newly revised hit biography *Aretha Franklin: The Queen of Soul*. His official website is: www.MarkBego.com. You can write to him at: MarkBego@aol.com.